FILIATION AND AFFILIATION

FILIATION AND AFFILIATION

Harold W. Scheffler
Yale University

Routledge
Taylor & Francis Group

LONDON AND NEW YORK

First published 2001 by Westview Press

Published 2019 by Routledge
52 Vanderbilt Avenue, New York, NY 10017
2 Park Square, Milton Park, Abingdon, Oxon OX14 4RN

First issued in hardback 2019

Routledge is an imprint of the Taylor & Francis Group, an informa business

Library of Congress Cataloging-in-Publication Data
Scheffler, Harold W.
    Filiation and affiliation / Harold W. Scheffler.
        p.   cm.
    Includes bibliographical references and index.
    IBN 0-8133-3761-5
    1. Kinship.   2. Kin recognition.   3. Matrilineal kinship.   4. Patrilineal kinship.
5. Affiliation (Philosophy).   I. Title.

GN487.S34   2000
306.83—dc21
                                                                                    00-043788
    ISBN 13: 978-0-367-31577-1 (hbk)
    ISBN 13: 978-0-8133-3761-6 (pbk)

CONTENTS

Illustrations

Introduction

One of the special tasks of social anthropology has been to detect the order that is inherent in the universal and often-extensive use of relationship by birth (kinship) in the constitution of human social orders. Notwithstanding the claims of a few contemporary skeptics (Needham 1971; Kuper 1982, Schneider 1972, 1984), progress in this area has been substantial, especially since clarification, around the turn of the century, "of the old confusion between kinship and descent" (Goodenough 1970:45; C. Harris 1990:22) or, in other words, between the genealogical relations of persons one to another and the allocation of persons to social groups or categories on the basis of their parentage or ancestry. Our understanding of this latter domain, of "descent," is still, however, more than a little untidy, and it continues to be a subject of much, often more heated than illuminating, discussion and controversy.

Since the late 1950s that discussion has focused from time to time on the questions of how best to define the categories "descent" and "descent groups," but there has been little progress toward a consensus. Indeed, some writers (e.g., Kuper 1982) have suggested that this whole area of inquiry, debate, and discussion is deeply flawed and should be abandoned altogether. That course of action is, however, no more necessary than it is possible—if, that is, we intend to continue to practice social anthropology. We cannot in good conscience turn our backs on the practices of our subjects who persist in organizing themselves into groups that are either wholly or in part genealogically constituted and that vary greatly in other aspects of structure and function. Nor can we in good conscience turn our backs on or routinely belittle the very substantial ethnographic and conceptual contributions of our predecessors. However much we may find fault with their general theoretical orientations, many of the projects they began can be brought to greater fruition.

The predominant tendency on the part of the critics (e.g., Schneider 1965, Dumont 1971, Holy 1976, 1996, Kuper 1982) has been to identify the root of the problem as the theoretical orientation known as structural-functionalism, which dominated social anthropology from the 1930s through the 1960s, and to call into question not only a number of empirical generalizations but also much of the ethnographic data produced under its influence. For all the attention and acclaim that polemic has drawn, its arrows have fallen rather wide of the mark. The principal impediments to progress in studies of descent, so-called, although certainly theoretical, are much more limited in scope. They have no special connection to structural-functional theory and their resolution is not tied to any of the various theoretical schools that now compete for anthropological attention and acclaim. They are simple conceptual inadequacies, but the damage they have done has been extraordinarily broad and deep and difficult to perceive as such.

One of those conceptual difficulties was identified by Meyer Fortes in 1959 as conflation, under the single term *descent* (or, in French, *filiation*), of the relation of child to parent per se and the relation of the person to his or her preparental antecedents or ancestors. This conflation, Fortes thought, was at the root of a number of disagreements about matters of ethnographic fact and empirical generalization. As a necessary step toward resolution of those disagreements, he proposed to designate the relation of child to parent per se as *filiation* and the relation of the person to his or her preparental antecedents or ancestors as *descent*. Doing that permitted him to argue that, logically and empirically, relations of descent can have jural or structural values only if either patrilineal or matrilineal and only in the constitution of groups and intergroup relations. Therefore, he proposed to reserve the designation *descent group* to describe only unilineally constituted (patrilineal or matrilineal) groups. Although often challenged, the argument is, I try to show herein, wholly sound.

A subsidiary difficulty, one made more readily noticeable by Fortes's introduction of *filiation* into our working vocabulary, is the practice of using the expressions *patrilineal* and *matrilineal* principally to describe any mode of allocation of social status, if from or through father to child or from or through mother to child. That usage is troublesome because there are three ways in which a kind of filial relation may be relevant to acquisition of a status (or, what is significantly different, of one similar to it) that is held by the parent. A kind of filial relation may be either

1. the necessary and sufficient condition, or
2. a necessary but not sufficient condition, or
3. a sufficient but not necessary condition for acquisition of that status.

Also, the relevant relation may be either

1. simple filiation without regard to the sex of the parent, or
2. patrifiliation, the relation of child to father per se, or
3. matrifiliation, the relation of child to mother per se.

Therefore, if we describe as a rule of filiation any rule that makes acquisition of a status contingent on a relation of filiation, the number of logically possible kinds of such rule is nine. The conventional terminology makes allowance for only two, the so-called patrilineal and matrilineal. That deficiency has been a potent source of descriptive imprecision, theoretical confusion, and much too often of not only profitless but also largely destructive controversy.

Consider by way of example the possibility that the set of groups described as patrilineal descent groups in the ethnographic literature includes not only one but at least three different kinds of groups, each differentiable from the others by the way in which patrifiliation is a condition for inclusion in a group. If it can be shown that those different kinds of rules of filiation and affiliation do exist and do have systematically different implications for the internal structures and the external relations of the groups they constitute, it can be shown also that any attempt to generalize across the board about such groups as equally patrilineal descent groups is bound to prove unproductive, and the consequences for anthropological theory of persisting to describe all such groups as patrilineal and as descent groups are bound to be wholly negative.

For many years, however, we anthropologists have been doing just that. We have been trying to use generalizations derived from the study of various but mostly a few African societies, wherein patrifiliation is the necessary and sufficient condition for inclusion in a group, to facilitate our understanding of what we take to be groups basically of the same kind in various other societies in the Pacific, South Asia, China, and so on. Yet the relevant ethnographic reports often contain many indications that in those other societies patrifiliation is either a merely necessary or a merely sufficient condition for inclusion in certain groups. Expectably, it has been a rather consistent finding that "Africa-derived models" of "patrilineal descent systems" are "inadequate" or "misleading" for purposes of cross-cultural comparison. Moreover, many observers (e.g., Buchler and Selby 1968:69ff.; Keesing 1975:58–59; Pasternak 1985) have concluded that the "failure" or "inadequacy" of "African models" in relation to "patrilineal descent systems" outside Africa must imply that those models are equally inadequate or misleading as representations of those African "descent systems" that were the prototypes for those models to begin with. As a consequence, there has been much reanalysis and rejection of the most relevant and influential African ethnographies such as those of Evans-Pritchard (1940, 1951) on the Nuer of the Sudan and of Fortes

(1945, 1949) on the Tallensi of Ghana, and also of the theoretical writings of so-called descent theorists and their intellectual predecessors. The upshot has been something rather less than progressive growth of theory and consequent refinement and enrichment of ethnographic understanding. Indeed, the self-inflicted incapacity to attain such goals is now sometimes lauded as a positive achievement of an interpretative or symbolic, or post-modern, rather than a scientific (realist) anthropology.

One purpose of this study is to re-establish the good sense of much that has been criticized and rejected under the name of descent or lineage theory. It is not, I want to stress, intended as a "critique" of (cf. Masquelier 1993:443), or as a contribution to, or an attempt to refine and salvage so-called descent or lineage theory. That theory is, or so it seems to me, a double fabrication on the part of its critics (mainly Schneider 1965; Dumont 1971). It is a loose aggregation of concepts and generalizations, not only assembled by but often also made up by one or another critic and then reiterated uncritically, third- or fourth-hand, by many others. It is, therefore, not a theory to which a contribution can be made. As Fortes (1969:280) once remarked in response to one of his critics (Schneider 1965), it is not a matter of defending a theory, or, worse yet, of defending anything so absurdly antithetical to sociological thought as a model of a type of society holistically defined; our real goal must be "analytical rigor" in structural analysis and comparison. That goal will be facilitated by distinguishing between relations of filiation and relations of descent, between the various ways in which a relation of filiation may be a condition for acquisition of a social status, and by describing as descent groups only those groups for inclusion in which patrifiliation or matrifiliation is the necessary and sufficient condition.

It has been argued (Schneider 1965:75) that it is not only useless, but also misleading and downright harmful, to suggest that significant sociological problems can be resolved by the word-magic of definitional fiat. Surely, though, it is by changing or clarifying definitions that we draw attention to structurally significant similarities or differences that have gone unnoticed or the implications of which have yet to be fully appreciated. In so doing we sometimes manage to resolve spurious conceptual and descriptive difficulties that stand in the way of intellectual progress in a field. In order to show why Fortes proposed to define "descent" and "descent groups" as he did, it is necessary first to undertake a critical review of W.H.R. Rivers's highly influential attempt, beginning in the early 1900s, to establish a uniform terminology for the description of genealogically ordered social conditions and processes. Any such proposal has a theoretical foundation or presuppositional basis, and it is arguable that the basis of Rivers's proposal is deeply flawed. Rivers must be dealt with here not only because he is still sometimes cited as the authority for the proper uses of *descent, descent group,* and some other widely used technical terms, but also because his and Fortes's proposals are often confused with one another although they are in fact quite different, and, finally, because some of the commonsensical assumptions underlying his proposals are at the root of many of our contemporary theoretical difficulties.

All of that is the subject matter of Chapters 1 and 2, the intention of which is not merely to settle a terminological or semantic dispute. Such disputes are frivolous and uninteresting except insofar as they are matters of disagreement about what is likely to be the more productive research strategy in a particular area of inquiry. The purpose of Chapters 1 and 2 is to advance our comprehension of the structural and functional similarities and differences between widely diverse modes of group organization. To do that it is necessary, as George Appell (1974) has already pointed out, to pay rather more attention than we have in the past to the jural, as well as to the "kinship," dimensions of group structure; and, as Fortes always stressed (see also Goody 1990), to the larger-scale political and economic features of the societies in which the groups occur. The conceptual work that is necessary, or at least at this point seemingly useful, for more effective treatment of the jural dimensions, is done in Chapters 3 and 4. Chapter 3 also spells out in the abstract the apparent structural implications of the various kinds of rule of filiation and affiliation for various features of intra- and intergroup relations.

The second part of this study brings the largely abstract argument of the first part to bear on the reinterpretation of a number of forms of group organization, all of which have been the focus of much theoretical controversy. It would be impossible though, without going on at tedious length, to exhaust the relevant empirical permutations and sociological ramifications of the reorientation of perspective being worked out in these pages. So, what is offered here is by no means an exhaustive treatment, but is only a preliminary account of what might be done along these lines.

SOME COMMENTS ON THE TYPOGRAPHICAL CONVENTIONS USED HEREIN

All expressions from languages other than English are italicized on their first use but not thereafter. English expressions also are italicized either for emphasis or where the reference is to the expression itself, rather than to a (notice that I do not say *the*) category it designates. When an English expression is used as a gloss for an expression from another language, it is placed between single quotation marks. A category designated by an expression is represented by that expression placed between double quotation marks. All of this is by way of being careful to make due allowance for the possibilities of polysemy (one expression having two or more related meanings, one derivable from another) and metaphor, and not incidentally to rule them out with careless prose. In much writing about descent and descent groups, as in much writing about kinship and many other things, the expressions *term* and *category* are used more or less interchangeably, and the reader is constantly confronted with remarks about "the category X" or "the meaning of the category X" such that, even if the possibility of polysemy is acknowledged by the author, its presence is difficult to perceive and even more difficult to describe (for a particularly egregious example of this error see Needham 1975 on "the category descent").

ACKNOWLEDGMENTS

Portions of this study first appeared in articles in *Man* and the *American Anthropologist* (Scheffler 1985, 1986). Over the years since I first published on the subject of descent (Scheffler 1962), I have benefited from the generous advice, commentary, and encouragement of numerous teachers, colleagues, and students; among them Fred Eggan, W. E. H. Stanner, John A. Barnes, Meyer Fortes, J. D. Freeman, Floyd Lounsbury, Michael G. Smith, Michael Allen, Jeremy Beckett, Les Hiatt, William Kelly, Roger Keesing, Keith Basso, George Appell, Andrew Strathern, Warren Shapiro, Morris Foster, John Cinnamon, Dorothea Schulz, and Jan Simpson.

Harold W. Scheffler

PART ONE

General Considerations

1

KINSHIP AND DESCENT

I

Genealogical connection or relationship by birth, although variously conceptualized (Malinowski 1963, Scheffler 1974), is a structural element in
all human social orders. It varies also in the ways and in the degrees to
which it pervades those orders. Because those ways and degrees have
had gradually to be discovered and differentiated one from another
through the use and adaptation of (Western) concepts and terminology
sometimes alien to them, conceptualizing this diversity has presented a
major challenge to anthropology, and it has been a major arena of theoretical disputation.[1] W.H.R. Rivers's contribution, in various publications between 1907 and his posthumous *Social Organization* (1924), has been
highly influential, perhaps because in some ways it does not depart
greatly from ordinary English usage of the key terms *kinship, relationship,
descent, inheritance,* and *succession*. Indeed, in the past several decades
Rivers has been widely cited as the authority for a distinction between
"kinship" and "descent" which, it is sometimes said, substantially ad-
vanced sociological analysis and comparison. Rivers himself did not explicate the rationale behind his proposals, so it has to be deduced from
some things he did say. When that is done it will be seen why his proposals have not achieved universal acceptance, and we will be led to a rather
different conceptualization of the social phenomena Rivers was trying to
understand and to represent.

II

Rivers was, by philosophical inclination, something of a positivist. He appears to have believed that progress in any science depends on clear, consistent, and unambiguous use of its key terms. He was especially troubled

by what he saw as vague, divergent, conflicting, uninformed and all too casual uses of *kinship, relationship, descent, inheritance,* and *succession.* As a solution, he proposed to use each of these terms in one and only one way.

Beginning, it seems, with a decision to distinguish between social states or conditions and social processes, Rivers (1924:85–88) proposed to speak of the condition of two persons being related by birth (as they themselves see it, of course) as *kinship.* He proposed to use *relationship* as a more general term, to encompass also the condition of being related by marriage. *Descent* he proposed to use in contrast with *transmission,* each to designate a kind of "social process." He defined "descent" as "the process by which a person becomes a member of a group [or category or class], either through the father or the mother." He did not define "transmission" itself, but he did say there are two kinds of it, "inheritance" and "succession." By *inheritance* he designated the process wherein one person acquires the property of another when that other person dies. By *succession* he designated the process wherein one person takes the place of another as the incumbent of an office or as the holder of a title or a rank, again when the other person dies or retires. Rivers proposed to describe these various processes as *patrilineal* where the legally relevant genealogical relationship is that of a person to his or her father and as *matrilineal* where it is that of a person to his or her mother (or mother's brother).

To understand why Rivers proposed to use those expressions in those ways, it is best to begin with *descent.* In nineteenth century anthropological and legal writings, descent was widely (though not exclusively) used in its most general ordinary English sense of "downward movement" to speak about the allocation, on the basis of genealogical connection, of social positions and their associated rights and duties. Virtually all such positions were represented as descending "from one generation to the next" or as being transmitted from one person to another, as from parent to child.[2] *Descent* and *transmission* were often used more or less synonymously. Also, many writers were given to making statements like "Among the Nuer descent [or kinship, etc.] is strictly patrilineal," statements that Rivers thought were hopelessly vague and uninformative, if not also seriously inaccurate. Taken out of context, and often even in context, it was not clear what they were intended to mean or even what they could mean. Moreover, and this was a point Rivers wished to stress, such statements tended to imply that in a particular society virtually all social positions allocated on the basis of genealogical connection come down, as it were, to a person from or through his or her father, or mother if it were said "descent is strictly matrilineal." As Rivers saw it, the ethnographic evidence is all to the contrary. In any society some kinds of social position are acquired "from or through the father" and other kinds are acquired "from or through the mother." Further still, it is questionable that there is any value or sociological good sense in saying about many kinds of social position or status either that they descend or that they are transmitted, and certainly not that they do so patrilineally or matrilineally.

There is, for instance, as Rivers (1924:86) observed, "little sense" in saying about persons' statuses as kin or as specific kinds of kin of other persons that they descend to or that they are transmitted to them. As each person is born he or she becomes a kinsman and a particular kind of kinsman of each of many other persons; but those identities are not transmitted (or transferred) to the person from or through any other person, nor may they be said to descend to him or her from or through any other person. The point will be obvious enough from one simple example.

John, let us say, is the father of Sam and as such has certain rights and duties in relation to Sam. In turn, Sam has a son, Mark, and as the father of Mark has rights and duties in relation to him that are similar to (indeed, identical in kind to) those John has in relation to Sam. We could say, speaking very loosely, that the status "father" and its associated rights and duties descended or came down from one generation to the next, but that could be only a way of saying that a kind of social position present in one generation is present also in the next generation. That is to say, the social order, insofar as it is made up of certain statuses and the rights and duties associated with them, does not (in this example) change from one generation to the next but has a certain intergenerational continuity. But it would be absurd to suggest that this continuity is maintained patrilineally. Sam's position as a father, which is in relation to Mark, does not descend or come down to him from or through his father, John, for John's status as a father is strictly in relation to Sam, and not in relation to Mark (of whom John is a grandfather). Sam's status as a father (specifically the father of Mark) did not exist until Sam begot Mark, so it could not come down to him either from or through anyone.

That is not to say that it is not possible for a person's identity as a particular kind of relative and its associated rights and duties to be transmitted, as it were, to another person. Succession to some kinship statuses is possible in some societies (see e.g., Fortes 1969:173–175; Cunnison 1956). By and large, however, such statuses do routinely die, as it were, with their bearers and, therefore, it was quite reasonable for Rivers to object to saying about them that they descend or that they are transmitted. As he saw it, such talk tends to conflate several quite different kinds of "social process."

Also, Rivers appears to have perceived that not all rights that may be said to descend from one generation to the next may be said also to be transmitted from one person to another. It seems clear enough from his definitions of "inheritance" and "succession" that, as he saw it, only certain kinds of right and duty are transmittable (or transferable) from one person to another. Those are rights and duties that are held exclusively by single persons and that must be relinquished by their bearers before they can be acquired by other persons. That is the process Rivers proposed to call transmission. It will be fairly obvious that, if we want to use transmission in that way only, we cannot say that the rights and duties that persons acquire when they become members of groups are transmitted to them. When a person is added to a set or group of which his or her father or mother is already a member, the status he or she acquires is not the status held by the parent but is only one that is similar (and identical in kind) to it. The father or mother retains his or her status as a member of the group and his or her rights and duties as such; the rights and duties acquired by the child are not the rights and duties of group affiliation held by the relevant parent but are, again, only similar (and identical in kind) to them.

It would seem, then, that by a process of elimination, Rivers came to use *descent* more residually than in any other way, although he gave a positive characterization of his usage. Beginning with its (over)use to designate virtually any mode of allocation of social status based on genealogical connection, he eliminated first those statuses that cannot sensibly be said to descend or to be transmitted. Then he eliminated those that may be said to be transmitted and also either inherited or succeeded to. As he saw it, that left only "the process by which a person becomes a member of a group [or a class], either through the father or the mother."

Focusing as he did on trying to establish a terminology for the description of "social processes," Rivers paid scant attention to another way in which *descent* was and still is widely used in anthropological and legal writing, as well as in ordinary English, that is to speak about ascendant genealogical connection or kinship itself (as pointed out in Forde 1963a). We say, for example, that one person descends from or is related by descent to another or that two persons are related by common descent from a third person. The Western folk concept underlying this use of descent is, of course, the idea that a person's flesh and blood are derived from the flesh and blood of his or her parents; they descend or come down to him or her from both of them and, moreover, through them from their parents and so on back. Being "related by descent" or by "common descent" is, therefore, much the same thing as being "related by blood" or "by birth," and persons who are so related are, we say, kin (or, nowadays, relatives) of one another. It is hardly unexpected, then, that in anthropological writing the phrases "relations of descent and marriage" and "relations of kinship and marriage" are often used interchangeably (see e.g., P. Bohannan 1963:58–59).

Rivers did not discuss this use of *descent* nor did he explain why we should discontinue it. Perhaps, because of his positivism, he thought it undesirable to use any scientific expression in more than one sense, even if those uses are in context readily distinguishable one from the other. He appears to have supposed that he had to make a choice between using *descent* to speak about a specific kind of social process or to speak about relations of ascendant kinship. He proposed to use it in the first way, but he said nothing about how we might then get by without using it also in the other way.

Many if not most anthropologists have found it virtually impossible to avoid using *descent* in that other way, sometimes even while endorsing Rivers's recommendation that it be used to designate "the process of becoming a member of a group, either through the father or the mother." Some of those who nowadays do claim to avoid using *descent* to speak about relations of ascendant kinship use it instead in the way that Rivers found most unsatisfactory, that is more or less synonymously with transmission and to speak about all modes of allocation of rights and duties "from one generation to the next." Those authors insist, however, that to talk about "generations" is not to talk also about genealogical connection or kinship (see e.g., Needham 1971; Parkin 1997). They say there is patrilineal descent (of rights or, as they put it, of "jural status") when a right passes from one man in one generation to another man in the succeeding generation, and that those men need not be related as father and son. They do not explain how, if those men need not be related in that way, it is appropriate to continue to talk about patrilineal descent. Also, what is the point of talking about descent or transmission of "jural status," given that, as shown above, in the vast majority of relevant kinds of instance no status, right, or duty does descend or is transmitted?

Indeed, if, as Rivers said, there is "little sense" or sociological value in saying of persons' identities as kin or as particular kinds of kin that they descend or that they are transmitted, there is equally little sense or value in saying of persons' identities as members of groups that they descend to those persons when acquired "through the father or the mother." Again, the status acquired by a person is not the status held by the parent; it is only one of the same kind. Therefore, no one's status as a member of a group is transmitted to or descends to anyone else. The status-type "member of group X" could be said to descend (from one generation to the next), but only in the sociologically trivial sense that it persists as a type over perhaps many generations.

None of this should be taken to imply that there are no social statuses that do descend, both from one person to another and from one generation to the next. They are, however, precisely those that may be said also to be transmitted from one person to another. But contrary to Rivers, although they do include all those that we may say are succeeded to, they do not include all those that we may say are inherited. Because an office or a title is (usually) an indivisible entity and is occupied by one and only one person at a time, it and the rights and duties vested in it remain intact when one person succeeds another as the incumbent of it. Thus an office, succession to which is governed genealogically, may well endure over several generations and be transmitted or descend, as it were, repeatedly from father to son (or in some other way). Much the same may be said of items of property and rights over them in some kinds of systems of inheritance. In his brief discussion of inheritance, Rivers (1924:87) did not distinguish between partible and impartible estates. In the latter, an object of property and some set of rights held in relation to it are not divisible and they pass intact to a single person. This and only this kind of inheritance is like succession to an office. In systems of partible inheritance, however, the object is divisible, and although there was originally only one owner, there may be several heirs. But what each heir acquires is not the property (fully intact) of the deceased but only some part of it. As a consequence, no heir acquires the rights held by the deceased but only rights of the same general kind. The original rights die with their bearer and are not capable of being transmitted or of descending.

It might be objected that, even in instances of impartible inheritance, the rights held by one person are not transmitted to another person but, as in instances of partible inheritance, "die" with their bearer. What the heir acquires are new rights of the same kind as were held by the deceased; they only "look like" the rights of the deceased because they have the same scope, and that is because the object of the rights remains intact. On that interpretation no status is ever transmitted from one person to another, nor does it descend from one generation to the next. Perhaps, however, we should allow for the possibility that the process may be conceived in either way. In some legal systems it may be conceived in the one way but in other legal systems in the other. In any event, most talk about statuses or rights and duties descending or being transmitted is only a vague and sometimes seriously misleading metaphor, and it is difficult to see how it could ever be made to have any genuine sociological value.

In view of these considerations, it seems fair enough to say that in choosing to use descent to designate a social process, rather than the condition of ascendant kinship, Rivers made the wrong choice. He could not reasonably expect to eliminate the practice of using the term in the second way, and using it residually to speak about "the process of becoming a member of a group, either through the father or the mother" was at best infelicitous. There is, it seems, no sociologically useful sense in which it may be said that such membership does indeed descend. Why, then, have Rivers's proposals been so often praised and endorsed?[3]

One reason is that when Rivers recommended that *descent* be used only to speak about the process of becoming a member of a social group, either "through the father or the mother," he said also "use of term is only of value when the group is unilateral . . . where . . . a child must belong to the group of the father or the mother, but cannot belong to both" (1924:86). The now orthodox interpretation is that Rivers intended to restrict *descent* to designation of the process of recruitment to membership of a group "automatically by birth," such that the person's affiliation is "permanent and involuntary," and such that the groups are nonoverlapping or mutually exclusive (Leach 1962). In other words, or so it is argued, Rivers intended to speak of descent only where it is necessary and sufficient for inclusion in a group to be a child of a male or, as the case may be, of a female member of that group. If so, it follows logically enough that Rivers intended also to exclude from the category "descent group" any group membership of which may be acquired in any other way. This latter apparent intention is the one that Leach and some other anthropologists have most strongly endorsed.

The sociological value and terminological good sense of restricting the use of *descent group* in that way has been much debated since the late 1950s, but in that debate two questions have been often confused and conflated (as in Schneider 1965:75). One is about how best to use the expression *descent group* or, in other words, how best to define the category "descent group"; the other is about how best to use *descent* itself. In effect, Rivers has been credited with resolving both questions at once. His proposal about the use of *descent* has been endorsed precisely because of its apparent association with and corollary implications for a definition of "descent group" that is alleged to have certain definite sociological merits (of which more below). There are, however, good reasons to suppose that Rivers did not intend to restrict use of *descent* to designation of the process of becoming a member of a group "automatically by birth," such that affiliation is involuntary, permanent, and irrevocable, and such that the groups are mutually exclusive.

When Rivers (1924:86) stipulated "use of the term [descent] is only of value when the group is unilateral," he went on immediately to observe that "use of the term has little sense, and consequently little value, in the case of [the kind of] bilateral grouping" that he proposed to call a "kindred," that is the category consisting of the totality of any specified person's relatives by birth (or kin). This shows that his first purpose was merely to stress again that the condition of being "of kin" to someone, or of being included in that person's kindred, is not a condition that is transmitted or that descends. To make his point, Rivers chose to contrast "unilateral groups" with "bilateral groups" or "groupings," but that was an unfortunate choice. From Rivers's perspective, the reason why there is "little sense" in speaking of descent in relation to a kindred is not that this is a bilaterally, rather than a unilaterally, constituted category, but that the statuses (and rights and duties) of persons as kin of one another do not descend and are not transmitted from one person to another (at least not usually).

Also, when Rivers (1924:86) said of "clans" and "moieties" that these are the groups to which descent "applies most definitely" because "a child must belong to the group of the father or mother, but cannot belong to both," the reason he gave for why the child cannot belong to both is "the principle of exogamy." That is, the two parents must belong to two different groups because the men and women of any one group are forbidden to intermarry. From this it follows that (by the rules at least) a person cannot belong to any one exogamous group of which his father and his mother are both members; but it does not follow that he cannot be included in two groups of the same kind, exogamous or not, of one of which his father is a member and of the other of which his mother is a member. Rivers did not distinguish between these two kinds of situation, perhaps because he was not aware that exemplars of the latter kind do exist.

Leach (1962:131) says, but cites no evidence to show, that Rivers was well aware that there are many societies in which there are overlapping (not mutually exclusive) and named sets of kin, or kin groups, to membership of which persons are recruited either "wholly or in part" through their fathers or their mothers. It seems more likely, though, that what Rivers was aware of was that rules of descent (in his sense) had been confused also with rules of post-marital residence. As a consequence, local groups whose male members are by and large related one to another through their fathers—because when men marry they bring their wives to live with them and their fathers—had been conflated terminologically, as patrilineal descent groups, with groups constituted by the rule that being the child of a male member is the necessary and sufficient condition for inclusion. It would be sociologically frivolous to say that membership of such a local group descends from father to son; and, certainly, Rivers would not have said its "male members are recruited largely by means of patrilineal descent" (as per Barnard and Good 1984:77, following Needham 1971:11; also Gottlieb 1986:698). To put it that way is to confuse "recruited" with "related" and to use *descent* to speak of the relation of child to father per se—and Rivers specifically wanted to avoid using the term in that way.

Even more telling are two other examples Rivers gave of contexts in which descent "has a definite meaning, and is useful." These are "the joint family" and "the simple family" (1924:86). As an instance of the latter Rivers cited "our own family system." This, he said, "might be regarded as an example of patrilineal descent, in that we take the name of the father; though it is hardly customary to use the term [descent] in this case."

Surely, Rivers was aware that, although in the first instance or at birth, each person does "automatically" take or is assigned the surname of his or her father (if "legitimate"), there are other ways in which such names may legally be acquired. Most notable of course is that on marriage women routinely take (or used to take) their husbands' family names. Also, a person may legally (or even informally) change his or her surname and to virtually any other name he or she chooses. (One of Rivers's students, A. R. Brown, informally changed his name to A. R. Radcliffe-Brown.) In other words, being the (legitimate) child of a man with a particular surname is a sufficient condition for acquisition of that name, but it is not also a necessary condition. In Rivers's terminology, a surname is not transmitted from father to child, for the father continues to bear the name and shares it with the child. Therefore, Rivers had to say that family names descend and that they do so patrilineally; but, plainly, he did not intend to say that descent is the only way a family name may be acquired.

The joint families, so called, of India and China are in some ways analogous. Women born into such families must marry out of them and become members of the families of which their husbands' (or their husbands' fathers) are the heads. But the men born into them remain for life (or at least until partition of the family estates) members of them. Therefore, although membership is "automatic by birth," it is not "permanent and involuntary" (Leach 1962:131). Being the child of a male member of a group is a sufficient condition, but it is not a necessary condition, for inclusion in that group. Even so, Rivers said descent "has a definite meaning and is useful" in this context. It may be that he said that because of the nature of ownership of, and of re-allocation of interests in so-called ancestral property, which interests cannot be said (at least not in Rivers's terminology) to be transmitted from father to son or inherited by a man from his father. In those families each son acquires at birth an undivided interest (equal to that of any other son) in certain assets (especially land) held individually or jointly by his father; he thus becomes a co-owner along with his father (and his brothers, if any) of those assets. When the father dies, or before that if he agrees, those assets are divisible equally between the sons. In many ethnographic accounts of Indian and Chinese joint-family organization, the sons are said to inherit or to succeed to the property when it is divided. But in Rivers's terminology (and as Indian jurists see it [Diwan 1978:149; Aiyar 1953:324–325]), the property is not inherited but is simply divided or allocated into definite shares. There is no inheritance here because (by definition) no one can inherit that which he already owns, which in this instance is an undivided interest in a kind of family estate. Moreover, because ownership is a condition that a man may share with his father, Rivers had little choice but to say that it descends and does so patrilineally.

III

Of course, what Rivers intended to signify by *descent* is not the basic issue here. What matters sociologically is not what Rivers said or thought but what he was trying to elucidate or uncover, namely, some of the dimensions of structural similarity and difference between, as he put it, various social conditions and processes, especially insofar as they are "determined" or regulated by considerations of relationship by birth or genealogical connection. In the process of discussing his terminology, we have uncovered several ways in which his perception of those dimensions was, if not mistaken, at least rather limited and inadequate. We have seen, for one thing, that having chosen to use *descent* to designate a kind of social process, he thought he could not use it also to designate the kind of genealogical relationship that figures in the rules that regulate that process. To do the latter job he used *patrilineal* and *matrilineal*, and he used them not only to qualify *descent* but also *inheritance* and *succession*, and even to qualify *kinship* or *relationship*, where two persons are related solely through males (fathers) or solely through females (mothers). As Rivers used them, *patrilineal* and *matrilineal* were equivalent in meaning to "relationship to or through fathers" and "relationship to or through mothers." Many anthropologists still use those expressions in those ways, but the consequences for ethnographic description and anthropological theory have been unfortunate at best.

A few writers have expressed dissatisfaction with Rivers's and others' rather indiscriminate use of *patrilineal* and *matrilineal*. Dumont (1957a:4), for example, proposed to use them only in conjunction with *descent*, and to use *descent* only with reference to "transmission of membership of the exogamous group." He proposed to speak of inheritance and succession "as being from father to son" or whatever. Dumont offered no reasons for his terminological preferences, but they are endorsed by Barnard and Good (1984:69), who say about them only that it is desirable to be terminologically precise. Even so, they then go on to follow Needham (1971) in using *patrilineal* and *matrilineal* as two of six terms by which to designate the various "possible avenues for the transmission of descent group membership, *or anything else*, from parents to children" (Barnard and Good 1984:70; emphasis added; "parents to children" is their phrasing, not Needham's). Fox (1967 [1983:47]) has said that *patrilineal, matrilineal,* and *unilineal* "really mean," not "using only one 'line' (male or female) in tracing kinship for some purpose," but "unisexual linkage" or computing relationship for some specified social purpose only through the male parent or only through the female parent. Goodenough (1970:53) makes a similar observation. But perhaps because Fox and Goodenough were focusing on the use of those terms in conjunction with *descent group* they did not notice that in many other kinds of context it is not appropriate to use them precisely because it is not a "line" of male parents (fathers) or a "line" of female parents (mothers) that is the critical desideratum. As Dumont appears to have perceived, in by far the vast majority of rules of inheritance, and in all rules of succession, the criterial relation is merely that of child to father or mother per se; and, patently, there is little to be gained by describing that relation as lineal. This appears to be the rationale behind P. Bohannan's (1963:59, 132) preference for use of *patrilineal* and *matrilineal* only in reference to unilineal descent groups, wherein "from any contemporary member, the line back to the founding ancestor is through a line of fathers or a line of mothers," and his observation that otherwise use of *patrilineal* or *matrilineal* is inappropriate "because the emphasis on lineality obscures the point."

The reason why such usage tends to "obscure the point" is this: To talk about patrilineal descent or transmission of something is to imply that it passes, not merely from a man to his child, but that it does that repeatedly so that eventually it is held not only by the first man's child but also by his son's child, his son's son's child, and so on. We have seen already, however, that most kinds of status cannot properly be said to do any such thing. Even in those few kinds of context in which it is appropriate to talk about the descent or the transmission of social statuses and their associated rights and duties, it is definitely not appropriate to talk about them descending patrilineally or matrilineally (see below).

There is a further difficulty for Rivers's use of patrilineal and matrilineal, even if restricted as per Dumont to description of rules of group affiliation. As pointed out by Goodenough (1970:53), parental sex may be only one among a number of different considerations relevant to inclusion in a group or, we may add, to acquisition of various other kinds of social status. Also, there are various ways in which parental sex itself may be a relevant consideration. It can be one among several considerations relevant to acquisition of a status such as "member of group X" only where being a socially acknowledged child of a male or, alternatively, of a female member is something other than the necessary and sufficient condition for inclusion in the group.

The logical possibilities are only three. Either a kind of filial relationship is necessary and sufficient, or it is necessary but not also sufficient, or it is sufficient but not also necessary. Also, the relevant relation may be either patrifiliation, matrifiliation, or simple filiation (without regard to the parent's sex).[4] It follows that the number of logical possibilities here is nine, and not only the conventionally recognized two, patrilineal and matrilineal. If these nine kinds of rules of allocation of status can be shown to have systematically different implications for other features of social structure, it follows also that glossing over the differences between them must have impeded rather than facilitated sociological analysis and comparison and must have given rise to spurious ethnographic and theoretical issues.

In discussing these nine logically possible kinds of rule and their social-structural correlates, it will be useful to have a common name for them. Certainly, it will not do to name them after a presumed common function, as it were, and to call them all rules of descent (of statuses or whatever). We have seen that it is only when describing a possible consequence of a rule of succession to an office or of impartible inheritance that it may be appropriate to speak of a right as descending or as being transmitted. We might, however, choose to use descent in the other ("ascending kinship") sense and to describe all nine rules as descent rules, on the supposition that each of them makes acquisition of a status contingent in some way on a relation of descent. If we do that we must then ask: Which if any should we call rules of patrilineal or of matrilineal descent? Also, what specific kinds of rule of descent are we to say the others are?

The answer to the first question must be that it would not be appropriate to describe any of those rules as a rule of patrilineal or of matrilineal descent. The reason, again, is that the *lineal* element implies that it is not simply relationship to one's father or mother but relationship through him or her and to one's father's father or mother's mother that is criterial. It implies that acquisition of something is contingent not only on a child/parent relation but also on a grandchild/grandparent relation. But none of the nine rules makes acquisition of anything contingent on such a relation, not even indirectly. Whether or not such a relation is implicated, even indirectly, is contingent not on the form of the rule alone but on that form in combination with a quality of the social condition that the rule governs.

If all that is accepted, it is difficult to see how any of the nine kinds of rule can be described as rules of descent. Indeed, it seems that the concept "rule of descent" or "descent rule" is one that, however defined, anthropology will be better off without. It does not follow, though, that we can and should do without any concepts of "descent" and "descent group."

If *descent* is to remain at all useful in anthropology, the category it designates must be, as Fortes (1959b, 1969) argued, narrowed in its range of inclusion so as to exclude the relation of child to parent per se. It must be used, at least in discussions of genealogy and social structure, only in reference to a series of child-to-parent relations, minimally the relation of a person to his or her parent's parents. To use it in that way would not be at odds with ordinary English usage, for the expression has always been potentially ambiguous in yet another way in ordinary and legal and anthropological usage. In some contexts of use it signals "ascendant kinship" in general, such that anyone's "relatives by descent" include his or her parents and their parents and so on back *ad infinitum,* all of whom are counted as his or her "ancestors." In other contexts, it excludes one's parents so that his or her "ancestral kin" include only his or her preparental and so-called lineal (as against collateral) antecedents. Noticing this, Fortes (1959b) suggested that it would clear up a number of anthropological muddles if we were to use *descent* only in the latter, somewhat more narrow sense.

Following that recommendation, we say here that one person is descended from another if and only if, minimally, he or she is a child's child of the other. The minimal "common descent" relation is the genealogical relation between two persons who have an ancestor (minimally, a parent's parent) in common. Also following Fortes, we adopt the expression *filiation* (from the Latin *filius* 'child') to designate the relation of child to parent per se.[5] For the relation of child to father per se, instead of the trouble-prone patrilineal descent we use patrifiliation, and for the relation of child to mother per se we use matrifiliation. We can then describe the nine kinds of rule mentioned above as rules of filiation because each of them makes acquisition of a status contingent on a relation of filiation.

In line with these recommendations, we notice that the closest relations of common descent are those of first cousins (who are second-degree collaterals), who do indeed have a parent's parent in common. One implication of this decision is that we do not count the relation of, say, mother's brother to sister's child as one of common matrilineal descent, or that of father's brother (or sister) to brother's child as one of patrilineal descent, and so on for any first-degree collateral relationship, the reason being that in each instance the apical linking relative is a parent (not an ancestor) of the genealogically senior party. Of course, any two persons who happen to be related as, say, mother's brother and sister's child will always have a common maternal ancestress (in the mother's mother of the mother's brother) and that fact may become an important desideratum in social relations between them. In that event, however, the situationally relevant relationship would not be that of mother's brother to sister's child, but a much more general relationship that would implicate also all other living descendants of the designated ancestress. Fortes may not have intended to argue otherwise when he said that in a society with matrilineal descent groups a man's rights and duties in relation to his sister's child "are based on the principle of descent" (1959b [1970:104]). The context of the remark makes it fairly clear that he was merely asserting that the mother's brother/sister's child relationship would inevitably have different jural, moral, and affective content in the presence of matrilineal descent groups than in the presence of patrilineal descent groups or no descent groups at all.

Various advantages of this conceptualization are developed here and there throughout this study. At this point, we may notice, once again, that in some contexts a right acquired by one person as a child of another may plausibly be described as the right held by the parent (rather than as a right of the same kind). That is where the right is one vested in an office or is to personal property in a system of impartible inheritance. It can happen, however, only on the condition that being a child of the bearer is necessary but not sufficient for acquisition of the right. If the rule were that being a child of the bearer of a right is necessary and sufficient for acquisition of that right (or of one similar to it), there might be several children and each would qualify as an heir. That would entail the necessity of one or the other of two arrangements. One is that the property-object is partible so that each heir acquires a portion of it and a property right similar to that held by the deceased. The other is that the property-object is kept intact and each heir is given some kind of right of co-ownership, and that would be a right different in kind from the right held by the deceased. If the rule were that being a child of the bearer is sufficient but not necessary, the consequences would be much the same except that persons other than children of the deceased also could acquire rights. Therefore, rules of succession and rules of impartible inheritance must be rules of filiation of the "necessary but not sufficient" kind.

If the rule specifies also that it is necessary to be a male and the eldest surviving child of the bearer in order to acquire the right, Rivers would have said that the right is transmitted and that it is patrilineally inherited or succeeded to; others would have said also that it descends patrilineally. There is nothing intrinsically wrong about talk of that kind, but it must be understood as a manner of speaking from an historical, rather than from a legal or, as Fortes often put it, a structural or jural perspective. An example will clarify the point.

Suppose that John is the incumbent of an office; he is the King of Zor. The rule of succession in Zor is that the king's eldest son becomes king when the incumbent dies or chooses to retire. As it happens, Sam is John's eldest son and eventually does succeed to the office. In turn Mark is Sam's eldest son and, eventually, he becomes King of Zor. Historically speaking, it would be at least somewhat appropriate to say that the kingship has descended patrilineally, from one man to his son and then to his grandson. That it has done so may be a matter of some pride to Mark and to his subjects who may accord him great prestige, not only as their king but also as a patrilineal descendant of a long line of illustrious rulers. From a strictly legal perspective, though, the fact that Mark is a patrilineal descendant of John and of all former kings of Zor is beside the point. He has to be that, because it is a logical implication of the rule of succession that he will be that.[6] Although we might, in ordinary English, say that he is a descendant, he is not a patrilineal descendant of Sam, his own father, and what is legally at issue in any instance of succession is simply who is the eldest living son of the immediately deceased incumbent of the office. If being a patrilineal descendant of John had any legal bearing on succession, Mark would have had no distinctive claim to succeed his own father, unless by accident he happened to be the only surviving patrilineal descendant of John at the time the succession opened. Otherwise, he would have had to compete for the office with other patrilineal descendants of John and, for that matter, with other patrilineal descendants of even earlier incumbents of the office.[7]

In short, Rivers's way of speaking and writing about succession and inheritance confounds historical and structural or legal considerations. What he needed was a terminology for description and comparison of rules or principles, and of elements of them, that govern the allocation or distribution and redistribution of statuses and their associated rights and duties. What he concocted was a terminology for description and comparison of some social conditions and some social processes, a terminology that in some ways at least is more suited to description of possible (but not inevitable) historical consequences of repeated application of certain kinds of rule of allocation. And even for that purpose it is rather misleading. It is difficult to see what special sociological value there is in saying of persons' identities as members of groups that they descend, or in saying of property rights in general that they are transmitted, for rights in partible property must die with their bearers.

Having established that there is little point in trying to restrict our use of descent to designation of any kind of "social process," be it broadly or narrowly defined, and also the distinction between relations of descent and relations of filiation, we may now consider, in Chapter 2, the implications for our talk about descent groups. First, it is necessary to add some remarks on the concept of "filiation" itself.

IV

So far, "filiation" has been treated as an unproblematic concept, defined simply as "the relationship of child to parent per se." Yet, as attested by the lengthy relevant discussions by Fortes (1969:250ff.), Goodenough (1970:20ff), and many others, "parent" is hardly an unproblematic concept in anthropology. How best to define it, and "kinship" more generally, for purposes of cross-cultural comparison has been a major cause of disagreement for many decades. It is fortunate that, for our purposes here, it is not necessary to review and evaluate the issues and positions. It will be sufficient to notice, as Evans-Pritchard (1945:19) did in discussing "paternity" among the Nuer, that societies may and often do "recognize" different "degrees" (or kinds) of paternity, and also of maternity, each in different kinds of social context and for different kinds of social purpose. Thus,

what counts as paternity and as patrifiliation for the purpose of group affiliation may vary from one society to another, though only within a fairly
narrow range. Indeed, setting aside the minor complications introduced
by the possibilities of adoption and fosterage, there are only two main
possibilities: the relevant relationship is almost always either that of the
child to his or her de facto genitor or that of the child to his or her de jure
genitor, the latter being the man whose right it is to beget offspring by the
child's mother. Societies differ, again within a fairly narrow range, in
what may be done when these identities belong to different men.

In many if not most societies, being married to a woman at the time she
may be presumed to have become pregnant is evidence of paternity of
her child, at least for certain social purposes such as (although not invariably) determination of the child's group affiliation. That evidence may be,
however, either disputable or conclusive. Where it is disputable—as it is
among the Yakö and other peoples in Nigeria (Forde 1950) and the Lozi
and other peoples of Central Africa (Gluckman 1950)—the de facto genitor of a child born to a woman married to another man may claim the
child as his own and it may become affiliated with some group by right of
being his child. In these instances the de facto genitor does not have to
"legitimate" his child by payment of a fee; and it would be nonsensical to
argue that he is the de jure genitor merely because he is the de facto genitor. He has, of course, to go to the trouble publicly to assert and to show
that he is the genitor. Although he may establish rights and duties in relation to his offspring and make it kin of his kin, the de facto genitor does
not become a de jure genitor, because he begot his child without having a
right to do so, yet even so he may be spoken of as the child's father. The
right to beget offspring by the mother belongs to the mother's husband,
but it does not guarantee him exclusive claim to the designation 'father'
in relation to any of her children. Neither does being the de facto genitor.
Among the Lozi at least, and perhaps among the Yakö as well, a child
claimed by a de facto genitor remains known also as a child of the
mother's husband and his kin remain the kin of the child as well. Perhaps
not incidentally, in the ethnographic instances so far alluded to, the
groups in question are not genuine descent groups (see Chapter 7).

Among some other peoples (such as the Nuer [Evans-Pritchard 1945,
1950a, 1950b, 1951] and the Zulu [Gluckman 1950]), marriage to a woman
at the outset of her pregnancy is conclusive or nonrebuttable evidence of
paternity of her child, again at least for certain specified social purposes.
In other words, no one is permitted even to attempt to produce evidence
to the contrary. In these societies paternity is fixed by payment of
bridewealth, part of which is regarded as establishing an exclusive claim
to the woman's childbearing potential, and any child subsequently born

to her is, for certain specified social purposes at least, known as a child of the man in whose name the bridewealth was given—even though it may be common knowledge that he is not or could not be the child's genitor (e.g., he may be deceased). In other words, the bridewealth transaction establishes the mother's husband as the de jure genitor and permits no division or replication of his rights as such. It does not, however, entail that he and only he can be known socially as the child's father. As Evans-Pritchard (1945) shows in some detail for the Nuer, a de facto genitor (who is not authorized proxy for the de jure genitor) may have few if any rights in relation to his offspring, but he may still be spoken of in some situations at least as the child's 'father,' whether or not he also acts as its "foster father" (i.e., takes an active part in rearing it). Among the Nuer, then, as among the Lozi, Zulu, and the Yakö, "the role of the father . . . is often split" (Evans-Pritchard 1945:19, 21), but in different ways in each society. Among the Nuer, the different kinds of 'father' have, as Evans-Pritchard put it, different and complementary "social functions," whereas among the Lozi and Yakö the different kinds of father may have similar "social functions" or roles.

In short, the ethnographic record strongly indicates the necessity to recognize the possible existence and social significance, in one and the same society, of multiple forms of paternity or fatherhood, and no doubt of maternity or motherhood as well.[8] Where more than one form is operative, they are typically complementary. The rights and duties of an unmarried genitor may be quite limited (or, it should be stressed, quite extensive if he demands them), in comparison with and different from those of a mother's husband, and they may or may not be relevant to group affiliation. For these reasons, it seems infelicitous to attempt to define "filiation," as Fortes (1959b:206) did, as "the relationship created by the fact of being the *legitimate* child of one's parents" (emphasis added). It seems sufficient to notice that, typically, the social values of parent/child relations are held to depend (in various ways and to various degrees) on the kinds of social situations in which they were established. The relationship that counts as patri- or matrifiliation may and does vary from one society to another; it remains to be seen whether or not that variation has any relationship to or bears any import for the kind of social-structural variation that is the principal focus of this study.

NOTES

1. See Malinowski (1929, 1930) for one man's view of the nineteenth and early twentieth century debates, and Fortes (1969), Needham (1971), D. Schneider

(1984), Scheffler (1974, 1976), and Harris (1990) for some divergent views on more recent developments.

2. On the legal usage, see the entries "descend" and "descent" in *Black's Law Dictionary*, first published in 1891 (5th ed. 1983:231–232).

3. It has been noticed already by L. Dumont (1971:48–49) that A. R. Radcliffe-Brown sometimes followed and sometimes quite significantly departed from Rivers's recommendations. They are followed closely in the 1924 essay on the mother's brother/sister's child relationship, but in the 1935 essay on patrilineal and matrilineal succession, *succession* is the cover term for "transmission of rights in general" (see Radcliffe-Brown 1950:22, 32).

4. In the interest of thoroughness it must be noticed that it is at least logically possible to take into account the sex of the child as well as that of the parent, and instances of so-called parallel or cross (or alternating) descent have been reported (e.g., instances in which a son is affiliated with his father's group or category and a daughter with her mother's). Those reports are, however, rather sketchy and often difficult to comprehend, and in some instances they have been demonstrated to be mistaken. See e.g., DaMatta (1973) on "parallel descent" among the Apinaye of Brazil and McDowell (1991) on "alternating descent" among the Mundugumor of New Guinea. It seems not at all improbable that "parallel" and "alternating" forms of "descent" are wholly anthropological fictions with no genuine ethnographic exemplars.

5. As Fortes (1969: 253, n. 7) noticed, this expression is widely used in French anthropological literature and with much the same ambiguity (and pitfalls) as *descent* is in English anthropological and legal writings. For some French examples see Augé (1975:62–68). That use of *filiation* seems to be uncommon in English anthropological writings, although Malinowski (1935, I: 36) provides one example. Another usage that occasionally crops up in social anthropology is as a sort of shorthand expression for "affiliation via filiation," as when P. Bohannan (1963:80) writes of "rights to filiate children to the husband's groups"; and J. D. Freeman (1958) of "utrolateral filiation" among the Iban of Sarawak.

6. Except of course in the event of an illegal coup that would ignore the constitutional rules of the system.

7. Fortes (1969:282–283) argues, I think rather unconvincingly, that succession to the British Crown is determined first by descent ("co-lineal . . . if we must have a name for it") and that filiation "serves as a secondary principle for differentiating among the eligibles." By his own definition of "descent," the monarch's child is not one of his or her descendants, yet it is a child (preferably the eldest son) who succeeds in preference to anyone else.

8. We need not at this point, because it is not critical to the general argument of this essay, enter once again into the hoary debate about whether or not or which of the various forms of paternity or maternity is or ought to be accorded some kind of "primacy," either within particular cultural systems or within a comparative anthropology (as in Goodenough 1970). I do, however, emphatically disclaim that the argument being made here is that "the concept of paternity (or maternity) is polythetic" (compare Needham 1975 on "descent").

2

DESCENT GROUPS

I

The questions of how best to define "descent" and "descent groups" came to the fore once again in the 1950s, in part as a consequence of a great expansion of academic anthropology and of ethnographic fieldwork following World War II, especially in the Pacific, South and Southeast Asia, and Africa. Until then most discussion of "descent" and "descent groups" had taken it for granted that such groups are necessarily either patrilineal or matrilineal. But with this intensification of ethnographic research it soon became evident that in many parts of the world people do organize themselves into sets or groups of persons who claim a common ancestry, although not one that is strictly either patrilineal or matrilineal. Many writers found it fitting to describe these as descent groups or, more specifically, as lineages or clans, and, in contrast with "unilineal descent groups," as "nonunilineal (or ambilineal or ambilateral or cognatic) descent groups" (e.g., Goodenough 1955; Firth 1957, 1963; Davenport 1959). Also, by then something of a body of theory about unilineal descent groups and structured sets of them (that is, "lineage systems") was being established (Fortes 1953) and it was possible to use that theory to try to understand, by contrast and comparison, how nonunilineal descent groups are structured and operate. One difference between those two general kinds of group and systems of intergroup relations became a major focus of attention.

Lineage or descent theory, as eventually it came to be called (largely by its self-styled critics), was formulated within the more general context of "structural-functional" theory. A major goal of that theory was to account for how particular institutions or social systems, and social systems in general, are constituted and function or operate so as to maintain their general forms over long periods or at least from one generation to the next, as it were. That seemed especially easy to do for certain kinds of unilineal descent system (which we must be careful not to confuse with whole social systems or societies). Because affiliation with a patrilineal or a matrilineal descent group is "automatic by birth," fixed and immutable, and is not a matter of individual choice and decision, such groups are (in principle at least) self-perpetuating. Their continuity and the continuity or persistence of organized sets of them "from one generation to the next" seemed, therefore, not especially problematic for sociological theory.

In contrast, affiliation with a nonunilineal descent group, although perhaps in some sense "automatic by birth," is not fixed and immutable but is or can be a matter for individual choice and decision. Also, such groups are not mutually exclusive; at least they are not made mutually exclusive by the routine operation of their genealogical rules of recruitment. As a consequence, in at least some systems of them it is possible for any person to be simultaneously a member of more than one such group. That entails the possibility of competition and conflict between groups for members and their loyalties, a kind of competition and conflict that cannot exist in unilineal descent systems (which, again, should not be confused with whole social systems or societies). Assuming that system continuity or persistence is dependent on minimizing or at least closely regulating and limiting interpersonal and intergroup conflict, it was assumed also that any attempt to institute and to maintain a system of nonunilineal descent groups must in due course confront this "problem" of intergroup competition and conflict. Such competition and conflict would have to be obviated in some way or, at the least, regulated to a degree sufficient to permit the social system as a whole to persist "from one generation to the next." That, it was supposed (somewhat erroneously), could be achieved only by making the groups mutually exclusive, at least in practice if not also in principle. The sociological problem then became to show how, in each ethnographic instance, such practical mutual exclusiveness is achieved.[1]

It should not be surprising that, given this orientation, it was soon proposed that, in many ways, the two kinds of groups and systems of grouping (the unilineal and the nonunilineal) are highly similar in structure and operation. Indeed, the argument went, the nonunilineal descent groups of at least some societies are "the precise functional analog" of the unilineal descent groups of some other societies (Firth 1963). In 1959, however, Fortes argued that such talk was at best seriously misleading, and, by way of attempting to show how and why, he suggested that only unilineally constituted groups be described as descent groups. Superficially, Fortes's proposal about use of descent group is similar to the one often attributed to Rivers. As a consequence, Fortes's views on "descent" and "descent groups" are often confused with and mistaken for the views attributed to Rivers. Further, Fortes is accused of trying to revive and then to ride an intellectual dead horse, all with the implicit goal of defending, from the dubious perspective of structural-functional theory, a particular conception of a particular "type of society" holistically conceived (Schneider 1965; Scheffler 1966; Dumont 1971; again, for his response, see Fortes 1969:280ff.). But, whatever Fortes's intentions may have been, he meant by *descent* something quite different from what Rivers meant. As noted already in Chapter 1, he meant the relation of a person to his or her preparental (and lineal or direct) antecedents per se, and not "the process whereby a person becomes a member of a group, either through the father or the mother." His reasons for arguing that only unilineally constituted groups should be described as descent groups were, therefore, quite different from any that could plausibly be attributed to Rivers. To show what those reasons were and why they must be regarded as compelling, it is best to begin by examining the only other systematic perspective on "descent groups" that is based on a similar use of *descent* itself.

II

Developing a line of theory that he began in 1955, Goodenough (1970:51–67) proposed that we describe as a descent group any group for inclusion in which being a descendant (of some specified kind) of the reputed founder is a condition. He recognized two main kinds of descent group, unilineal and nonunilineal. The unilineal he divided into the patrilineal and the matrilineal, and there may be, he said, "unrestricted" and "restricted" varieties of each kind and of nonunilineal descent groups. An unrestricted patrilineal descent group includes all and only patrilineal descendants of its founder; a restricted patrilineal descent group may or must include only some patrilineal descendants of its founder and may not include any person who is not a patrilineal descendant of the founder. As Goodenough put it, an unrestricted patrilineal descent group is one that a person has both a right and a duty to be a member of, because he or she is a patrilineal descendant of its founder; a restricted patrilineal descent group is one that a person has either a right or a duty to be a member of, again because he or she is a patrilineal descendant of the founder. As Goodenough saw it, where affiliation is both a right and a duty the person has no choice with regard to group affiliation. Where affiliation is a right (but not a duty) the person may choose whether or not to be a member. Where affiliation is a duty (but not a right) the group itself does the choosing; it may demand that a person identify himself or herself as a member or, alternatively, it may refuse to concede that status to him or her.

One difficulty for this model is that it is not clear how a person could have a right and a duty, or a right, or a duty to be a member of a group.

We are dealing here with groups that are sociologically interesting only insofar as becoming included in them normally entails acquisition of certain rights and duties. Therefore, to say that a person has a duty to be a member of a group is to say also that he has a duty (of one kind) to have a duty (of another kind) or a right of some kind. Similarly, to say that a person has a right to be a member of a group is to say also that he has a right (of one kind) to have a right (of another kind) or a duty of some kind. But people do not have and, in any imaginable world, could not possibly have rights to have rights or have duties to have duties, much less have rights to have duties or have duties to have rights. They either have or do not have certain rights or duties because they are or are not persons who have the social identities (Goodenough 1965) to which those rights or duties attach. Having or not having such an identity (such as, "member of group X") may or may not be a matter of personal choice. It is, for example, not a matter of personal choice whether or not a person belongs to his or her father's group where patrifiliation is the necessary and sufficient condition for inclusion in that group. Such a rule does not entitle or oblige anyone to be a member of any group; it *stipulates* that anyone who is a child of a male member of a group is *ipso facto* also a member of that group. It follows from that condition that he or she simply *has* whatever rights and duties are entailed by being a member; not that he or she is entitled to have such rights, but that he or she may exercise them.[2]

It is possible to revise Goodenough's scheme and to differentiate between unrestricted and restricted descent groups by distinguishing between whether a kind of relation of descent is the necessary and sufficient condition, or a merely necessary condition, or a merely sufficient condition for inclusion in a group. From this altered perspective, an unrestricted patrilineal descent group is a group for inclusion in which it is necessary and sufficient to be a patrilineal descendant of the founder, for such a group includes all and only patrilineal descendants of the founder. Similarly, a restricted patrilineal descent group is one for inclusion in which it is merely necessary to be a patrilineal descendant of the founder, for such a group includes only patrilineal descendants of the founder but need not include all of them.

What about the third kind of group, for inclusion in which it is merely sufficient to be a patrilineal descendant of the founder? Goodenough did not discuss groups of this kind, or even notice that they may exist. But, given his stipulation that a group is a descent group if being a descendant (of a specified kind) of its reputed founder is a condition for inclusion in it, it would seem that they should be classified as descent groups. In practice they have been so classified by numerous ethnographers working in the highlands of New Guinea—but largely on account of failure to notice or to understand Fortes's distinction between descent and filiation.

Although something like this approach to defining "descent groups" has been advocated by various anthropologists (Schneider 1965; Scheffler 1965, 1966; Keesing 1975), there are some substantial difficulties for it. One is that it assumes that it is logically and empirically possible for a kind of relation of descent to be the necessary and sufficient, or a merely necessary, or a merely sufficient condition for inclusion in a group. That assumption has only rarely been put in those terms (cf. de Lepervanche 1968:173) and it has gone unexamined. But on close scrutiny it cannot be sustained. As Fortes perceived, for a kind of relation of descent to be a condition for inclusion in a group, a kind of relation of filiation must be logically a prior condition. That is to say, any rule of descent and affiliation must be also and more fundamentally a rule of filiation and affiliation. All rules of descent, so called, are describable more accurately as rules of filiation—but not the other way around. The reason is that not all rules of filiation jurally implicate relations of descent in the internal or external relations of the groups they constitute, however much such relations may be present between members of a group constituted by such a rule.

III

The practice of describing rules of filiation and affiliation as rules of descent has promoted the practice of describing the groups constituted by those rules as descent groups, especially if the rule is such that the group may not include anyone not "born into" it. The presumption has been, at least implicitly, that we should describe such groups as descent groups not only because they are de facto sets of persons with a common ancestor, but also because they are *constituted* as sets of persons with a common ancestor (Scheffler 1965, 1966) and relations of descent are somehow structurally significant in the internal and external relations of those groups.

Fortes (1959b) was highly skeptical. As he saw it, unless patrifiliation or matrifiliation is the necessary and sufficient condition for inclusion in one of several groups of the same kind, relations of descent cannot have any "jural values" or "structural significance," either in intragroup affairs or in intergroup relations. Therefore, if we pay attention to and place any analytical weight on features of group constitution *in addition* to rules of affiliation, we will not describe any group as a descent group unless patrifiliation or matrifiliation is the necessary and sufficient condition for inclusion in it. Otherwise defined, the category "descent group" is not likely to be one about which it will be possible to formulate any coherent sociological generalizations—or so Fortes argued.

To show what Fortes was getting at, it is necessary to survey in a more systematic fashion than we have already the structural (and for the most

part simply logical) implications of the nine possible kinds of rule of filiation and affiliation. For expository convenience the present discussion is
restricted to the three kinds of rule of patrifiliation. It is summarized in
Table 2.1.

Patrifiliation: Necessary and Sufficient

Where patrifiliation is the necessary and sufficient condition for inclusion
in a group, each group includes all and only the offspring of its male
members and, if it is presumed to have had a unique founding ancestor,
all and only his patrilineal descendants. Such groups are nonoverlapping
or mutually exclusive; no one can be a member of more than one group of
the same kind. Also, affiliation is "automatic by birth" and is in principle
unchangeable and irrevocable. No one can choose whether or not to belong to such a group, nor does a person ever have a choice which group
to be a member of. Any member of such a group has certain rights and
duties as a member, either vis-à-vis other members or vis-à-vis outsiders,
and having rights and duties entails having choices. The relevant choice
here is whether or not to exercise one's rights or to fulfill one's duties as a
member of a particular group. To the extent that a person does exercise
those rights and fulfill those duties, he is an active member of the group;
to the extent that he does not exercise those right or fulfill those duties, he
is an inactive member of the group. But whether or not he exercises those
rights or fulfills those duties, he remains a member of his father's group.
That is a social identity that the person bears irrespective of his or anyone
else's choices and decisions.[3] If the group is presumed to have had a
unique founder, each member is related to each other member and to the
apical ancestor wholly and solely through men or fathers. They are all related by patrilineal descent to the apical ancestor and they are all agnatic
kin of one another.[4] Further, no patrilineal descendant of the apical ancestor is not a member of the group, and no member of the group has an agnatic kinsman (at least within a certain range) who is not also a member
of the group.[5] Any rights and duties that persons may have or share as
members of a group, they have or share by virtue of their common patrilineal descent from the apical ancestor. The rights and duties of co-members vis-à-vis one another are co-extensive with and indistinguishable
from the rights and duties of agnatic kin in general (at least within a certain range) vis-à-vis one another.

Patrifiliation: Necessary but Not Sufficient

Where, in contrast, patrifiliation is a merely necessary condition for affiliation, each group includes only offspring of its male members but it need

TABLE 2.1   Implications of Rules of Filiation and Affiliation

1. Patrifiliation necessary and sufficient (e.g., Nuer, Tiv, Tallensi, Gusii).
   (a) Each set includes all and only children and descendants through males of all male members.
   (b) All members of a set are related agnatically one to another and not to any nonmembers.
   (c) There can be no recruitment from the outside; change or loss of affiliation is not possible; there can be no conflict between sets for members and their loyalties; nor can there be conflict within sets for membership and its privileges.
   (d) Such sets are suited to be (but are not inevitably) jural entities (i.e., right- and duty-bearing units); they may have special rights (*in personam*) vis-a-vis one another and may be highly solidary.
   (e) Relations of descent may have jural values in intra- and intergroup relations.

2. Patrifiliation necessary but not sufficient (e.g., Swat Pathan, joint family systems, and so-called lineages of China and India).
   (a) Each set includes only, but not all, children and descendants through males of some male members.
   (b) All members of any set are related agnatically one to another, *but* some or all may be related agnatically to nonmembers as well.
   (c) There can be no recruitment from the outside and, therefore, no conflict between sets for members and their loyalties. But there can be conflict within sets for membership and its privileges. Change of affiliation is not possible but loss of affiliation is.
   (d) Such sets are ill-suited to be jural entities but may be jural collectivities or aggregates; likely to be racked with internal conflict, they are unlikely to exhibit political/military solidarity.
   (e) Relations of descent can have no jural values in intra- or intergroup relations.

3. Patrifiliation sufficient but not necessary (e.g., Yakö, New Guinea Highlands [Enga, Chimbu, Melpa, Siane, Mende]).
   (a) Each set includes all but not only children of all male members.
   (b) Although some members of any set may be related agnatically one to another, co-members of any set may be related genealogically in any way or not at all.
   (c) There may be recruitment from the outside, change of affiliation, and, therefore, competition or conflict between sets for members and their loyalties. Conflict within sets for membership and its privileges is unlikely.
   (d) Such sets are ill-suited to be either jural entities or collectives, but *may* be jural aggregates, and are unlikely to exhibit political/military solidarity.
   (e) Relations of descent can have no jural values in intra- or intergroup relations.

not (and perhaps cannot) include all of them; and it includes only patrilineal descendants of its founder but, again, it need not include all of
them. Such groups also are nonoverlapping or mutually exclusive, and
affiliation is not changeable, in that once established it cannot be relinquished and replaced with a similar status in another group, but it is not
necessarily irrevocable. That is because it is not "automatic by birth." To
be counted as member of his father's group a person has to meet some
condition in addition to being a child of a male member. Doing that may
or may not be a matter of personal choice, so a person might be able to
choose whether or not to become identified as a member of his father's
group. There would be, however, no possibility of choosing to affiliate
with another group of the same kind. By choosing not to become or by
otherwise failing to become a member of his father's group, a person
would choose also not to become a member of any group of the same
kind. It might be possible to acquire but then to lose such an identity, by
losing or relinquishing the necessary additional qualifications. A person
who fails to acquire, or who acquires and then loses membership of his
father's group, will have no rights and duties as a member of any group
(of a certain kind) and will be, so to speak, "a person without a country,"
because he will lack at least that kind of citizenship.

As in a group of the first kind, in a group of this second kind the members are necessarily all patrilineal descendants of the founder and agnatic
kin of one another; the difference is that, here, some patrilineal descendants of the founder may not be counted as members and anyone may
have some, perhaps many and even close agnatic kin who are not members of his or of any other group of the same kind. As a consequence, relations of co-membership, relations of agnatic kinship, and relations of
common patrilineal descent need not overlap in any systematic fashion.
They may overlap to some degree, which may vary from group to group,
but the critical consideration here is that any set of rights and duties attributed to the group or allocated to persons as members of it cannot be
attributed to common patrilineal descent or to agnatic kinship. Any rights
and duties ascribed between persons of common patrilineal descent, or to
or between sets of such persons, or between agnatic kin would be distinct
from any set of rights and duties ascribed between co-members per se.

Patrifiliation: Sufficient but Not Necessary

Where patrifiliation is a merely sufficient condition for affiliation the situation is radically different from either of the two already described. As
where patrifiliation is the necessary and sufficient condition, initial affiliation is "automatic by birth," for each person becomes identified at birth as
a member of his father's group. But here affiliation is not in principle un-

changeable or irrevocable. Any person's filial status does no more than establish his natal status as a member of a group, and that status need not persist throughout his lifetime. Because it is not necessary to be a child of a male member of a group in order to gain admission to it, anyone can opt out of the group into which he was born and then acquire membership in another group of the same kind; such groups are in principle open to recruitment from the outside. As a consequence, a person born into one group may later elect to become instead—or in addition, because such groups are not in principle mutually exclusive—a member of another group of the same kind. The children of a man who ends up in a group into which he was not born will be members of the group to which he belongs at the time of their birth. In this kind of situation any group may include all, some, or very few persons who were born into it, and the members of it need not be related one to another in any particular way. Some or many may be agnatic kin of one another, but in principle they need not be. Unless recruitment from the outside is restricted to kin of established members, some members may not be related by birth in any way to some or many other members. Similarly, if such a group were represented as having a founder, it could in principle include all, some, few, or—for that matter—none of his patrilineal descendants. It would be stretching a point to describe such a group as a kin group (that is, as a group constituted of kin) or even as a group of kin (that is, as a group that happens to include only persons who are kin of one another).

Here some portion of anyone's agnatic kin may be co-members of his group, but the remainder will be members of perhaps several or many other groups. Therefore, as where patrifiliation is necessary but not sufficient, social relations between agnatic kin will be distinctly different from social relations between co-members of a group. Indeed, because there is in principle no correlation between relations of co-membership and any kind of relation of kinship or of common descent, the rights and duties of members vis-à-vis one another could have no basis in any particular kind of relation of kinship or of common descent.

In summary: Unless patrifiliation is a necessary condition for affiliation, relations of patrilineal descent need not even occur within a group. That makes it quite inappropriate to describe as a patrilineal descent group any group in which patrifiliation is a merely sufficient condition for inclusion. The only reason that could be offered for describing it that way is the mere possibility that some members of the group may be related by common patrilineal descent. In such a situation relations of patrilineal descent or common descent could have no jural or structural values, in either intra- or intergroup affairs. Where patrifiliation is a necessary (but not sufficient) condition for affiliation, the members of the group must have it in common that they are patrilineal descendants of the group founder, but there may be other similar descendants of the founder who are not included in the group. Therefore, whatever the derivative rights and duties of group affiliation may be, having and sharing them is not also a function of patrilineal descent or common descent. Although we might describe such groups as "patrilineal descent groups de facto" because their members must be patrilineal descendants of the founder, we cannot reasonably describe them as "patrilineal descent groups de jure," because relations of descent can have no right and duties values or structural significance in either intra- or intergroup affairs. Only groups for inclusion in which patrifiliation is the necessary and sufficient condition can properly be described as "patrilineal descent groups de facto and de jure."

Matrifiliation

It is hardly necessary to repeat the argument taking matrifiliation, rather than patrifiliation, as the principal variable. Although it has been both argued and demonstrated at considerable length and in considerable detail that "matriliny" has some structural implications and poses some organizational complications that "patriliny" does not (cf. Schneider and Gough 1961), none of that has any immediate bearing on the present discussion. We may conclude then that only groups for inclusion in which matrifiliation is the necessary and sufficient condition can properly be described as "matrilineal descent groups."

Simple Filiation

The situation with regard to simple filiation (without regard to sex of the parent) is clearly much the same where simple filiation is either a necessary (but not sufficient) condition or a sufficient (but not a necessary) condition for affiliation. It is somewhat different, however, where simple filiation is the necessary and sufficient condition for inclusion in a group. In that kind of situation, too, relations of descent can have no jural or structural values in either the internal or the external relations of the groups. It is, as Fortes (1959b) so strongly insisted, wholly inappropriate to describe such groups as descent groups of any kind (be it cognatic, nonunilineal, or ambilineal).

Where simple filiation is the necessary and sufficient condition for inclusion in a group, the groups—perhaps it would be better to say sets—constituted by that rule are widely overlapping. Any person is included in as many sets as he or she has ancestors who are recognized as founders, or as having been members of, different sets. The number of different sets in which any person is included might vary greatly from one person to another and from one society to another, depending on a number of factors such as the number of such sets, their scale, and the rules and practices of interkin marriage. It could even come down to this, that every person is counted as a member of every set. The sets would then be socially meaningless categories, for there could be no rights and duties entailed by inclusion in them. Everyone would be simply a kinsman of everyone else, irrespective of inclusion in a set. The only way to structure social relations on the basis of relationship by birth would be egocentrically, that is by dividing each person's kin into a number of categories, inclusion in each of which would entail certain rights and duties in relation to that person.

We need not go so far as this to make the essential point. Whatever the extent of the overlap, in any small-scale society it is bound to be sufficient to make it virtually impossible to institute a set of rights and duties between co-members that is distinctively different from the set of rights and duties entailed by the condition of two persons being kin of one another. The named categories or sets consisting of all of some person's descendants, whether through men or through women, could not be anything more than named cognatic stocks.[6] Convenient perhaps as devices for reckoning kinship per se, they would necessarily be devoid of jural significance in and of themselves. Only if we were content to use group itself in a sociologically trivial fashion could we describe them as "descent groups de facto"; nothing would justify description of them as "descent groups de jure."

It is warranted then to say, as Fortes did, that only unilineally constituted groups should be described as descent groups, and those are groups for inclusion in which it is necessary and sufficient to be a child of a male or, as the case may be, a female member. Moreover, and as Fortes put it, it is only in such contexts that relations of descent can have jural values or structural significance. In other words, there can be no such thing as a "rule of descent" or a "descent rule" that is not also a rule of group affiliation. That point is easy to miss or to misconstrue, especially if it is lost sight of that by descent Fortes meant the relationship of a person to his or her preparental (and direct as contrasted with collateral) antecedents, thus excluding the relation of child to parent per se. If that is understood, Fortes's point will be obvious enough.

If a kind of relation of filiation is the necessary and sufficient condition for inclusion in a category, that category will be in principle a multimember set. Eventually, it must include not only all offspring of the focal person but also the offspring of some of those offspring (e.g., the offspring of the males if patrifiliation is the relevant relation), and so on. In other words, in due course it will include a number of persons related by some form of common descent. Ipso facto, allocation of a jural status (a set of rights and duties) via the rule that a kind of relation of filiation is necessary and sufficient for acquisition of that status must establish a descent group or, in other words, a set of persons who are related by common descent and who share a jural status. There can be no one-member category (except by demographic accident) that is "defined by descent" and therefore no single-person status that is acquirable "by descent." Finally, if the categories or sets overlap (as they must where simple filiation is the necessary and sufficient condition for inclusion), the jural implications of inclusion cannot come to much, if anything at all. Because of this overlap, even if it were logically possible to institute a set of rights and duties distinctive of the social relations of co-members per se, in order to avoid conflicts of right and duty that are in principle irreconcilable, those rights and duties would have to be so severely limited in scope that, again, they could not amount to much.

Fortes's point that there can be no such thing as a "rule of descent" that is not also a rule of affiliation has been obscured not only by the failure of others to remember his stipulated definition of "descent," but also perhaps by his own failure to keep clearly in mind the implications of that definition for our use of ancestor, and conversely descendant. At one point Fortes (1959b:208) asked: Where a sibling inherits or succeeds in preference to a child or a sister's child, is the critical factor a relation of descent or a relation of filiation? Much earlier Rivers (1924:88) had found it necessary to say that inheritance or succession by a brother in preference to a child or a sister's child may be described as patrilineal or matrilineal, depending on whether it is a man's child or his sister's child who inherits or succeeds in the event there is no surviving brother. Fortes's answer was that descent must be the critical factor because a sibling is closer to the "source" of the deceased's "estate"—"a common ancestor"—than is a child or a sister's child. Here Fortes seems to lose sight of the possibility that in the matter of private property the source of the deceased's estate may have been only the deceased himself, who may have acquired the property not through inheritance but through purchase, exchange, or gift. Even if he had acquired it by inheritance from his brother, father, mother, or mother's brother (who may have acquired it through purchase or gift), the source would still not be one of his ancestors. The critical factor where a sibling inherits or succeeds in preference to a child or a sister's child may well be, in some instances, that a sibling is genealogically closer to the source of the deceased's estate than is a child or sister's child; but none of this necessarily implicates any relations of descent or of common descent.

This is not to say that there can be no such things as patrilineal or matrilineal rules of inheritance—though, certainly, there are not and cannot be patrilineal or matrilineal rules of succession (to offices and other similar kinds of social position), and most so-called rules of patrilineal inheritance reported in the ethnographic literature are in fact (in the language of this essay) either rules of filiation and affiliation or simple rules of inheritance by one or another kind of close kin. One possible example of genuine matrilineal inheritance is provided by Fortes himself. Among the Ashanti of Ghana, when a person dies his or her private property becomes the "corporate" property of all his or her matrilineal kin within a certain range (Fortes 1969:173–176). One consequence of that rule is that private and therefore inheritable property is converted into "corporate" and therefore not inheritable property.

IV

The questions focal to this and the preceding chapter—how to define "descent" and "descent groups"—have seemed to some anthropologists trivial and even "merely semantic" issues. Indeed, it has been argued repeatedly over several decades that there are no such things as descent groups, as that category was defined by Fortes, and therefore that "the theory of unilineal descent groups," or descent or lineage theory, is much ado about nothing. But the claim that there are no empirical tokens of the type "unilineal descent group" rests in large part on the observation that in many instances recruitment to membership of "lineages" is not wholly and solely "from the inside" or "automatic by birth." It can be shown, however, that where "recruitment from the outside" does indeed occur, the rule of affiliation is not that patrifiliation (or matrifiliation) is the necessary and sufficient condition for affiliation. That is to say, the set of all groups described ethnographically as unilineal or, more specifically, as patrilineal or matrilineal descent groups, is a structurally heterogeneous set only some of the members of which are genuine unilineal or, more specifically, patrilineal or matrilineal descent groups, as that category was defined by Fortes. Therefore, ethnographic data about many of them cannot reasonably be held to reflect negatively on so-called descent or lineage theory. This point is elaborated upon in Chapters 5 through 8.

Other writers (e.g., Appell 1974, 1983, 1984) have complained, somewhat more justifiably, that there is more to group constitution than rules of recruitment (or affiliation) and that a typology of groups based on their respective rules of affiliation can have only limited sociological utility. It has not been my intention, though, to assert or to imply that (for example) patrilineal descent groups as defined herein are in all respects a unitary class, such that a proposition about the structure and operation of any one such group or set of groups will be applicable in a straightforward fashion to any other. Far from it. Constructing a typology of groups based on their respective rules of filiation and affiliation can be only a first step in constructing a more general understanding of group structure and operation, and it must be supplemented by consideration of other features of group constitution if it is to have any general sociological utility. Some such features of group constitution are discussed in detail in the next chapter. It does seem, however, that construction of a typology of groups based on their respective rules of filiation and affiliation is an essential first step. We have seen already that there are correlations between the genealogical-constitutional and the jural-constitutional features of groups. More such correlations are exhibited in the next chapter.

NOTES

1. The problem is clearly stated in Freeman (1960); see also Peranio (1961) and Scheffler (1965, 1966), both strongly influenced by Freeman.

2. By way of clarification of this point we may note that virtually anyone has a right or is at least free vis-à-vis Yale University to apply for admission to the student body of Yale College, but this is not a right to have any rights, etc. If it were, there would be no need to apply or petition for admission. If an offer of admission is made and accepted and the applicant is actually matriculated, thus becoming a member of the student body, certain rights and duties immediately accrue to him or her. Those rights and duties are not constitutive of membership of the Yale College student body; they constitute (some of) the significance of membership of that group. The defining feature of being a member of the student body of Yale College is that one has been formally inducted (matriculated) into that status by persons who have the power to so act.

3. Feinberg (1990:86) muddies the waters. He acknowledges that "in a system of unilineal descent, one lacks the flexibility to affiliate with a variety of groups," but still, he says, a person "may choose whether or not to activate group membership at all, and that decision . . . is based on extragenealogical criteria." This, he goes on to argue, implies that "descent may be viewed as a necessary but not sufficient condition for membership in both unilineal and nonunilineal descent groups." The argument is unwarranted and depends entirely on confusing being a member with being an active member of a group, thus quite arbitrarily ruling out the possibility that there could be someone who is an inactive member of a group. Yet on the same page, Feinberg takes note of that possibility in relation to at least one category designated *pare* in the language of Anuta atoll.

4. Note that I wrote *agnatic*, not *patrilineal*. We need a simple expression to signify the way in which all members of a patrilineal descent group are related to one another, but it is no longer possible to say that it is patrilineally, because there is no lineal relationship between child and father; nor is it possible to say they are related by common descent, because that relationship exists only between second- and higher-degree collaterals. P. Bohannan (1963:59;131,134, n.4) has pointed out that many anthropologists use *agnatic* and *patrilineal* as virtual synonyms, to mean relationship to or through the father. He uses *patrilineal* only in reference to unilineal descent groups but he uses *descent* itself in the sense of ascending kinship and thus continues to use *agnatic descent* and *agnatic kinship* interchangeably. Because

herein we use *descent* in a more restricted sense, we can use *agnatic* only to modify *kinship* and, in effect to mean, relationship to or through fathers only. Correlatively, *uterine kinship* means relationship to or through mothers only.

5. The significance of the parenthetic qualification "within a certain range" is missed by Feinberg (1990:86). He argues as though when one lineage divides to become two segments of a higher-order lineage, such that persons who were (and still are) members of one lineage are then describable also as members of different lineages, we may say that "shared agnatic descent is a necessary but not sufficient condition." He obfuscates the issue by substituting "shared agnatic descent" for "patrifiliation," which in his ethnographic example remains necessary and sufficient for inclusion in a certain kind of group.

6. "All the descendants of a man and his wife counting descent through females as well as males" (Radcliffe-Brown 1950:22; cf. Freeman 1960:199–200; Fortes 1969:287).

3

JURAL STRUCTURES I

I

Rules of filiation and affiliation are commonly described as "jural rules" and they and their implications for the conduct of persons and groups are discussed as though they were regulative rules, that is as rules that specify what persons should or must do and that may be followed or broken or violated. Indeed, social rules in general are often discussed as though they all prescribe or proscribe certain forms of conduct (see e.g., Edgerton 1985). Rules of filiation and affiliation are, however, neither jural nor regulative rules. They are *constitutive* (Searle 1969:33–37; 1995:43–50) or *defining* rules, rules that create social categories or groups, the internal and external relations of which are established and regulated by jural and other kinds of rules.

Jural itself means "of or pertaining to rights and duties." Therefore, a jural rule is a specification of the rights and duties entailed by occupying a specified social position or by having a specified social status. In exercising a right a person is not following a rule that prescribes or proscribes a form of conduct, because to have a right is simply to have a sanctionable claim to do or to be exempt from doing something in relation to some specified person or persons. In other words, a right is a kind of permission to act. If a kind of conduct is prescribed or proscribed, it is not one's right but one's duty to do or not to do it, and then perhaps only if the corresponding right holder elects to claim that which it is his right to claim— or is "in the right" when he claims it but not "in the wrong" when he does not. Jurally regulated conduct is inherently variable, and it is a fundamental sociological error to think of it narrowly as a matter of following, breaking, or violating regulative and prescriptive or proscriptive rules.

More specifically, and as discussed at length in Fortes (1969:87–92), jural denotes not only rights and duties but also how they are sanctioned.

It excludes what we usually describe as morally or metaphysically sanctioned relations and activities, and it includes those relations and activities that we usually describe as legal. More broadly, though, it includes relations and activities based on rights and duties that "have the backing of the whole society," that "derive their sanction from the political framework of the society" and thus "have 'public' legitimacy in contrast to the 'private' legitimacy of rights and capacities based solely on moral norms or metaphysical beliefs." Characteristically, according to Fortes, "breach of jural norms disrupts a person's relations with society rather than with individuals only" (1969:89). In the context cited, Fortes provides several excellent examples by way of clarification. Perhaps needless to say, "jural" is not a tightly defined category that is unambiguously either applicable or not in any and all situations; but then neither does it need to be that in order to have considerable anthropological value.

Jural rules certainly do regulate or govern social action or conduct, and they do that by specifying the rights and duties of persons or of sets of persons vis-à-vis one another. Rights and duties, however, always attach to particular social positions or statuses, which themselves must be defined, and the rules that define them comprise a class of constitutive rule. Rules of recruitment, so called, belong to this class, because they specify the conditions for inclusion in a group and thereby define its boundaries or constitute it. In so doing, like the rules that constitute games, they establish features of the social contexts within which people may act, by choosing to do or not to do whatever it is that they may rightfully do, or that they have a duty to do, if and when called upon.

Because rules of recruitment are often thought of as prescriptive, they are often thought of also as rules that leave no room for "choice and decision," in some matters at least, on the part of the persons whose actions they are said to govern or regulate. If we think of them, however, as constitutive rules we can see that the kinds of social context they help to define also vary in the kinds of choice and decision that they make possible. Because social actors are right and duty bearing, they are continually confronted with the necessity to make choices and decisions, but the options open to them vary in kind from one society to another. This brings us to one of the major systematic implications of the formal differences between the various kinds of rule of filiation and affiliation.

II

Reasonably enough, Fortes, Leach, and others have made much of the fact that, where patrifiliation or matrifiliation is the necessary and sufficient condition for inclusion in a group, a person has no choice in the matter of group affiliation. The rule of affiliation establishes a patrilineally or a matrilineally constituted group, and membership of such a group is indeed prescribed: A person has no choice whether or not to belong to such a group and no choice as between groups. This must not be misconstrued, as too often it has been, as implying that every person is deprived of all capacity to choose or to decide to act in one way or another. One such misinterpretation (also a particularly flagrant misrepresentation) is Schneider's (1965:46, 74) undocumented assertion that it is a major tenet of "descent theory" that "The whole man has to be in one and only one group, so that the group can be a physical as well as a conceptual group" and that "The unilineal descent rule . . . allocates a whole man to a group." It was precisely to avoid any such sociological nonsense that Rivers, Radcliffe-Brown, and others were at great pains to distinguish between kinship and descent and to insist that the former is necessarily "bilateral" and the latter either "patrilineal" or "matrilineal." As Fortes (1969:287) replied, unilineal descent is not a device "for neatly sorting all the members of a society . . . into discrete 'groups,' like apples in a stack of boxes." What we are dealing with here is merely a culturally constituted incapacity to make a choice about having or not having a particular social identity and, therefore, about having or not having the rights and duties that are entailed by having that identity. A person may have no choice in the matter of whether or not he or she is a person of a particular kind yet (it should not even need to be stated, much less emphasized) still have a choice in many other matters. Further, although membership itself is prescribed, any member of a group still has a choice whether or not to exercise the rights or to fulfill the duties entailed by being a member of a group. Again, he can choose between being an active or an inactive member of the group. What he cannot do is choose between groups in which to exercise rights and to fulfill duties of the kind entailed by being a member.

Depending on the nature of those rights and duties and of the benefits to be gained or lost, the choice to be an inactive rather than an active member may be of more or less consequence, both for the person making the choice and for other persons who may be affected. But if the rights are such that they confer or have the potential to confer substantial benefits, it may be very difficult for a person to avoid being an active member. More specifically, it may be difficult for a person to avoid fulfilling the duties entailed by being a member, if and when called upon to fulfill them. By refusing to fulfill his duties, he would be refusing to render unto others something they have a right to demand of him, and he would be giving them reason to refrain from fulfilling their duties to him, if and when he tries to exercise his rights. And, because he can have no rightful claims of the same kind elsewhere, he would be, for all intents and purposes, relinquishing his ability ever to make rightful claims of a certain and at least potentially valuable kind.

A relevant example from Ashanti is provided by Fortes (1963:61). An Ashanti man was born and reared in his father's matrilineage community and chose to remain there as an adult. Although he could never achieve political office in that community, he could continue to reside and to prosper there as long as he continued voluntarily to subscribe to its communal levies. But when the head of his matrilineage died and he was elected successor, he had little choice but to assume the office, even though doing so entailed not only the inconvenience of moving his household but also a substantial loss of income. Otherwise, he would have had to relinquish all the rights of matrilineage affiliation and to risk the anger of the ancestral spirits of his matrilineage.

Up to a point, much the same thing could be said about being a member of any group. A person who does not fulfill the duties entailed by being a member is liable to be denied the rights; and sometimes a person who refuses to fulfill the duties (or who wrongs other members) may be not merely denied the rights and allowed to remain a member "in name only," but formally expelled from the group. But where patrifiliation or matrifiliation[1] is the necessary and sufficient condition for inclusion in a group, expulsion is in principle impossible, at least as long as it is socially acknowledged that the person is a child of the relevant kind of group member. Being a child of a male member of the group, a person simply is a member, too. Therefore, if it comes to that, expulsion can be accomplished, but only by first establishing, contrary to a previous judgment and perhaps by ritual means, that the offending party is not a child of the relevant kind of member of the group (see also Chapter 5).

Putting much of this in another way, we may say that the constitution of a society in which patrifiliation is the necessary and sufficient condition for inclusion in a group is such that change of group affiliation is not an option that is open to anyone, at least not in relation to that kind of group. In this kind of situation, no one can pick and choose between groups (of a certain kind anyway), nor can the members of a group choose to admit to their ranks a person whose father and father's father is or was not one of them (except via adoption as the child of an established member). It is not merely that people are prohibited by cultural rule from doing such things. It is instead that those forms of social action do not exist in those societies, just as the form of social action known as "making kula" in the Trobriand Islands (engaging in a certain kind of exchange of certain kinds of object; Malinowski 1922) does not exist in the United States. That is not because we do not know about it, but because our forms of social life are not constituted such that we could engage in it. We do not have in our cultural repertoire the kinds of social statuses and the

associated modes of conduct or the kinds of object that it takes to play, as
it were, that particular kind of social game. Similarly, "change of affiliation" is not a kind of event that can occur in a society where patrifiliation
is the necessary and sufficient condition for inclusion in a group.

This last statement may seem to fly in the face of ethnographic fact.
Numerous ethnographic reports have it that change of affiliation is possible and does occur, even rather frequently in some societies wherein,
nominally at least, patrifiliation or matrifiliation is the necessary and sufficient condition for inclusion in a group. We are often told something like
the following. A man, let us call him Sam, whose father was known as a
member of group X, is born and reared in the country and company of
group Y, his mother's natal group. Sam does not associate much if it at all
with the Xs but is only nominally one of them because his father was.
Instead, through his close association with the Ys, he becomes known as
one of them; he is permitted to exercise the rights and is called upon to
fulfill the duties entailed by being a Y. As many ethnographers have put
it, Sam is assimilated to or becomes incorporated in group Y; he has
changed his affiliation from X to Y. In the process, or so we are told, the
parties to the event have failed to follow or have broken or violated one of
their own jural or cultural rules. Assuming for the moment that this kind
of recruitment from the outside does in fact occur, the first thing to notice
is that it might be more appropriate to say that the parties to the event
have assented, in effect at least, to suspend or ignore one of the constitutive rules of the "game" that is their form of social life. They have assented either to "play at" that "game" (rather like playing at the game of
baseball by deleting the shortstop or the centerfielder because there are
too few people on hand at the moment to make up the proper two teams),
or to "play" a different kind of "game," at least for the moment and at
least in relation to Sam. It is shown in Chapter 5, however, that there is little reason to suppose that the "game" of social life is ever "played at" in
that way. If it were, the probable long-run consequence would not be a
"loosely structured patrilineal descent system" or a "system of quasi-
patrilineal descent groups" (for those are oxymoronic conceptions), but
something other than a system of patrilineally constituted social groups.

The situation envisioned in the example of Sam being born an X and
becoming a Y during his lifetime, and for which there is little reliable
ethnographic evidence, must be distinguished from a rather different
kind of situation for which there is much substantial ethnographic evidence. It is one in which during his lifetime Sam remains known to one
and all as an X who always lived with the Ys, and so did his sons and
sons' sons; but eventually after the passage of several generations they all
become known (many of them *post mortem*) as Ys and, via some genealogical gerrymandering, their female link to Y is or may eventually be con-

verted into a male link. In that way Sam and his agnatic descendants are incorporated into group Y as one of several small lineages within it. This process is discussed more fully in Chapter 5.

The more general point derivable from these observations is that where patrifiliation is the necessary and sufficient condition for inclusion in a group, the possibility of competition between groups for members and their loyalties is precluded. Also precluded is the possibility of competition and conflict within a group on the matter of membership status per se. Or, perhaps more accurately, the only point on which there can be conflict is whether or not a particular person is a child of a male member. The only way to prevent someone from becoming a member and from having, therefore, certain rights and duties, is to challenge his or her filial status, just as that is the only way to expel someone from the group. Of course, that is not to say that in this kind of system there can be no intragroup conflict, but only that it must be about other things, such as nonfulfillment of the duties entailed by membership or claiming more than one is entitled to claim, and not about the condition of membership itself.

III

The situation must be significantly different where patrifiliation is necessary but not also sufficient for inclusion in a group. This rule of affiliation is no less prescriptive, as it were, than is one that makes patrifiliation both necessary and sufficient. It is merely that the conditions necessary and sufficient are not wholly and solely genealogical. If the groups are to have anything like recognizable boundaries, that is if people are to be able to say of someone that he or she is or is not a member of a particular group, there must be some quality in addition to the filial that the person must have in order to qualify for inclusion. If he has that additional quality he is ipso facto a member of his father's group; if he does not have it he is ipso facto not a member. As noticed in Chapter 2, having or not having the additional quality may or may not be a matter of personal choice. If meeting the additional necessary condition is not something over which the person himself has control, it may be within the control of the established members of the group and they can then choose who to admit to their ranks, by conferring the additional qualifications on some persons but not on others. They would be limited, however, to choosing between the offspring of the male members of the group. If the person himself can choose to have or not to have the additional necessary quality and he chooses to have it, he becomes ipso facto a member of the group. If he chooses not to have it, he remains a nonmember, and not merely a nonmember of his father's group, but also of any group of the same kind. He thereby precludes for himself the possibility that he may exercise the rights or that he may be asked to fulfill the duties entailed by being a member of such a group—again, not only of one such group in particular but of any such group. Depending on the nature of the rights and duties (if any) entailed by being a member of a group of that kind, being a person who has no such rights or duties may be a matter of little or no social consequence. Where it is, however, we may expect that whenever possible anyone who has the necessary filial qualification will try to acquire also the additional necessary nonfilial qualification and, if he succeeds, to become ipso facto a member of his father's group.

In this kind of situation the only choice (in the matter of group affiliation) open to a person is whether or not to become a member of his father's group. He may also have the corollary choice, once having established himself as a member, whether or not to remain in that condition, because it may be possible to relinquish the additional, nonfilial qualification and, thereby, to relinquish one's identity as a member of the group. Also, if having that qualification is under the control of the group itself, the group may be able to expel one of its members by depriving him of the requisite additional quality. But, as where patrifiliation or matrifiliation is necessary and sufficient, "change of group affiliation" is not an option that is open to any person or set of persons. No one can elect to be a Y rather than an X, and the Xs cannot choose to assimilate a Y to their ranks.

This absence of even the possibility of change of affiliation has an important social and sociological corollary. It entails that there can be no competition or conflict between groups for members and their loyalties. Again, that is not to say there can be no intergroup competition or conflict, but only that there can be none of a certain kind. The Xs cannot "raid" the Ys, either physically or rhetorically, with the intent to remove a person or persons from Y and to make him or them members of X. It would be pointless to try to do that, even if it were conceivable, because there is no culturally constituted way in which anyone can be assimilated to membership of a group other than that of his father. In contrast, however, to situations in which patrifiliation is the necessary and sufficient condition, there can be competition or conflict within a group on the matter of affiliation per se. This may have some significant social and sociological implications. Suppose, for example, that whatever it is that a person has to have or to be, in addition to being a child of a male X, is some attribute, thing, or good that is for some reason in short supply and not readily available to every person whose father is an X. If this additional good is itself something of value for possession of which people are likely to compete, or if the benefits of being an X are substantial, the consequence may be that persons who are already Xs or who are partly qualified to be Xs (because their fathers are) will enter into competition and conflict for acquisition of that good. Depending on the degree of scarcity of the good and on the degree of severity of the competition for it, the factionalism or even atomism thus engendered could seriously compromise the ability of any such group to act as a body or unit in any kind of social situation. It might also make it difficult to institute or to enforce a body of duties of persons vis-à-vis one another as co-members of such groups.

It was argued in Chapter 2 that groups of this kind should not be described as descent groups. The main reason offered there was that the rights and duties (if any) of members vis-à-vis one another could not be the rights and duties of agnatic or uterine kin, or of persons of common patrilineal or matrilineal descent, vis-à-vis one another. We now have a reason to suspect that the "if any" was not an idle insertion. If membership itself is a matter of little or no jural significance, as it could turn out to be in that kind of social context, there will be few if any rights and duties even between those persons of common descent who happen to be also co-members of a group. That is, relations of agnatic or uterine kinship, or of common patrilineal or matrilineal descent, would have no jural significance even if only within groups.

IV

Turning now to situations in which patrifiliation is a merely sufficient condition for inclusion in a group, we may notice that the social order thus constituted is, again, one in which persons have certain kinds of choice, but not other kinds, open to them. Indeed, the range of choice or of kinds of choice is considerably greater, for in this kind of situation it is not limited to the choice between being an active or an inactive member of a particular group, or to the choice between being identified as a member of one particular group or of no such group at all. Instead, it encompasses the possibility of "change of affiliation." Here, no one is bound to remain a member of the group into which he or she was born. Although born an X, a person may later elect, perhaps pending the consent of the already established Ys, to become a Y instead. If the groups were in principle mutually exclusive (on other-than-genealogical grounds), that would entail giving up the identity X; otherwise it would be possible to be an X and a Y at the same time. That, however, would require that the duties entailed by being an X are not in conflict with those entailed by being a Y.

In any event, because change of affiliation is permitted, in this kind of situation there can be intergroup competition and conflict for members and their loyalties, and also intragroup competition and conflict on the matter of membership status per se. But precisely because there can be that kind of competition and conflict between groups, that kind of competition and conflict within groups is likely to be muted. Because no one is bound, by constitutive rule or by duty, to maintain the group affiliation acquired at birth, each person is free to some degree anyway to relinquish membership of one group and then to acquire membership of another.

Assuming, however, that the established members of a group have some interest in its continued existence, they will want to retain the persons (and their loyalties) who were "recruited from the inside" (that is, by filiation), and, as a hedge against possible losses of such persons, as well as against downward demographic fluctuations, they will want to attract and to retain persons "from the outside." Surely, one advantage in having groups that are in principle open to recruitment from the outside is to be as inclusive, rather than as exclusive, as possible whenever the social circumstances seem to warrant it. One consequence of all this is that there is likely to be competition between groups for members and their loyalties. But, if a particular group is to engage at all effectively in such competition, it can ill afford to promote invidious distinctions within its own ranks and thereby run the risk of alienating some of its members.

Therefore, in systems of group organization of this kind it is difficult if not impossible to institute jural differentiation between members born into a group and members recruited from the outside. No group could afford to try to distinguish between those two kinds of member by granting to the former rights that are in some way superior to the rights granted to the latter. If that were done, the latter would have to settle for being "second-class citizens." They might do that in the expectation that their children, who would be persons born of members (even if only second-class members), will be themselves first-class citizens. But possible advantage for someone else and in the long run may not be an adequate incentive and it is, therefore, likely to be counterproductive to try to institute such an arrangement. The probable long-run condition is one in which "a member is a member," there are no grades of membership, and relations of agnatic kinship or of common patrilineal descent have no jural significance in the internal affairs of groups. Lacking that kind of structural significance, neither could they have any in the sphere of intergroup relations.

All of this is likely to mitigate the jural significance of group affiliation itself by limiting rather severely the quality and the scope of the rights and duties entailed by co-membership. For one thing, the ability of persons to pick and choose between groups with which to affiliate, even if not entirely ad lib, implies that if the duties of membership of any one group become burdensome, some or many members of that group may vote with their feet, as it were, and desert it for other groups. In the competition between groups for members and their loyalties, one successful strategy will be to diminish the costs of membership by diminishing the duties (and, conversely, the rights as well). For another thing, the persons who belong to any one group and who have kin and in-laws of certain kinds within it may well have other kin and in-laws of the same kinds in other groups. To the degree that such kin and in-law relations cut across group boundaries, either they or relations of co-membership per se must suffer a corresponding diminution in jural significance, because otherwise the two kinds of relation would be in chronic conflict. Yet social relations between kin and in-laws who are members of different groups are likely to be precisely the social relations on which people depend when considering changes of group affiliation.

V

These observations and hypotheses—about how different rules of filiation and affiliation have systematically different implications for other features of group constitution and therefore group operation—suggest some more hypotheses.

We have seen that where patrifiliation is necessary and sufficient for inclusion in a group, both change of and loss of affiliation are precluded; as a corollary so also is the possibility of intragroup competition and conflict on the matter of membership status per se, and so is intergroup competition and conflict for members and their loyalties. But not all kinds of intragroup and intergroup competition and conflict are precluded. Indeed, the mutual exclusivity of these groups, coupled with the impossibility of change or loss of affiliation, entails the possibility of competition and conflict or cooperation between them. It is not merely that several or many persons who happen to be members of one group may unite in opposition to or in cooperation with outsiders, perhaps several or many persons who happen to be members of another group of the same kind. It is instead that such groups are uniquely suited to act as bodies or wholes vis-à-vis outsiders, including other groups of the same kind. They are so suited because in a system of groups of this kind it is possible to institute and to sanction effectively a distinctive set of rights and duties of members vis-à-vis one another, including duties of a kind that would effectively unite those persons into an active body. That would be possible because no one can have rightful interests of the same kind, or be duty-bound in the same way, to more than one group. Thus, in situations of intergroup competition or conflict no one would have any cause to be uncertain about where his loyalties should be, at least in principle. As already pointed out, a group member called upon to fulfill his duties to other members may well find it difficult to refuse, for if he does refuse he stands to lose the benefits of the rights of membership, rights he cannot replace simply by joining another group of the same kind.

Where patrifiliation is necessary but not sufficient, change of affiliation is precluded but loss of affiliation, or failure to obtain an affiliation, is not.

As a corollary, although intergroup competition for members and their loyalties is precluded, intragroup competition on the matter of membership per se is not. That may make it difficult to institute a body of mutual rights and duties between members because intragroup factionalism may make it difficult to sanction duties from within the group. One implication of that is that no group will be able to act as a body in opposition to any other, or to unite as a body with another group, in opposition to one or more other such groups. Not only are these groups unable (for constitutional reasons) to engage in competition and conflict for members and their loyalties, they may not be able to engage in any kind of competition and conflict.

The claim here is not that there can be no intergroup conflict in societies where a kind of relation of filiation is a necessary but not a sufficient condition for inclusion in a group. It is instead that there can be no conflict between groups of that kind. If in the same society there are groups or sets of another kind, they may be able to engage in competition and conflict and to combine with other such groups or sets in the process, depending of course on how they are constituted.

Where patrifiliation is merely sufficient for inclusion in a group, change of affiliation is a possibility and, as a corollary, groups may engage in competition and conflict for members and their loyalties. As suggested above, one likely consequence of that is that it will be difficult to institute a distinctive sets of rights and duties between members of a group because it will be virtually impossible to sanction such rights and duties from within the group. That is not so much because of factional tendencies (as where patrifiliation is merely necessary), as it is because of the freedom of persons to come and go from one group to another should the duties of membership of any one group become burdensome. The ultimate sanction of expulsion from the group for failure to fulfill one's duties as a member might well be inoperable in this kind of context, because it is always possible for a person to change his or her group affiliation and perhaps even to better his or her life situation in the process. Again, one likely implication is that a group of this kind will not be able to act as a body in opposition to or in cooperation with outsiders, including other groups of the same kind.

In a situation of this kind it might appear (to the ethnographic observer) that groups do act as bodies in opposition to or in cooperation with one another. Although membership itself may entail little in the way of rights and duties vis-à-vis other members, many members of such a group will be various kinds of kin (or in-laws) of one another and, as such, will have various rights and duties vis-à-vis one another. Being kin (or in-laws) who have chosen to be also co-members of a group, they may choose also to cooperate with one another, either to advance the private interests of one of them (which interests may have implications for the private interests of the others), or to advance the similar (but not shared or joint) interests of each. Because they happen to share the identity "member of group X" they might even represent themselves as "Xs"; and the other party, similarly constituted, could represent itself in a similar fashion as "Ys." It might then appear to an outsider, such as an anthropologist who does not yet fully understand how things are done in that society, that group X is acting as a unit in opposition to or in cooperation with group Y. It would not be, however, "the Ys (in toto)" who are doing something together because they are duty bound to do so, but only "(some of) the Xs" who are doing something together because it is in the interest of each of them to do it that way rather than individually, or because it cannot be done individually. As shown in subsequent chapters, ethnographers have often mistaken collaborative activities organized in that way for joint or corporate activities. They are misled by a local sort of "shorthand" way of speaking into thinking that they are dealing with groups that are also jural entities (corporate groups) or jural collectivities when, as it happens, those groups may not be even jural aggregates.

This introduction of the distinction between jural entities, jural collectivities, and jural aggregates (which is elaborated in Chapter 4) brings up another general topic that must be discussed before proceeding to the ethnographic chapters. So far in this discussion of the structural and functional implications or correlates of the different kinds of rule of filiation and affiliation, the focus has been on the possibility of instituting and sanctioning a distinctive set of mutual rights and duties between co-members of a group. It must now be noticed that individuals' rights and duties as members of groups may be not only vis-à-vis other members but also vis-à-vis outsiders, and not only individuals but also groups may be right- and duty-bearing entities. Again, there are systematic relationships between these possibilities and the different kinds of rule of filiation and affiliation.

NOTE

1. Hereinafter let the "or matrifiliation" be understood without having to be restated.

4

Jural Structures II

Rights and duties in general are divisible into two main kinds, general rights (also called rights *in rem* or "as against the world") and special rights (also called rights *in personam*) (Stoljar 1984). A special right is a sanctionable claim against a particular person or a delimited set of persons and it imposes a duty on that person or set of persons and to the bearer of the right. A general right is a sanctionable claim against an indefinitely large number of persons. Such rights establish the possibility of certain kinds of wrong or injury that may be done to the right holder and done by virtually anyone. Some such rights are also claims to things or to services, and they impose duties on virtually all other persons not to interfere with someone's property. Other such rights provide claims against actual or possible wrongs or injuries to their holders by prohibiting other persons from harming them or from interfering with their not-unlawful activities.

The holder of a general or of a special right may be either a single person or a set of persons or some other culturally constituted kind of entity. One example of the latter is an office, because the rights and duties vested in an office belong, as it were, to the office *per se* and not to the incumbent or officer. Stoljar (1984) suggests that instead of saying that the incumbent or officer has certain rights and duties, we say that he or she has certain powers and limitations. Trusts, foundations, and the like also are culturally constituted entities that are neither single persons nor sets of persons yet are right and duty bearing. The assets of a trust (for example) must be managed by some person or set of persons (who have certain powers) and for the benefit of some other person or set of persons. But neither the trustees nor the beneficiaries are owners of those assets. The owner is the trust itself. Similarly, a religious shrine or temple may be a right- and duty-bearing entity, rather than the property of an officer (such as a parish priest).

The focus of this study, however, is on social sets or groups and, in particular, on those constituted by rules of filiation and affiliation. Like other kinds of social group (Appell 1974, 1976, 1983, 1984), these may or may not be right- and duty-bearing units, that is *jural entities*, and if they are jural entities the rights attached to them may be either special or general or both. If they are not jural entities they may be sets of persons each of whom holds in severalty (i.e., individually) a right (or rights), either special or general, that is similar to the right held by each other member of the set. If the right is general and is to some item of property, the members of the group are co-owners of that property, and, as Appell (1976:67–69) has pointed out, relations between them and other persons or sets of persons may be organized in one or the other of only two ways. In response to a violation of their rights, either one or more members of the group is permitted to initiate a jural action such as a suit for restitution, damages, or compensation *on behalf* of the other members, or each right holder must represent his own individual interest. Following Appell, a group of the first kind is here described as a *jural collectivity* and a group of the second kind as a *jural aggregate*. After discussing these categories in some detail we consider whether or not it is possible for each of the various kinds of set constituted by the various kinds of rule of filiation and affiliation to be either a jural entity, or a jural collectivity, or a jural aggregate.

II

The prototypical right- and duty-bearing unit or jural entity is the single person or individual who has general rights to the integrity of his or her person, to conduct his or her not-unlawful affairs without interference from other persons, and to possess property, and who therefore may be a party to special jural relations with other persons. Social groups and other culturally constituted kinds of entity may be treated jurally as person-like by attributing to them some of the same jural capacities. Perhaps the most person-like kind of jural entity is the kind described in Western legal terminology as *corporate*.

The concept of corporateness has a long and tangled history and the word *corporate* is used by diverse anthropologists in diverse ways, many of them, alas, merely ornamental. For many anthropologists corporateness is, by definition, an attribute of groups and any group is corporate that exhibits some degree of "solidarity," that is if its members, or even only some of them, sometimes act together vis-à-vis outsiders. In this usage, property holding is not an essential feature of corporateness. That, however, is a sociologically trivial and, again, merely ornamental use of *corporate* and it is best avoided in favor of more precise description and analysis.

Another usage, one derived from the sociologist Max Weber, also treats corporateness as an attribute of groups, and a corporate group is one that in principle "never dies" or is perpetual. Groups constituted by the rule that patrifiliation (or matrifiliation) is the necessary and sufficient condition for inclusion are corporate in this sense, whether or not they exhibit any sort of solidarity or hold any property, because they continue to exist independently of the existences of their individual members, so long as at least some of those members (of the appropriate sex) continue to reproduce. So-called ethnic groups also are corporate in this sense (see e.g., M. G. Smith 1974). Groups that are corporate in this sense may or may not have any legal or jural status, but that, of course, does not prevent them from being socially and sociologically significant in many different ways and degrees.

In Appell's (1984) terminology, almost any jural (that is, right- and duty-bearing) entity other than a single person is some kind of corporation, and any property-holding group is a corporate group. As Appell points out, the members of a property-holding group are not co-owners of its property, but they do have rightful interests in relation to that property, and they must be organized among themselves not only to manage those interests and thereby to reduce the potential for intragroup conflict, but also to enhance and, if necessary, to protect the group's property. They must, that is, have certain rights and duties vis-à-vis one another. They may have also certain rights and duties vis-à-vis an office, the incumbent of which manages intragroup relations and represents the group in its external affairs. One of the duties of that officer will be to sue, in the name of the group, any person or set of persons who violates the group's property rights; and Appell treats the capacity of a group to sue in its own name as the distinctive feature of its corporateness.

In Western law, however, there is more to corporateness than property holding and the capacity to sue. To be corporate, an entity other than a single person must possess a "common fund" or set of assets that may be proceeded against in a suit by another jural entity. That is, it must be capable of being sued, as well as capable of suing, and in suits against it liability is limited to the extent of the common fund that is the corporate asset.[1] The individual members of a corporate group cannot be made liable with their personal assets for the group's debts;[2] nor can the group be made liable with its assets for the private debts of its individual members. That implies that the group's property must be such that the whole or a part of it is separable from the group and transferable to another jural entity in settlement of a claim. Otherwise there would be no point in attempting to sue the group rather than its members either jointly or jointly and severally.

The suggestion that there can be property that is not jurally alienable and transferable to another jural entity may seem strange and unacceptable. In Western societies virtually anything that can be owned can be also transacted, that is bought and sold, exchanged for something of comparable value, or alienated by way of gift, and much of our legal system is designed to facilitate such transactions and the profit-making they may entail. In many other societies, however, some kinds of thing are not transactable. Land is especially notable in this respect. The purpose of holding or possessing it as against all other persons may be only to use it for growing or collecting food or for grazing animals, and people may have no interest in being able to alienate the land they control in exchange for items of other kinds. Indeed, land may not be a scarce good and there may be no need jurally to regulate access to it or to provide for kinds of transaction in relation to it.

In many societies areas of land are controlled by village communities, and portions of those areas are used by the inhabitants for their own subsistence. The land itself is never bought, sold, exchanged, or given away. It is not that transactions in land merely do not occur, but rather that they cannot occur because that is not a culturally constituted kind of jural activity. Yet if in those societies land is "owned" by anyone, it must be by the village community, for rights to use of it are contingent on being a member of the community, and when a person leaves the community he loses all rights to use of any portion of the land it controls. While he holds a portion for his own use he has the power to permit another member of the community to use it or some part of it, but he has no power to let a nonmember do so, much less to alienate it completely from the village community.[3] Thus, to the extent that there is ownership of land in such a society, land is owned by village communities, yet it is jurally an inalienable possession. Nonjural alienability by forcible dispossession is, of course, another matter altogether.

It follows that unless the group *per se* owns some other kind of jurally alienable property, there would be no point in attempting to sue it, rather than its individual members jointly or jointly and severally. Also, for what actions could such a group be sued? Most such communities are constituted for the mutual cooperation (and protection) of their members in making a living off the area of land they occupy and exploit, and they have no collective purposes in the pursuit of which they (or some of their inhabitants acting representatively) could commit wrongs or inflict injuries on other jural entities. Although it would be wrong to trespass on the group's land, and trespass might lead to a suit, neither the group itself nor anyone acting in its name can commit a similar offense or, of course, be sued for it.

It may seem odd also to suggest that an entity may be capable of suing yet not capable of being sued. Certainly, from the perspective of the prototypical right- and duty-bearing unit, the single person or individual, especially one who has the full complement of the rights of a citizen, it seems anomalous to suggest that possibility. But other kinds of jural entity are not persons or even fictive persons.[4] They are only entities that are legally person-like insofar as they are attributed certain rights and duties. Because they are not persons and are not capable of acting in all respects like persons, they cannot have the full accoutrement of a person's jural attributes. The degree to which they are person-like depends on the purpose or purposes for which they are constituted and, therefore, on the kinds of action that are proper to them. An entity's character may preclude it taking any action that would constitute a wrong or injury to another entity.

The village communities of the Rungus of Borneo, as described by Appell (1976:76–77) provide an example. Each of those communities includes several longhouses, the inhabitants of which recognize a headman who represents them against trespassers on the "village reserve." Such a trespasser may be warned off or even fined, but there is no village common fund into which the fine can be paid; it is kept by the headman as his private property. To all appearances, the community itself is not and cannot be held liable for any offense. Because it has no common fund, it would make little sense to think of it, rather than of its inhabitants jointly, as capable of doing a wrong or inflicting an injury and therefore as potentially liable to pay damages or to make compensation. In short, the concept of corporate liability has no place here, and therefore neither does the concept of corporateness itself—at least not in its long-established Western legal sense.

Appell (1976:76–77) does say, however, that the Rungus village community is a "ritual entity," and he describes it as "ritually corporate" and as conducting "corporate ceremonies." The point, though, is only that certain ceremonies are carried out in the name of the community as a whole, and their purpose is to renew the fecundity of the village's land and of its inhabitants. Also, the villagers are required to observe certain behavior restrictions, violation of which would loosen certain malicious spirits who would then harm some or all the villagers indiscriminately. If a violation occurs, the village headman extracts a fine of a pig, which is used as a sacrifice either to perform or to reperform the appropriate ritual. Clearly the village community is treated as a unit or entity in ritual, as well as a property-holding unit; but that is not sufficient to make it a corporate group—again, at least not by the standards of Western law.

The important point here is not simply terminological. It is that it is essential to distinguish not only (as Appell has clearly shown) between jural entities, jural collectivities, and jural aggregates, but also to notice that there is much sociologically significant structural variation within each of those general categories. For some sociological purposes it may be satisfactory to draw a line within the category of jural entities between single persons and all other kinds, and then to describe the latter as kinds of corporate entity. For other purposes, though, it may be especially important to stress that some jural entities may sue but not be sued whereas others may sue and be sued. In the discussion that follows, *corporate* is used in the stronger, less inclusive sense. So, whereas for Appell all groups that are jural entities are corporate groups, herein only some groups that are jural entities are also corporate; herein *corporate* signals not only property owning, but also the capacity to sue and to be sued, with group liability limited to the extent of its common fund. It is a likely consequence of that choice that we will have to acknowledge that corporate groups, though perhaps not corporate entities of other kinds, are or were rather uncommon in the "tribal" world. Saying (or acknowledging) that will annoy those anthropologists who are given to decorative overuse of *corporate*, but it does have the advantage of permitting us to say (or acknowledge) also that corporateness has a political-economic history. It is a part of that history that whereas perpetuity was once, and still is by some parties, insisted upon as an essential feature of corporateness, it no longer has that status in Western law, as Appell (1983, 1984) and others have pointed out. There is such a thing as a "limited-life corporation," that is a corporation the charter or constitution of which explicitly provides for its dissolution at some specified time or on the occurrence of some specified event, on which occasion its property is transferred to another jural entity or entities (as when a trust expires and the beneficiary becomes the owner of its assets). Perpetuity, then, is an incidental feature of corporateness (in the legal sense).

From this perspective we must differ from Fortes (1959b [1970:111]) who observed that "theoretically, [descent groups] are necessarily corporate groups, even if the corporate possession is as immaterial as an exclusive common name or an exclusive cult." What Fortes was getting at is that in principle descent groups are perpetual social units; they persist for as long as their members continue to reproduce; and, if they are also jural entities, their external jural relations persist unchanged despite the continual turnover of their personnel. But there are no reasons why descent groups must be jural entities (rather than, say, jural collectivities or aggregates) or, if they are jural entities, why they must be also property owning, much less corporate (in the sense intended herein). Another possibility is that a right (or duty) held by a descent group may be special or personal, one that imposes a duty specifically on some specified person or definite set of persons. For example, in segmentary lineage systems proper (see Chapter 5), the jural constituents of the lowest-level lineages are individual persons, but those lineages (and not those persons) are the jural constituents of lineages at next level up, and so on up to the level of the maximal or highest-order lineage. Thus lineages at all levels are jural entities. It is highly significant, however, that the rights and duties they have are strictly in relation to immediately adjacent collateral lineages at the same structural level. Those rights are special rather than general; they are not property rights, so the lineages are corporate only in the sociologically rather trivial sense that they sometimes act "as bodies" (again, see Chapter 5).

Finally on the subject of jural entities, it may be obvious now why it was important for Rivers to distinguish between the "social processes" he called descent, inheritance, and succession, even if not especially in those terms. Many social entities described by anthropologists as descent groups are also property-holding entities, even if not corporate groups. Where patrifiliation or matrifiliation is necessary and sufficient for inclusion they are also "perpetual" groups, that is groups the continued existence of which is guaranteed, as it were, by the "rule of recruitment," because the group and its jural relations persist even as individual members leave it through death or join it "by birth." As already noticed, anthropologists often talk about membership of such a group and about the rights and duties entailed by it as being inherited by a person. But, because the property in which an individual acquires an interest when he or she becomes a member of such a group is group property, that property is not inheritable by anyone. Any one person's interest in it derives from being included in the group, and that membership is not itself a heritable condition.

It is possible, however, for a member of a property-holding group to acquire a more specific rightful interest in some part of the group's property and for that interest to be passed on to his child or sister's child. For example, where a group owns an area of land, each of its members may be entitled to equitable use of such a portion. That portion is not his personal property because his rights in relation to it are not general or "as against the world," but are only as against other members of the group, each of whom has a duty to refrain from interfering with his use of that portion and for a specified or unspecified period of time. His special interest in that portion derives from his special right as a member of the group to use of a portion of its land, which right derives in turn from the group's general right to the land itself. Such derivative rights, often called "rights of use," may be succeeded to. For example, a man's sons may be allowed to claim for their own use the land that had been allocated for his use. If, like Rivers, we restrict our use of inheritance to talk about reallocation of individuals' general rights (personal rights in rem), we may not say that special, derivative rights of use are inherited, but that they may be succeeded to—for, in effect, Rivers intended to restrict *succession* to description of reallocation of individually held special or personal rights. No matter how we look at it, though, there is no inheritance of or succession to ownership of the land or to any portion of it. That is vested in the group itself and cannot be inherited or succeeded to.

In summary: In the terminology employed herein there are many kinds of jural entity, not only single persons and corporations (groups, trusts, etc.). At this point it is not yet clear that we need any special terms by which to distinguish between the possibly diverse kinds of groups that are jural entities but not corporate groups.

III

There are potentially many different kinds of jural collectivity. The rights held in severalty by each member of a group may be special or general or both, and they may be not only similar but also necessarily equal to those of each other member. Where they are similar and necessarily equal the parties have, in Western legal terminology, *joint* rights and duties.

Jointness

In anthropological writings jointness is often confused with corporateness. For example, A. R. Radcliffe-Brown (1935 [1952:44–45]) once wrote, "the establishment of . . . joint rights immediately establishes . . . a corporation." Also, J. Goody (1990) describes Chinese and Indian "lineages" as corporate and their members as having joint property rights. We have already seen, however, that a corporation is itself a right- and duty-bearing entity, that the members of a corporate group are not co-owners of its property, and that they are not joint owners but are *corporators*. In contrast, joint owners are genuine co-owners, each with his own distinct general rights in the joint assets, and the rights of each are equal in extent to the rights of each other member of the group. In other words, each is "an owner of the whole," subject to the equal rights of the others.

One reason why it is easy to mistake jointness for corporateness, or a set of joint owners for a corporate group, is that no member of either kind of group is free to alienate any portion of the group's assets without the unanimous consent of the other members, unless of course he is an officer of the group who is acting within his powers as such. The reason a joint owner is not free to do that is that his rights are in relation to the undivided whole of the assets, and not in relation to any specific portion or proportion of them. Therefore, he could not alienate his own interest without alienating also the interests of the other joint owners. Because they are equal co-owners, when one of them is allocated his interests as a specific portion or proportion of the joint assets, the others must be allocated theirs also, and that partition of the joint property terminates their jointness.

Another similarity between a corporate group and a set of joint owners is that jointly held assets, like corporate assets, cannot be inherited or succeeded to. When a joint owner dies, his rights in relation to the whole of the jointly held property are not inherited or succeeded to by one of the surviving joint owners, for that would make the survivors unequal in status and terminate their jointness; nor could it be presumed to pass to all of them jointly, for that would have no effect (each of them being already "an owner of the whole") and so would be a nonevent. Neither could it pass to one of the deceased's sons or to all his sons jointly. That would violate a corollary of the equality of joint owners, that is that no one can be introduced into a set of joint owners without the unanimous consent of all parties.

None of that should be taken to imply that a set of joint owners cannot persist "from one generation to the next," for in some legal systems it is permitted to introduce new members "by birth" into a set of joint owners, though not by inheritance or succession. But it does imply that, unlike a corporate group, a set of joint owners can hardly be a perpetual group. The reason is that jointly held assets are ipso facto partible assets, and because of that (and by way of prior use of the terms in Anglo-Hindu law) anthropologists often describe holders of joint rights as *parceners* or *co-parceners* and a set of joint-right holders as a *co-parcenary*. In the Common Law of England from which those terms ultimately derive, they designated persons who *inherit* jointly. That was possible by testament only, and the joint heirs were legally obliged to divide their jointly held assets and to convert them into estates held in common or into wholly separate individual estates, which could then be inherited. In this scheme, no man could be described as a co-parcener with his sons, because they could not hold jointly, and no co-parcenary could endure for even a single generation.

In some other societies, however, jointness between a man and his sons is not merely permitted but is legally enjoined. We may say, with reference to such systems, that men and their sons are parceners or co-parceners, insofar as each is equally an owner of the whole. It is not a problem that, in some systems, when the family estate is partitioned during the lifetime of the father, he is not entitled to an equal share along with each of his sons (see also Chapter 9). What we need to recognize is that partition takes place between the survivors of a co-parcenary, and a father who retires or who is forced to retire by pre-mortem partition of the joint estate is jurally no more a survivor than is one who dies.[5] We may, therefore, continue the long-established anthropological practice of describing a jointly held estate as a parcenary. a set of joint owners as a co-parcenary, and the individual joint owners as parceners or co-parceners.

In the Common Law of England, joint inheritances were (obligatorily) partitionable but joint tenancies were not. That was because tenancies included (but were not confined to) special rights and duties to a lord, and it was forbidden to introduce anyone into a joint tenancy either by birth or, as it was put in the Common Law, "by descent" (i.e., a son could not take his deceased father's place in a joint tenancy). The purpose of those restrictions was to place a limit, if not one of a specified number of years, on the life or term of such a tenancy, so that the lord would be able sooner or later to reapportion use of his estate. In the so-called joint family systems of India and China, however, each of a man's sons becomes at birth a co-owner of his property, especially of any property he acquired in the same way. When he dies or retires his sons are not his heirs or successors but are the surviving members of a co-parcenary (again, see Chapter 9).

It may seem that in principle this process could go on *ad infinitum*, thus creating generation after generation—demographic contingencies permitting—a genealogically ever deeper and broader set of sets of co-parceners. But it must not be overlooked that co-parceners have equal interests in their jointly held assets. As a corollary, each person has a right vis-à-vis the others to benefit equally from those assets and a duty vis-à-vis the others to contribute equally to maintenance and enhancement of them. Unless great care is taken to insure equality of benefit and contribution, and even if it is taken, the likely outcome sooner or later is tension and dissension within the group. Either the members must go on living somehow with that tension and dissension or the group must divide, either into lesser groups of the same kind or by converting each jointly held right into a separate personal estate (which becomes again a joint estate as soon as its owner has a son). As a consequence, in legal systems that recognize joint rights it is typically the arrangement that no one can be compelled to remain joint against his will, at least not with anyone other than his father and sometimes not even with him. Therefore, any co-parcenary broader than the set of a living man and his own sons is likely to be legally a voluntary association and subject to dissolution on demand by any one of its members. Or, if legally more stable than that, it will be a group from which anyone can withdraw more or less at will.

Jointness and corporateness are similar also in the matter of liability. As indicated above, corporate liability is limited to the extent of corporate assets. The creditor of a corporation can recover only to the extent of those assets. If they are insufficient he cannot sue for the balance to be paid from the private assets of the individual corporators; that is one of the great advantages (in some kinds of society anyway) of corporateness. Strict joint liability is similar in that, if co-parceners (or their legal representative) contract a debt against their joint assets and if those assets are insufficient to pay the debt, the creditor will be able to collect only to the extent of the joint assets and will not be able to claim the balance from the private assets of the individual co-parceners.

Ownership in Common

Another kind of jural collectivity already mentioned is that in which rights are held in common. Appell (1974) has pointed out that Radcliffe-Brown (1935 [1952:44]) erred when he wrote that the distinctive feature of this kind of jural collectivity is that each of its members holds a right that is "similar and equal" to that held by each other member. That is what is characteristic of jointness. The difference between joint rights and rights in common is that the rightful interest of each joint owner is in the undivided whole of some thing and not in any specific portion or proportion of it, whereas the rightful interest of each holder of rights in common is in a specific portion or proportion of the undivided whole of some thing. For example: Because of the rule of survivorship, until the time of partition a joint owner has no definite portional or proportional interest, so if there are three of them at the moment they do not each own one-third of the joint assets. In contrast, each holder of a right in common does have a definite portional or proportional, and not necessarily equal, interest in the common assets. If there are three of them one may own one-half of the undivided whole and each of the others only one-quarter, or one of the others may own one-eighth and the other three-eighths. As a corollary, and because owners in common may have quite disproportionate interests in their common assets, the potential for conflict of interest between them may be high and difficult to contain within tolerable bounds, short of terminating the relationship. Therefore, jural collectivities of this kind tend to be fragile, both legally (being terminable on demand) and practically. Each right holder is usually free to transfer his interest, even without the consent of the other owners, and each person's interest is inheritable.

When Radcliffe-Brown described rights in common as "similar and equal" he confused rights *in* common with rights *of* common (Appell 1974). As an example of rights in common he mentioned that each member of a "tribe" may have the right to graze his cattle and to water them anywhere within the tribal territory, "grass and water are common." Because he presented this example in a discussion of rights in rem (general rights), it seems that he regarded these grazing and watering rights as property rights. But many peoples say about resources such as grass and water or uninhabited forest or uncultivated portions of an area controlled by a group that they "belong to no one," thus making it clear, not that access to them is a free-for-all, but that anyone's right of access to and use of them is not a general property right but is only a special or personal right vis-à-vis other members of a group. It is, in other words, a right that derives from group affiliation and that regulates social relations within the group. The area within which those rights may be exercised could be the property of a group that is some kind of jural entity or jural collectivity, or it could be the property of an office such as a kingship or chieftainship.

IV

A jural aggregate, like a jural collectivity, is a set of persons each of whom has a similar right, either general or special, but it differs from a jural collectivity in that none of its members may act on behalf of or represent the interests of the others. Each member of a jural aggregate must make his own rightful claims and fulfill his own duties.

An example is Appell's (1976) description of a Rungus (Borneo) tree-owning unit. A fruit tree or one usable for building materials is the private property of the person who plants it. When the owner dies all his children and their children and so on inherit interests in the tree, but not as a corporate group or jural collectivity. Each person holds his or her right in severalty; and each person must make his or her own claim to produce from the tree or to the proceeds resulting from a legal action should the tree be damaged or destroyed. When damage or destruction occurs, each person must appear and make claim for compensation along with any other right holders who wish to do the same. A right holder who does not appear and make a claim is not entitled to share in the compensation. No one may make a claim to a portion of the produce of the tree, or to a portion of the compensation paid for damage to it, on behalf of anyone else. The number of shares (but *not* the number of unit members) at any one time is equivalent to the number of active claimants rather than to the number of potential claimants. Such a set or group must have some sort of internal organization; otherwise there could be conflict that is in principle not resolvable over access to its assets. The arrangement here is that the person living closest to the tree, who is in the best position to look after it to the benefit of all the co-owners, takes the responsibility for doing that and, in return, has the right to the first harvest of its fruit. He must also notify the other co-owners if the tree is damaged or destroyed so that they may participate with him in arbitration proceedings to obtain compensation. He is not their leader or representative and may not seek to obtain compensation to be paid to persons who do not appear in person to represent their own rightful interests.

V

The preceding section dealt with, among other things, kinds of co-ownership wherein each of two or more persons has general rights of the same kind in relation to some thing. It is possible also for two or more persons (or other kinds of jural entity) each to have *different kinds* of rights in relation to some thing, in which case we may speak of divided rights and perhaps even of divided ownership.

One way to divide rights in relation to some thing is to allocate to one party all general rights in relation to that thing and to give to the other party certain special rights in relation to the first party that are also but indirectly rights in relation to that thing. For example, John Critchley (1978:16–18) points out that, at one period in the history of Roman law, if person P contracted with person Q to rent or lease some of Q's land, and if person R were to interfere with P's use of that land, P could not take legal action against R to have the use of the land restored to him. Only Q, who is the owner of the land and the other party to the contract with P, could do that. Also, if Q were to sell the land, say to R, and in that contract make provision for P to continue to use the land, if R later tried to evict P then P would have to depend on Q to attempt to enforce the terms of the sale. The most P himself could do was try to recover for damages if he or his own property were injured by R. Roman law at that time recognized divided rights but not divided ownership.

Another possibility is to divide the set of all general rights between two or more parties, so that each party has not only some general rights in relation to some thing but also some special rights and duties vis-à-vis the other party. There are, it should be pointed out, some kinds of arrangement that can appear to be of this kind but that are in fact somewhat different. In some legal systems, although person P is recognized as the owner of some thing, say an area of land L, P is not at liberty to dispose of some part of or the whole of L as he alone sees fit. Instead, as the owner of L he has an obligation to at least some of his kin, especially to his potential heirs, to preserve and enhance his property so that they, too, may continue to benefit from his possession of it. Before disposing of his property P is obliged to consult with them, and if he does not, that may be grounds for voiding the transaction. So, if ownership of something includes the right to dispose of it, that right is not necessarily wholly unqualified; it may be *entailed*.

Joint ownership is perhaps easy to mistake for an arrangement of the kind just described, because often a set of joint owners has a manager whose powers permit him, at least in certain circumstances, to alienate some of the jointly owned property, but even then usually only after adequate consultation with the other joint owners. Where the manager is also the father (or a mother's brother) of the other joint owners, he may be able to alienate rather freely, especially if the others are still jural minors and cannot readily oppose him. But they are nonetheless joint owners, and not merely prospective heirs who must be consulted by a single owner.

Where the set of general rights in relation to some thing is divided between two or more persons (or other kinds of jural entity), it is sometimes the arrangement that eventually all those rights will revert to one of those parties, as for example at the expiration of a lease. But the subsidiary right holder might well have the power to sell his (albeit limited) rights, or to sublet to another party. That was one arrangement in the feudal systems of Medieval Europe, where it was sometimes possible for tenancies to be perpetuated over several generations between the heirs of the landlord and the heirs of the tenant. At least certain kinds of tenancy were inheritable. A tenant could not, however, dispose of his rights "with no strings attached," because he had not only certain rights in respect of his land but also certain duties in relation to his lord, and anyone who took over his rights had also to take over those duties.

As pointed out by Gluckman (1965) and Critchley (1978), similar arrangements are quite common, and it is useful to conceptualize them all as consisting of "estates of administration" and "estates of production" (Gluckman 1965:77–79, 90–91). An estate of administration is a set of rights (and of related duties) held in relation (usually) to an area of land and the persons living on it and "covering powers to allocate the land further, ... to dispose of it, to control and regulate its use, and to defend it against trespassers." Having those powers entails the possibility that the bearer himself may put the land or some part of it directly into production; but it entails also the possibility of creating two or more lower-level estates of administration, the holders of which then stand in a special jural relation to the holder of the primary estate of administration. They may put the land or some part of it directly into production or they may allocate estates of administration or of production to still other persons. Typically, the holder of an estate of administration undertakes to guarantee the tenure of those immediately below him and, in return, they are obliged to render to him some form of payment or service.

Gluckman (1965:85–86) stresses that the individual producer's right to land is more than a mere right of usufruct ("to take the fruits" of the land). It may be that there is no one with a greater right to use that land than its present cultivator, provided that he fulfills the duties entailed. Those duties may be to someone who holds an estate of administration, perhaps an official such as a chief or village headman, or to the other members of a social group such as a village community that may hold an estate of administration either autonomously or in relation to a lord. Where the village community holds in relation to a lord or other official, it is not necessarily as a corporate group. Stoljar (1973) pointed out that the village communities of Medieval Europe were not corporate groups, because they had no common fund against which a creditor could proceed. The payments to the lord were met by a levy on each holder of an estate of production, and if payment was not forthcoming the lord could not sue the community as such, for again it had no common fund. Instead, the members of the community were treated as jointly and severally liable for the debt, and the lord sued some of the wealthier members of the community and left it up to them to recover from the others.

VI

The terms *corporate* and *joint* are widely used in anthropology with reference not only to forms of ownership but also to forms of liability for debts, wrongs, or injuries, and they are sometimes used more or less interchangeably, along with *collective liability*. Here, however, *corporate liability* means the liability that a corporation may incur in the pursuit of its declared and designated purposes, and limited to the extent of its common fund.

Unlike corporate liability, joint liability is not necessarily associated with joint ownership. Where joint owners contract a debt jointly, each is liable for the debt to the full extent of his interest in the property, so he and the other joint owners may stand to lose all that they hold jointly. If the joint property is insufficient to cover the debt, the joint owners cannot be made to pay the balance from their private funds. Persons not owning jointly may undertake a debt jointly; if the creditor names only one in a suit the one named may compel the other to join him as a co-defendant. If the party named does not do that, he alone is responsible for the debt, and necessarily with his own funds. Alternatively, persons who are not joint owners may contract a debt with joint and several liability. If they default, the creditor may proceed against any one or more of them, at his discretion. If he names only one in the suit and that person is compelled to pay, he may later seek to be indemnified by the others. Where it is not a debt but a wrong or injury that is at issue and two or more persons acting in concert are responsible, liability must be joint and several, rather than strictly joint, because (in the commission of an illegal act) there can be no legally binding agreement beforehand about whether liability is to be joint or joint and several. So, if one of two possible defendants is found guilty of an offense, that does not prevent the possibility of later trying the other for it also—but without increasing the amount of the assessed damages or compensation.

It is common in the world of small-scale communities that an established social group, perhaps a "descent group" or a village community or hamlet, may become implicated either formally or informally in the wrongdoings of one or more of its members, even if no one supposes that the wrongdoer acted as an agent of that group. Anthropologists commonly describe such arrangements rather indifferently as matters of corporate, joint, or collective liability, often alas without sufficient ethnographic documentation to make it clear exactly how liability is allocated, although that documentation is especially critical where it seems that the group itself has no assets held either corporately or jointly whereby it could settle a suit against it. Fortunately, T. Elias (1956) and S. Moore (1972) provide a large number of helpful examples and sophisticated analyses of them and of their import for comparative law and social anthropology more generally.

As Moore (1972:89) explains, it is possible, perhaps inevitable we might add, that "even in a society which stresses that ultimate liability is entirely individual . . . for social collectivities to be vulnerable to seizures of property or other attacks by outsiders because a member has defaulted on his obligations" or committed a wrong against a member of another such collectivity. It is possible, and perhaps inevitable, especially where in dealing with derelictions of duty or other jurally actionable offenses it may, in the end, be necessary to employ self-help (which, as Moore carefully explains, is always itself regulated by societal norms that are highly sensitive to the nature of pre-existing social relations between parties to a conflict). In other words, if the aggrieved party cannot get satisfaction via negotiations carried out by himself or others, he may be permitted to resort to, for example, recovering stolen property or extracting payment for damages done to his own property by helping himself (with the assistance of some other members of his own group) to some of the property of some member of a group to which the accused belongs. In a more extreme instance, parties with a right or duty to take revenge for a homicide may not be required to seek out the killer himself and to take their revenge specifically on him, but may be free to take it on one of his close kin or virtually any member of some specified kind of group of which he is a member.

Where, as Moore (1972:89) puts it, "every member of a . . . group has the power to commit it in this way to a collective liability," the groups themselves must organize internally so as to be able to control their members' conduct both internally and externally and to "discipline, expel, or yield up to enemies members who abuse this power or whom [the group] does not choose to support in the situation in which he has placed them."

That power itself arises, of course, out of the general political-legal situation in which self-help is the final legal resort precisely because there is no one who can compel an aggrieved party and his allies to limit their actions strictly to the accused party or his personal property. The aggrieved party and his allies seek their satisfaction where they can most readily find it with least risk to themselves, and they leave it to the consociates of the culprit to get from him restitution for property or lives lost, or to do with him what they will.

A not uncommon organizational feature of groups who find themselves in this kind of predicament is to act as "pooling units" (Moore 1972; Robbins 1982) which provide a kind of "liability insurance" for members, provided they do not abuse the privilege. This may be a formal or an informal arrangement. In the informal situation a person who is, let us say, fined for an offense but lacks sufficient funds of his own to pay it is free to solicit contributions from his consociates, and they are obliged to help him to the extent they, individually, judge possible or appropriate. In the formal situation, some agent of the group is empowered to levy contributions (not necessarily equal) from other members. The point to be emphasized in conclusion is that none of this makes those groups or their liability corporate (at least not in the sense of corporate intended herein) or joint; although joint and several could pass as a description in reference to the more formal arrangements.

VII

So far we have seen that it is possible to classify social sets or groups constituted by rules of filiation and affiliation in at least two ways. One is according to the nature of the constitutive rule itself, and from that perspective there are only nine logically possible kinds of set or group. The other way is according to the jural structures of those sets, and from that perspective there are at least six logical possibilities. Either the set is a jural entity, a jural collectivity, or a jural aggregate and the relevant rights are either general or special (or both). Combining these two typologies would yield a large number of different hypothetical kinds of set or group. But are all those hypothetical types also logically possible types, or is it that some of these dimensions of difference are in fact logically incompatible one with another? And, of the presumably logically possible combinations, is it that some do not occur or are relatively rare? If so, why?

To some extent the answers to those questions were anticipated in Chapters 2 and 3. It was argued there that different rules of filiation and affiliation have different implications for other features of group constitution (and composition), for the kinds of social relations between members of a group, and for kinds of intergroup relations. We may now summarize those observations by saying: A group constituted by the rule that patrifil-iation (or matrifiliation) is necessary and sufficient for inclusion can be a jural entity, a jural collectivity, or a jural aggregate (or, of course none of these because it need not have any jural attributes). A group constituted by the rule that patrifiliation (or matrifiliation) is a necessary but not a sufficient condition for inclusion could perhaps be a jural aggregate, but not a jural collectivity or a jural entity. Any other group constituted by a rule of filiation and affiliation (i.e., a group of any one of the other five kinds) can be nothing more than a jural aggregate (if that). These conclu-sions or hypotheses could be developed in the abstract, but it will be more compelling and informative to turn now to reconsideration of sev-eral especially relevant ethnographic instances.

NOTES

1. Fortes (1969:277–308) includes an extensive discussion of "descent and the corporate group," in which he emphasizes the perpetuity of corporations and their jural personhood, but he also alludes to Maitland's observation that "what we personify is not the associated group of men but the purpose for which they are associated." He goes on to point out that the significance of "purpose" in this context lies in the implication that "corporations have a reality, have capacities to act as units, to exercise rights and fulfill obligations, *to sue and be sued*, are even, ul-timately, capable of moral and religious wrongdoing and are not merely a con-trivance of the law" (1969:303, emphasis added). Many of the descent groups he mentions in the course of his discussion of corporateness simply do not have the capacity to sue or to be sued.

2. This is or has become something of an oversimplification. Inventive attor-neys are working hard, or so I read occasionally in the *New York Times*, to find ways to "pierce the corporate shield."

3. For an exceptionally well done description and analysis of such an arrange-ment and its operation in the Trobriand Islands, see E. Hutchins's *Culture and Inference* (1980).

4. There is, I know, a long tradition in Western law of attempting to understand corporations as fictive persons. The jurists' metaphors are not without their own difficulties, but they are in any event not binding on anthropologists, who may wish to treat them as ethnographic data, of the same order as, say, Tallensi, Tiv, and Ashanti observations about their lineages that they are in some kinds of social situation "one man" or "one person" (where, by the way, it is *not* corporateness that is at issue).

5. That is precisely why pre-mortem partition is (again see Chapter 9) so very problematic. Although the father and mother are morally entitled to support by their sons, they have no jural (only moral) recourse once the father relinquishes control of the family estate.

PART TWO

Specific Instances

5

PATRIFILIATION NECESSARY
AND SUFFICIENT

I

Where patrifiliation is necessary and sufficient for inclusion in a group, that group includes all and only offspring of its male members. Such groups are nonoverlapping and mutually exclusive; affiliation is automatic by birth and is unchangeable and irrevocable. Although no one can choose to be or not to be a member of such a group or which group to be a member of, anyone may choose between being an active or an inactive member of the group into which he was born by choosing whether or not to exercise the rights or to fulfill the duties of a member of that group. If those rights have the potential to confer substantial benefits, it will be difficult for a person to refuse to fulfill those duties, if and when called upon to do so. Because of all that, and because descent groups are self perpetuating and of indefinite duration, such groups are better suited to be also jural entities or jural collectivities than are groups for inclusion in which patrifiliation is merely necessary or merely sufficient. Indeed, one mode of intergroup relations, the "segmentary lineage system," is uniquely dependent on the ability of patrilineal descent groups to be also jural entities and, in particular, for them to have special rights and duties vis-à-vis one another.

That kind of lineage system is of special importance for the purposes of this study because it is the one that has been most especially under consideration when, over the past several decades, it has often been asserted that the structural correlates outlined in the preceding paragraph do not and cannot not hold true in any society. It is now widely accepted as well-established ethnographic fact that recruitment from the outside to membership of nominally patrilineal groups is commonplace; and textbook

wisdom now has it that there may be and often are wide discrepancies between principle and practice, or between "dogma" or "ideology" and
"what people actually do." All that has led some scholars to conclude that
descent or lineage theory, so-called, is wholly irreparable and should be
junked with no further ado. It is almost always both difficult and misleading to pick out one from a complex tangle of issues and to identify it as
the crux of the matter. In this instance, though, it does appear to be the
chronic confusion between "descent" and "residence," or "lineage" and
"locality," and the impulse analytically to subordinate one to the other,
usually lineage to locality, that has bedeviled social anthropology virtually from the outset.[1]

II

It was pointed out by Fortes in 1953 (1970:91), and it has been confirmed
by numerous studies since then, that "lineage and locality are independently variable and how they interact depends on other factors in the social structure." Descent groups and local groups are conceptually and empirically two quite different kinds of social entity, and no good can come
of confusing one with the other. There are, though, many ways in which
the composition of local groups, their internal organization, and their relations with other local groups may be affected by the presence of one or
another kind of descent group. As Fortes observed, a descent group need
not be a compact residential unit in order to be an effective social entity,
and the degree to which descent groups tend to be compact or dispersed
depends on the nature of the purposes for which they are constituted and
on the derivative rights and duties of persons as members of them. Where
those rights and duties are of a kind that can be exercised or fulfilled in
one and only one place, there is likely to be a tendency for members (of
one sex) of each group to reside at or near that place, but otherwise not
(see also Firth 1959:213–216).

Where lineages are land-owning and a person's most secure claim to
land to use for purposes of subsistence derives from his or her lineage affiliation, it is expectable that the members (of one sex) of each lineage will
tend to reside on or near the lineage holdings and will as a consequence
form a more or less compact local group. It should not be expected that all
members (of one sex) of all lineages will do that. Having the right to reside in some place does not entail (but is contrary to) having a duty to do
that; and neither does it follow that only lineage members will be able to
reside on lineage land and to make use of lineage resources. The persons
who may reside and labor at some place by right of birth normally have
also the power to permit other persons to reside and labor with them at
that place, too, either for a specified period or indefinitely. It is common-

place in the ethnographic literature to notice that, where patrilineal groups are land-owning and therefore to some degree localized, children of the sisters of male members are often welcome as short-term or even life-long guests; and, where the land-owning groups are matrilineal, children of the brothers of female members are similarly welcome—but without becoming, contrary to group constitution, members of those lineages. That kind of arrangement is fully expectable for a number of reasons, only one of which is that the growth or decline of lineage groups is perhaps rarely in direct proportion to growth or decline in the quantity and quality of their subsistence resources. As a consequence it will often happen that some persons find it more attractive to live and to work with nonlineage kin on land belonging to other lineages than to live on their lineage lands and to work with their lineage mates. Being granted permission to do that is not at all the same thing as being made a member of a lineage by means other than birth. Nor is it (contrary to the rather loose language of many ethnographers) the same thing as being given the rights or even some of the rights of a lineage member.

Virtually without exception, though, when anthropologists complain about how descent or lineage theory fails to take into account and to account for recruitment from the outside, the groups under consideration are local groups which, it is said, are represented by their members as descent groups or lineages. As a consequence, it has become widely accepted that, as Barnard and Good (1984:77) put it, purporting to cite Sahlins (1965:104), "in general there need be 'no particular relation between the descent ideology and group composition.'" What Sahlins claims to demonstrate, though, is the more modest generalization that "in major territorial descent groups, there is no particular relation between the descent ideology and group composition." He concedes that, in "ritual lineages," in simple descent categories, and in "small, land-holding corporations," a disparity between constitution and composition is not likely to arise (Sahlins 1963:42). But, he argues, where lineages are also "political blocs," group constitution and group composition not only may be but must be "out of joint," and the more they are at odds the stronger will be the actors' insistence that their groups are what they are supposed to be.

More specifically, Sahlins has in mind those "acephalous" segmentary political systems wherein, as he sees it, the lowest-level or minimal territorial segments are represented as patrilineages that are related patrilineally one to another, and that (in principle at least) combine with or oppose one another according to their relative genealogical proximity (see Figures 5.1 and 5.2). In such systems, Sahlins argues, it will be virtually impossible to maintain 100 percent (male) agnatic composition of the minimal lineage-cum-territorial segments. If recruitment were strictly "automatic by birth," different minimal level segments would grow or decline in size independently of the quantity and quality of their subsistence resources, and in the long run some would be threatened with extinction and others with insufficient resources. To cope with such problems some groups must open themselves up to recruitment from the outside and others must somehow slough off some of their excess number. But it is necessary also to continue "ideologically" to maintain that each lowest-level residential and proprietary segment is in fact a patrilineal descent group, for it is as such that (in principle) those groups combine with one another to form higher-order patrilineal groups for purposes of defense and aggression. So, as Sahlins (1965:105) sees it, "The most probable long-run condition is paradox, . . . an inverted relation between commitment to agnation in principle and commitment to it in deed."

It might be thought that, if it does become difficult to maintain 100 percent (male) agnatic composition, and recruitment from the outside does become necessary, surely the appropriate thing to do is to change the ideology (i.e., the constitution) to bring it into line with de facto group composition. Sahlins argues "not so." He explains that it may well be useful to persist with an "agnatic ideology" (that is, patrilineal constitution) long after it has ceased to correspond (if ever it did) to the facts of group composition. Suppose, for example, that a group declining in size indulges in too much recruitment from the outside and threatens to deplete its subsistence resources. In that event, "authentic lines" consisting of genuine agnatic descendants of the group founder could argue that some or all persons recruited from the outside are not really members of the group after all and should remove themselves to another place. Sahlins does not explain how a patrilineally constituted group could go about recruiting from the outside without in the process revising its constitution, nor does he explain how anyone could be persuaded to throw in his lot with a group some other members of which could, at any time and for any reasons, deprive him of his membership and its benefits, even if voluntarily he had been fulfilling the correlative duties.

By way of ethnographic evidence Sahlins cites C. D. Forde (1963b) on the Yakö of southeastern Nigeria, M. Meggitt (1965) on the Mae-Enga of the New Guinea Highlands, and E. E. Evans-Pritchard (1940, 1951) on the Nuer of southern Sudan. It can be shown, however, that although the ethnographers do describe certain Yakö and Mae-Enga groups as patrilineages, in neither society is patrifiliation necessary and sufficient for inclusion in any group; it is instead merely sufficient (see Chapters 7 and 8). Among the Nuer, though, there is a kind of group (*thok dwiel* in the Nuer language) for inclusion in which patrifiliation is the necessary and sufficient condition. Therefore, even if we were to grant that certain Yakö and

Mae-Enga groups are in some sense descent groups, we would have to grant also that the Yakö and Mae-Enga rule of filiation and affiliation is distinctly different from that of the Nuer, and that the Yakö and Mae-Enga data cannot fairly be used to support the proposition that there is no particular relation between the constitution and the composition of "major territorial descent groups." The compositions of those Yakö and Mae-Enga groups are wholly consistent with their constitutions.

We are left then with Sahlins's use of Evans-Pritchard's reports on the Nuer, from which reports, it must be acknowledged, it is possible to extract various statements of ethnographic fact or of analysis and conclusion to support the contention that there is, in that instance anyway, no particular relationship between group constitution and group composition. Yet there are also many other statements that may be cited as evidence to the contrary, and we must, or so it is argued here, give greater credence to the latter than to the former, both as expressions of Evans-Pritchard's intent and as accurate reflections of certain aspects of Nuer social order. One of the main themes of Evans-Pritchard's most general conception of Nuer society is that, although there is much seasonal and other short-term variation and fluctuation in the composition of local groups, there is very little or none of that in the composition of Nuer descent groups, and so they provide whatever stability and continuity there is in Nuer social life. We need not defend the plausibility of the last assertion. What matters here is that, had Evans-Pritchard believed that change of lineage affiliation is both possible and frequent among the Nuer, even if "against the rules" as it were, he could not have sustained that view. What needs to be done, then, is not only to construct out of Evans-Pritchard's Nuer data a coherent account of those aspects of Nuer social life that are especially relevant to the thesis of this study, but also to account for those statements that are so often used in evidence against so-called descent or lineage theory.

That is not an easy task. The primary ethnographic literature on the Nuer is vast and it may be dwarfed by the derivative commentary and commentary on commentary on Evans-Pritchard's ethnography and its largely unstated theoretical foundations. No doubt many anthropologists (and their students) are by now quite tired of the Nuer and of Nuerology. Yet it is precisely because of the influence of Evans-Pritchard's Nuer studies and of the commentary on them, and because there is still much to be learned from them, that the Nuer must be dealt with here, and in some detail. In an effort to keep the discussion from becoming entirely too arcane, commentary on commentary is kept to a minimum.

Briefly, the argument of this chapter is this: Evans-Pritchard had considerable difficulty conceptualizing the relationship between lineage affiliation and local-group affiliation in Nuer society.[2] He experimented with various phrasings of his understanding of that relationship and they are sufficiently different that there are major inconsistencies, not only between one and another of his accounts, but even within any one account. In some large part his difficulties can be attributed to the subtlety of the relationship he was trying to capture, but he compounded the problem by not always distinguishing as carefully as he might have between a lineage and a "lineage homeland"—in the Nuer language, between a *thok dwiel* and a *cieng*.

With that difference kept carefully in mind, it can be shown that we have no good reasons to suppose that the composition of any Nuer lineage, or of any Nuer community, is inconsistent with its constitution. Perhaps it would be more convincing to be able to assert that we have good reasons to suppose that, consistent with their constitution, Nuer lineages are 100 percent agnatic in composition. But that proposition cannot be affirmed because we have no numerical data on Nuer lineage (thok dwiel) composition. The numerical data that several observers (e.g., Sahlins 1963, 1965; Holy 1976, 1979a, 1979b; Southall 1986) have treated as "the most relevant data" provided by Evans-Pritchard on the matter of "Nuer agnation" are data on the composition of several Nuer village communities and cattle camps, *cieng* and *wec* in the Nuer language. Evans-Pritchard never claimed that Nuer represent local groups as thok dwiel, but only that they speak of them as, or as though they were, lineages. They do that, or so he thought, by sometimes using cieng "with the meaning 'lineage'" and when they use a lineage name when referring to a local group. As a consequence he often used *lineage* as a gloss not only for Nuer thok dwiel, which is entirely suitable, but also for Nuer cieng. That has been a major source of misunderstanding, both of Nuer society and of Evans-Pritchard's accounts and interpretations of it.

III

It is appropriate to begin, as Evans-Pritchard (1933, 1940) did, with consideration of the nature of the physical distribution of the two-hundred thousand or so Nuer, who, in 1930, occupied a vast expanse of savanna in the far south of Sudan and whose economy is mixed pastoral and horticultural.[3] When the savanna is flooded during the rainy season, the Nuer and their cattle reside in village communities of varying size on low sandhills and ridges, where they also plant their crops. As the rains subside they (or at least many of the men and boys) spread out into cattle camps that are more widely dispersed over the savanna, only to congregate once again at the height of the dry season in large groups around the more permanent sources of water. Thus, Nuer communities (cieng) are and could hardly be anything but somewhat unstable aggregates of people related

Tribe											
Primary Section					Primary Section						
Secondary								Secondary			
				Tertiary	Section						
				Villages							

FIGURE 5.1 Territorial Segmentation, Nuer

one to another in various ways, either by birth or by marriage, and the composition of any community may vary to one degree or another, not only from year to year but also from season to season. Appropriately enough, because of their *in principle* highly variable composition, Evans-Pritchard stated repeatedly (e.g., 1950a:387) that although village communities are "groups of kin" (and of in-laws), they are not, as the Nuer see it, "kin groups" of any kind; certainly, they are not *in principle* sets of agnatically related men and their wives and children, or, in other words, localized patrilineages. He did, however, often say that they usually or typically include at least a few members of the locally "dominant" lineage.

Everywhere in Nuerland the areas occupied by several contiguous village communities taken together make up a higher-order region—in the Nuer language, again, a cieng, "place" or "home"—and several of those make up yet another and higher-level cieng.

Evans-Pritchard found that although the exact number varies from one part of Nuerland to another, there are at most five such levels of territorial division, ranging from the "tribe" at the top, down through "primary," "secondary," and "tertiary tribal sections," to the level of the village community at the bottom (see Figure 5.1). *Tribe* is the name he chose to designate that regional level of organization within which, according to his informants, it is in principle (though not always in practice) possible to pay compensation in the event of a homicide and, in so doing, to avoid blood revenge and a protracted feud.

Somewhat parallel to this spatial mode of segmentation, Evans-Pritchard describes another mode of segmentation, of patrilineal descent groups into patrilineal descent groups of lower order; or, looked at from the bottom up, he describes an aggregation of small patrilineages into successively high-order lineages—called thok dwiel at all levels (see Figure 5.2).

He reports that Nuer insist that each and every child becomes at birth a member of his or her father's lineage, and it is not possible for a Nuer to become a member of any other lineage, even by adoption as the child of a

Clan							
Maximal Lineage **A**				Maximal Lineage **B**			
Major		Secondary		X		Y	
			Minor	Lns **X1**	**X2**	**Y1**	**Y2**
			Minimal Lns			**Z1**	**Z2**

FIGURE 5.2 Descent Group Segmentation, Nuer

Nuer man. Thok dwiel can be rendered literally as "door of [a woman's] hut," and patrilineally constituted groups are so called because the Nuer practice polygyny and each of a man's wives has her own hut within his compound. It is from those different huts that the several lineages within a higher-order lineage often derive. That is because when a minimal lineage divides into two or more minimal lineages, it is likely to be into sets composed of the sons of the different co-wives or successive wives of one man. It is, moreover, quite typical of systems of segmentary patrilineal grouping that the line of cleavage between immediately-adjacent groups at the same level of segmentation is between men who are paternal half-siblings, who have the same father but different mothers (for Evans-Pritchard's comments on this point see 1940:247; 1951:127, 140–141).

A minimal lineage among the Nuer (and more generally as well) is at least three generations deep. As Evans-Pritchard (1940:195–196) points out, it cannot be maintained that "the smallest lineage are the sons and daughters of one man," because "the Nuer do not refer to them as a thok dwiel," but describe them, along with the mother, as a family (*gol*), and it is analytically crucial to distinguish, as the Nuer themselves do (but as many anthropologists fail to do in similar circumstances), between lineage affairs and domestic affairs. Often, but again not always, the lineage name is formed by prefixing to one of the names of the apical or founding ancestor either *gaat* 'children of,' or *gaatgan* 'grandchildren of,' or *ji* 'people of.' Thus, *Gaawär*, the lineage Wär, from *Wär* plus *gaat* with the final consonant deleted. To avoid the confusion that might arise because of this name-sharing relationship between some lineage groups and some local groups, Evans-Pritchard adopted the practice that will be followed here of writing the clan or lineage name in uppercase letters, thus GAAWÄR the lineage and Gaawär the territorial section.

Each minimal lineage is only one of two or more segments of a higher-order lineage, which itself is a segment of a still-higher-order lineage, and so on up to and, occasionally, above the clan. *Clan* is the term Evans-Pritchard (1940:192) uses to designate the highest-level lineage that is also in principle exogamous (that is, between members of which marriage is forbidden). He found that in general (though not without some exceptions) the clan level of lineage segmentation corresponds to the tribal level of territorial segmentation; that is to say, there is a correspondence (the nature of which will become clear in due course) between the territorial level (tribe) within which there may be compensation rather than revenge, and the lineage level (clan) within which marriage is prohibited.

The exact number of levels of lineage segmentation varies somewhat from place to place, but Evans-Pritchard found that there are at the most three levels of lineage between the minimal lineage and the clan. He termed them, in descending order, "maximal," "major," and "minor" lineages (again see Figure 5.2). He found also that in general, although again not without some variation, each tribe has a clan associated with it as its *diel* (singular *dil*). He describes this as the "dominant" clan of the tribe, and he describes its members who happen to be resident in that tribal area as that tribe's "aristocrats." Howell (1954) and Hutchinson (1988) gloss diel, somewhat less grandly, as "firstcomers." There are, however, as Evans-Pritchard often pointed out, some clans that are not associated in that way with any tribe. A member of one of those clans is not a dil in any tribal region but is everywhere a *rul*, a "stranger" or (per Hutchinson) a "latecomer." Similarly, each tribal section at each level of segmentation has associated with it a lineage of the dominant clan which is, as it were, dominant in that tribal section. The men of that lineage when resident in that section are its *gaat tuot*, 'sons of bulls.'

There is some ambiguity in Evans-Pritchard's accounts about whether the dil/rul contrast applies not only within the tribe and in relation to the clan but also within each tribal section in relation to the lineage associated with it. Howell (1954:18) appears to indicate that the dil/rul distinction is seldom invoked and operates mainly or only at the tribal level, whereas the more commonly heard gaat tuot/gaat nyiet distinction (in effect between members of a lineage and their sisters' or daughters' children) is applied at all levels of territorial segmentation. Because the difference seems to be not vitally important for the purposes of this discussion, it is assumed in what follows that the dil/rul or aristocrat/stranger (or firstcomer vs. latecomer) contrast is applicable at all levels of territorial segmentation.

Evans-Pritchard (e.g., 1933:42) describes the dominant clan or lineage of a tribe or tribal section as the "owner" of that area and its natural resources, and he says occasionally that strangers live where they do "on sufferance." But he states also that clans and lineages never act "corporately," that is, as unified bodies, and he presents no evidence to show that members of the dominant lineage of a community ever attempt to exclude other people from peaceful residence within it on the grounds that they are 'strangers' and have no right to be there. Resident members of the dominant lineage of a tribal section appear to have no rights or duties in that section or in relation to its resources that would set them off, as somehow specially privileged, from the other people who also live there. Indeed, the relation of a dominant clan or lineage to a tribe or tribal section appears to be little more than strictly "nominal."[4]

Even so, that relationship is quite significant for what Evans-Pritchard termed Nuer "political organization," that is, relations between territorial sections. The proper names of tribes and tribal sections are often (but by no means always) the names also of the clans or lineages that are dominant in them. A contrary instance is the tribe and tribal region named Lou, the clan associated with which is named JINACA, from *ji* "people of," and *Nac*, the name of the founding ancestor. Evans-Pritchard made much of this "nominal" relationship between some clans and lineages on the one hand and tribes and tribal sections on the other hand, because he found it, at first at least, quite difficult to comprehend, and because he believed that failure to comprehend it had resulted in considerable confusion in other accounts of Nuer social organization (1933:22–26; 1940:203–205). The difficulty is that, as a consequence of this relationship, and of the freedom of Nuer to move about and to settle wherever they will (so long as they have kin or in-laws already in the place), it cannot be deduced from a knowledge of where a Nuer lives or which place (cieng) he tells you he is from what his lineage and clan affiliations are. Moreover, Evans-Pritchard reports that it can be quite difficult to get a Nuer to report on his lineage and clan affiliations, as distinct from his tribal and tribal section affiliations. It is not that any Nuer is ever uncertain about his clan and lineage affiliations; nor is it, as Kuper (1982:84) has asserted, that "the Nuer do not clearly distinguish 'lineage' from 'local groups,'" or between territory and agnation; it is instead that, in contrast to his tribal section and village community affiliations, his clan and lineage affiliations are "irrelevant" (1940:204) to the conduct of everyday social life within his community. So, if you want to know a man's clan and lineage affiliations, you have to find out how he aligns himself in the conduct of those few affairs in relation to which clan or lineage affiliation is the critical consideration—that is, certain ritual and ceremonial activities, relations of exogamy, and, to a limited extent, participation in feud (but *not* in blood revenge).

There is, however, another way in which the lineage system, as distinct from an individual's lineage affiliation, is socially significant. *The Nuer* focuses on "political structure," defined as social relations between territorial segments, and it deals with the Nuer lineage system only insofar as it figures in the Nuer political system, and that, as it turns out, is only as a kind of "framework" or "skeleton" for social relations between territorial segments. It does that via the conception that each tribal region and section is the place or home of, because first settled by, a particular clan or lineage group. In addition, at each level of segmentation, immediately adjacent tribal sections tend to have associated with them as their dominant lineages just those lineage segments that are also immediately adjacent genealogically one to the other.

In the lineage system proper, immediately adjacent lineages have certain mutual ritual and ceremonial rights and duties vis-à-vis one another. Those rights can be exercised and those duties can be fulfilled virtually anywhere because they are in no way tied to the lineage homeland and can be exercised or fulfilled representatively by one or a few members of the relevant lineages. Evans-Pritchard is quite definite that no lineage at any level of segmentation, not even the minimal, is a "corporate" group, by which he means that the group as a whole never convenes to take collective action in its own name. There are no indications that any lineage at any level of segmentation, even the minimal, has a responsibility to protect its members or to exact compensation or to take revenge in the event of an injury to or a killing of one of them.[5] The right and duty to take revenge or to exact compensation in the event of a homicide falls jointly and severally on close agnatic kin, principally the victim's father, father's brother, brother, or son (who are not except per accident even a minimal lineage), and liability to be killed in revenge or to assist in payment of compensation is similarly restricted to those close agnatic kin of the killer. Lineage affiliation does figure in "feuding," but not above the level of the minimal (1940:160) or the minor lineage (1934:55). Feuding, or "blood feud" as Evans-Pritchard sometimes calls it, is not, however, a matter of shedding more blood, but of the lineage mates of the killer and of the victim having to avoid one another for fear of further violence and because they are forbidden to eat or drink with one another or to use utensils used by the other. This, Evans-Pritchard points out, is a rather onerous burden, because Nuer are not segregated into lineage-based communities and because Nuer of the same or adjacent communities are constantly visiting one another and eating in one another's homes. The avoidances of the feud thus sharply curtail the normal conviviality of community life, in which the Nuer are constantly "holding open house."

Despite all that, the lineage system does figure in relations of conflict between groups, but the operative groups are territorial units (cieng), and not the lineages (thok dwiel) themselves. Evans-Pritchard does sometimes say that Nuer often speak of the operative groups as lineages, or as though they were lineages, but he gives us no reasons to think that what he is getting at when he says that is anything but this: In many instances, though again not always (because not all lineage names are also lineage-homeland names), the Nuer have no way to speak of a particular tribe or

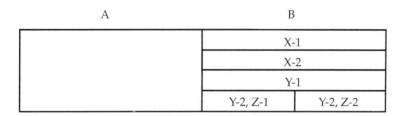

FIGURE 5.3   Dominant Lineage Relations, Nuer

tribal section other than by use of an expression that is the name also of a clan or lineage.

The general principle seems to be that, in the event of a dispute between two tribal segments, each has the right to call upon certain other tribal segments to come to its aid, in particular those tribal segments in which the dominant lineages are the immediately adjacent collaterals of its own dominant lineage. Should there be trouble between two adjacent village communities, Z-1 and Z-2 in Figure 5.3, the dominant lineages of which are immediately adjacent in the structure of the dominant clan of that tribe, the conflict would be defined as between Z-1 and Z-2 only.

Neither of the groups would have the right to call upon members of communities in tribal section Y-1, nor would a Y-1 community have a duty to aid one of the Z communities if asked, because the dominant lineage of Y-1 is equidistant from the dominant lineages of 2-1 and 2-2, and therefore the inhabitants of Y-1 have no formal grounds on which to take sides. Similarly, if a village community in tribal section A were to attack a village community in tribal section Z-2, the conflict would immediately be defined as one between tribal segments A and B, because their dominant lineages are, again, immediately adjacent in the structure of the dominant clan of the tribe. Members of those dominant lineages who are not themselves resident in those communities are not duty-bound to come to the aid of their lineage mates. That is because the two sides are defined and represented not as lineages or even as though they were lineages, but as tribal segments, and the level of tribal segment implicated in a conflict depends on the genealogical relations, if any, between the dominant lineages of the villages or of the higher-level communities of the principal parties.

Evans-Pritchard (1933:17; 1940:144) reported that in the accounts of actual intergroup conflict that he was given, the combinations of groups "were not always as regular and simple as they were explained to [him]."

Some anthropologists have taken his observation and the relevant data as indications that the Nuer "political system" does not actually work in the way that Evans-Pritchard and the Nuer say it does (Holy 1979b, 1996; Kuper 1982; Southall 1986). Yet, as Lucy Mair (1974:124) observed, Nuer accounts of actual intergroup conflicts are just as much a part of their view or representation of "how the system works" as are their generalized statements. The difficulty appears to be that Evans-Pritchard's critics take his informants' observations about which groups would come to the aid of or oppose other groups as regulative and prescriptive rules. Therefore, what impresses these critics is the degree to which actual intergroup relations "fail" to correspond to those rules. It seems rather more probable, though, that the informants' statements should be taken to indicate that certain groups (tribal segments) have certain mutual and special rights and duties vis-à-vis one another, because of the relations of inclusion between their dominant lineages. Those jural relations do not preclude the possibility of offensive or defensive alliances between territorial segments the dominant lineages of which are held to be related in other, nonagnatic, ways—although to form alliances of that kind may be to run the risk of expanding the conflict. Evans-Pritchard (1940:144–145) makes it clear that what we have to deal with here are special rights and duties between tribal segments, and not with regulative and prescriptive rules, when he observes that, if any section of one tribe is at war with a section of another tribe, the other sections of the two tribes "may leave them to fight it out if they are well matched and do not appeal for assistance."

Further on this point it must be noted that in such a system of intergroup relations, it is hardly to be expected that the parties to a conflict will neatly correspond to the inhabitants of certain territorial sections. For one thing, as we have already seen, these are not stable sets of people and their members are related by important ties of kinship and marriage to persons who are members of other such sets, often just that set that is at the moment the nominal enemy. As already noticed and elaborated upon by Gluckman (1955) and Mair (1962, 1974), this implies conflicts of allegiance that tend to mitigate or to dampen the impulse to intergroup conflict. On the one hand persons who are not implicated via their group affiliations may choose to ally as individual kin or friends with one of the principal parties to a conflict; on the other hand, persons who are implicated via their group affiliations may try to find reasons and ways for their groups not to participate or to find ways to make peace; or, if in the end they have to fight, they will avoid doing so directly with their kin, in-laws, and friends on the other side. All of this, too, is a part of Nuer politics.

To summarize the argument so far: As described by Evans-Pritchard, the relation between lineage and locality in Nuer society is that they are, as Fortes said about lineage systems generally, independently variable. There is, however, a definite relationship between particular lineage groups and particular local groups. The lineage (thok dwiel) affiliation of a Nuer is determined at birth and cannot be changed or altered, and that is in stark contrast to a person's local group affiliation which, if not wholly free from any sort of constraint, is at least readily changeable. Village communities, although fluctuating in composition from year to year, usually contain at least some members of the local 'firstcomer' lineage as a sort of core population to which various kin, in-laws, kin of kin, and various Dinka (a neighboring people) attach themselves, either temporarily or for an indefinite period. Many of those persons are children or grandchildren of female members of the dominant lineage. These "children of daughters" can never become members of that lineage, but they suffer no disadvantages and are not in any way discriminated against as a consequence of being "strangers" in a community.

Because lineage groups and local groups are constituted as quite different kinds of social entity, the rights and duties of lineages vis-à-vis one another are wholly different from the rights and duties of territorial segments vis-à-vis one another. Otherwise the categorical distinction between lineage groups and local groups would be itself quite meaningless. The rights and duties of lineages vis-à-vis one another and of persons as members of them are narrowly confined to certain ritual and ceremonial affairs, to relations of exogamy, and, up to the level of the minor lineage, to relations of avoidance entailed by the feud. Within each local community social relations are governed by the categories and rights and duties of kinship and of relationship by marriage, and differences in lineage and clan affiliation are irrelevant in the conduct of social life. Although local groups are not lineage groups, social relations between them are structured by the lineage system via the homeland relation between certain clans and lineages and certain tribal-territorial sections. Neighboring tribal sections are typically the homelands of lineages that are genealogically immediately adjacent to one another, and in periods of intergroup conflict those tribal sections have the right to call upon one another for assistance. That does not preclude offensive or defensive alliances between tribal segments held to be related in other ways. Nor does it entail that a party's right to ask for assistance will be exercised, or that the corresponding duty will be fulfilled when the request is made.

IV

Nothing said in III is inconsistent with anything said in the first paragraph of this chapter. But if there were no more to it than that, there would be no grounds for the claim that there are gross incompatibilities between descent or lineage theory, so called, and Evans-Pritchard's Nuer data. There is, however, another line of interpretation of the relationship between lineage and locality that runs throughout Evans-Pritchard's Nuer ethnography.

This other representation is similar to the first in maintaining that Nuer communities are quite diverse in composition, and for the conduct of everyday life within the community that diversity is kept discretely in the background and is not used to make invidious comparisons between neighbors. That is done, not (as the first interpretation has it) by treating lineage affiliations as irrelevant and favoring the categories and norms of kinship and of relationship by marriage as the bases of community life, but by treating the stranger Nuer "as though they were born into the community," as though they were members of its dominant lineage and therefore have as much right as anyone else to be resident in that tribal section. "In speech," says Evans-Pritchard (1933:48), the strangers "are assimilated to the dominant lineage"; later (1934:4) he says that is done by sometimes referring to the strangers as aristocrats. (He does not, alas, give any examples of or generalize about the kinds of social context in which that may be done.) Moreover, he often writes quite graphically of how "small lineages" of stranger or Dinka origin "attach" themselves to, or "incorporate" themselves into, or "graft" themselves onto "the growth of" the lineage that is dominant in a tribal section. Some of those statements seem designed to make the (now at least) rather obvious point that strangers and Dinka can become closely associated with some members of a locally dominant lineage in the conduct of everyday village life, and not themselves become or even need to become members of that lineage, because lineage affiliation is quite irrelevant to the concerns of ordinary, everyday village life, Yet there are, it must be admitted, many places in which it seems clear that another proposition is being asserted.

By way of example, immediately after remarking on how village composition is always changing and how, sooner or later, most people return to live with some of their agnatic kin in the tribal sections that are their lineage homelands, Evans-Pritchard writes:

> There is always a tendency in Nuerland to stress the dominant line of descent, that is to say the lineage which counts as diel, and if this happens to be the mother's line she is often regarded as though she were a man in the genealogy of her descendants. In this way people who are really unrelated in the male line to the dominant lineage of their district come to regard themselves and to be regarded as though they were truly members of it (1935:78).
>
> One does not call 'strangers' people who share one's daily experiences. They count as equivalent to members of the lineage because they carry out many of the major obligations of blood relations (1935:80).

[Writing of a woman's children who live with her brothers:] In the course
of time a maternal link of this kind may be treated as though it were a paternal link and therefore within the genealogical structure of the principal lineage of the community. . . . In this manner cognation comes to be regarded,
for ordinary purposes within community life, as equal to agnation. . . .
[W]hen people live together as members of the same small community female
links are often given equivalence to male links in a genealogy (1950a:373).

. . . Outside ritual situations, being gaat nyiet ['children of daughters'] to a
dominant lineage gives people complete equality with it. . . . It is, however,
common practice for children of strangers who have been brought up at the
home of their maternal kinsmen, who are aristocrats, to regard themselves a
members of their mother's lineage, except in ceremonial situations, and to
consider its members rather than their father's lineage as their true kinsmen
(1940:228).

And, finally, a simulated conversation (1933:29), in which cieng is used,
according to Evans-Pritchard, "with the meaning 'lineage'":

Thok dwillun e mith? "What is your lineage?"
Thok dwillan e cieng Rue. "Our lineage is the RUE lineage."
Cieng Rue babdien coaledi? "What is the lineage of which the RUE lineage
forms a part?"
Babdien e cieng Nyajkany. "They form a lineage of the NYAJEKANY
llineage."

However it may have been intended, some of this simply cannot be
taken at face value. We can be quite certain that if there really is a process
whereby a Nuer not born into a particular lineage can become a member
of it, it is hardly so simple as a mere act on his part of (somehow) treating
the woman through whom he is related to that lineage "as though she
were a man." We can be certain that it is not possible for a man to make
himself a member of a lineage to which he is linked through a woman
simply by moving into the homeland of that lineage and declaring that
the linking kinswoman was or is in fact a man. That would make a farce
of the distinction between aristocrats and strangers. In one place, Evans-
Pritchard (1945:65) appears to say that the process of assimilation into
one's mother's lineage begins when a woman's son comes (as any first-
born son should) to live with and to grow up among her kin. Her kin then
use her name, rather than his father's name, to refer to him (as "child of
so-and-so"), and, if her name is not distinctly a female name, it may in
time be lost sight of that her son's link to the dominant lineage in the
community was through a woman. Eventually, his agnatic descendants
will become a lineage that is agnatically collateral to the dominant lineage. But in every specific instance mentioned by Evans-Pritchard, the fe-

male link is still represented as such, and it is far from clear in what sense it might be said that she is being treated as, or as though she were, a man.

It is significant, too, that in some of the relevant passages Evans-Pritchard drifts from appearing to assert that a child of a female member of a lineage may become within his own lifetime known as a member of her lineage, to describing a much longer social process wherein, if a small lineage "grows up" in the homeland of another lineage and clan, the first lineage may become known as an agnatic collateral of the second. Yet, in other places he asserts that neither process is possible or that he has no reasons to suppose that it ever occurs:

> A lineage is a group of agnates, i.e., everyone descended through the male line from a given individual. A man cannot, therefore, be a member of his mother's lineage (1933:30).
>
> It may sometimes happen that a stranger of pure Nuer descent is given *buth* by [i.e., made a collateral agnate of] neighbours with whom he has taken up his residence and of whose group he considers himself, for purposes other than those of descent, to be a member, but I should be inclined to doubt whether this happens often and I have no definite knowledge of it ever occurring at all (1934:30).

He does not mention having any knowledge that such a process has ever in fact occurred; nor does it seem likely that he ever intended to imply, much less to assert, that a Nuer may acquire membership of his mother's or of any other lineage (thok dwiel).

Attached as a footnote to the statement that a man cannot become a member of his mother's lineage is the qualification, "Except when a woman founds a line of descent, . . . [and] even then descent is traced through males to the ancestress of a lineage" (1933:30). He does not explain what he means by that. He could hardly be alluding the possibility that the brideprice for a woman may be paid by another woman, so that the second becomes, specifically for the purpose of determining the lineage affiliations of children subsequently born to the first, the 'father' of those children. Although a woman may thereby "found a line of descent," it is not as the mother, but as the "pater" (legal father) of the other woman's offspring (see especially Evans-Pritchard 1945, 1951). He might be alluding to the way in which immediately adjacent lineages typically derive from the co-wives of one man; but, if so, it is rather misleading to describe the situation so simply as one in which "a woman founds a line of descent."

Finally, and much more likely, he may be alluding to myths that seem intended to account for how it happens that two or more maximal lineages belonging to different clans have in some instances come to occupy adjacent sections of the same tribal region (and thus of course to present a departure from the more common pattern of association of one clan with one tribe). One such myth (1933:46; 1940:229–230) has it that one of three lineages derives from a son and two others from daughters of the apical ancestor of a clan. The father, so the story goes, once consoled the son when his two brothers had been eaten by a monster, so that he had no companions, by telling the son "let your two sisters be your brothers." As a consequence, the three lineages are now companions who share a tribal region, and the two lineages deriving from the sisters and their sons have no external agnatic connections because the fathers of those sons are un-known. But, on Evans-Pritchard's own testimony, this is most definitely not a matter of incorporating a man into his mother's lineage, not even a great many generations after his death. As he then goes on to stress, the two lineages founded by the sisters and their sons "form separate exoga-mous groups since they cannot be members of the clan of their ances-tresses" (1933:46; 1940:230). It is not helpful for him to add: "However, in some respects the original daughter who gave birth to the stranger's lin-eage is treated as though she had been a son." She is so treated (in the in-formation presented by Evans-Pritchard) *only in the myth* and only for the purpose of being a companion to her brother. Again, as Evans-Pritchard goes on explicitly to state, she is most definitely not treated as though she were a man for the purpose of including her descendants in the lineage of which she and her brother were members.

It is noted below that there are lineage systems wherein a lineage stem-ming from the son of a female member may, many generations after his death, be incorporated into her natal lineage. But, to all appearances, the Nuer lineage system is not one of them, and it does appear to be true, as Evans-Pritchard often asserted, that among the Nuer no one can become a member of his or her mother's lineage, even temporarily or for some so-cial purposes but not others, or even many generations after his or her death, and no lineage can be moved from one clan to another. At most, a dwindling lineage group can attach itself to and eventually merge its identity with a close collateral lineage in its own clan, with which lineage it is already in a buth or collateral agnatic relationship (Evans-Pritchard 1940:211).

Evans-Pritchard sometimes says that, for purposes of everyday social life, strangers in a community "count as equivalent" to members of the dominant lineage of that community "because they carry out many of the major obligations of blood relations" (1935:80) , as though integration into the local community is necessarily via inclusion, even if only temporarily, in the dominant lineage. But he sometimes says just the opposite, that is that lineage groups and local groups, even though they may share their proper names, are by no means the same thing, and that recruitment from the outside to membership of a lineage is simply impossible. Consistent with that he sometimes describes local communities as "'groups of kin,' but not 'kin groups,'" and he says that life within them is ordered by the values (the concepts and norms) of kinship and of relationship by marriage, and not by "lineage values." Indeed, he often stresses that "lineage relations" are strictly inter-group, and not inter-individual in the way kinship relations are. If that is true, it cannot be true also that strangers count as equivalent to members of the dominant lineage because they carry out many of the major obligations of blood relations (that is, kin).

To compound the confusion, Evans-Pritchard sometimes appears to take yet another position. Immediately after stating that a Nuer community is not composed exclusively of a single lineage and their wives, nor do all members of a lineage live in the same community, he writes:

> In any large village or camp there is represented an agnatic lineage of one or other order and into the growth of this lineage are grafted, through the tracing of descent through females, branches which are regarded in certain situations and in a certain sense as part of it and in other situations and in a different sense as not part of it (1950a:386; 1951:23).

Here he seems to say that for certain (though unspecified) social purposes lineages are agnatically constituted, but for other (unspecified) social purposes each lineage consists of those agnatic descendants of the founder who are resident in its homeland plus those of their kin and in-laws who are residing there with them. In effect, the claim is that there are two kinds of membership of a lineage or two kinds of lineage.

That, however, is an incoherent notion. We must remember that lineage is our expression, and not one taken from the Nuer language. It is employed herein as it was by Evans-Pritchard himself on the presumption that it is the most suitable English gloss for Nuer thok dwiel, because (and Evans-Pritchard is totally consistent about this) patrifiliation is necessary and sufficient for inclusion in a group of that kind. Nowhere does he say that it is possible, nor does he anywhere provide information that could be taken to show that it is possible, for a Nuer to gain admission to a thok dwiel other than by birth. The kind of group for inclusion in which patrifiliation is not necessary and sufficient (and for that matter neither necessary nor sufficient) but which does, according to Evans-Pritchard, center both normatively and normally on a small set of agnatically related men, is designated cieng in the Nuer language.

So, it is not that Nuer represent one and the same kind of group, especially the kind they designate thok dwiel, sometimes as agnatically constituted and sometimes as constituted in some other way. It is, instead, that as Evans-Pritchard saw it, in many instances when a Nuer wishes to refer to a tribal segment he has no choice but to use "the name of a lineage" and in so doing he speaks of that tribal segment "as a lineage" or "as though it were a lineage." Significantly, though, there are many instances in which there is no such "nominal" correspondence between lineage group and local group, and there are therefore many instances in which a Nuer may speak, without danger of ambiguity, of a lineage group or a local group simply by mentioning its name.

Evans-Pritchard sometimes says also that Nuer use the expressions thok dwiel and cieng "interchangeably." Yet when he explicates what he means by that it always turns out that, as he sees it, the Nuer sometimes use the expression cieng "with the meaning 'lineage.'" He nowhere says that thok dwiel is used where cieng would be more appropriate or precise because of its "territorial connotations." So, when a Nuer speaks of, let us say cieng Rue, Evans-Pritchard would have us believe that he may be referring, not to the place with that name, but to the agnatically constituted social group with that name. That, according to Evans-Pritchard, is what the imaginary informant did when, in answer to the question *thok dwillun e mith?*, "What is your lineage?," he replied *thok dwillan e cieng Rue*, "Our lineage is Rue lineage."

There are several fatal difficulties for that line of interpretation. One is that it seems unwarranted to say that when a Nuer speaks of a tribe or tribal section using an expression that is also the name of a clan or lineage, he is, whether or not he intends to, speaking of that local group "as a lineage" or "as though it were a lineage." First, as already stressed, not all tribe and tribal-section names are also lineage names, so that in some instances no Nuer can speak of a tribe or tribal section as, or as though it were, a lineage. Second, any Nuer knows, as Evans-Pritchard himself eventually learned, that the rights and duties of lineages and of persons as members of them are quite different from the rights and duties of local groups and of persons as members of them. As a consequence, knowing what kind of social relations are being talked about will usually suffice to make it obvious whether, in that context, the referent of a proper name is a lineage group or a local group or place. From that it follows that using a "lineage name" when speaking of a local group is not at all the same thing as speaking of that group "as a lineage" or "as though it were a lineage." We might as well say, indeed it would be much better if we did say, that certain proper names are both lineage and local-group names, and the context of use is quite likely to make it wholly transparent which way they are being used.

We need to be skeptical also of the claim that cieng is often used "with the meaning 'lineage,'" so that the appropriate gloss for cieng in the context of, for example, *thok dwillan e cieng Rue*, "our lineage is Rue," is 'lineage.' Immediately following the passage quoted above, Evans-Pritchard writes:

In their collective relations with other communities, and as seen collectively by the members of these communities, there is a fusion of the attached elements with the lineage. They are incorporated into it, and the resultant whole is spoken of the cieng or wec, community, of the lineage, . . . (1951:23).

It is significant that although Evans-Pritchard here says the "attached elements" are "incorporated into" the locally dominant lineage, he makes it clear enough that what they are "incorporated into" is not an entity of the kind designated thok dwiel, but an entity of the kind designated cieng or wec. The result is, as he here acknowledges, not a lineage but, much more accurately, a sort of "lineage community" or, in other words, a community that includes (and perhaps must include) some members of the locally dominant lineage. Moreover, Evans-Pritchard finishes the paragraph with this observation:

Within the community itself there are occasions when a formal distinction between the lineage and its incorporated elements has to be made and the status of its members has to be defined to the exclusion of the rul, strangers; the gaatnyiet, the children of daughters (of the lineage), and the affines (1951:23).

In other words, from time to time within a community a person's lineage affiliation does become the critically relevant social identity, as when a family must make a ritual sacrifice and, to do it, must make use of the services of a man (its *gwan buthni* or, as Evans-Pritchard puts it, its master of ceremonies) from a collateral lineage. Co-resident persons who are not members of the lineage of the person making the sacrifice are not entitled to participate, nor are they entitled to a share of the sacrificial meat; but collateral lineages are entitled to such shares.

There is, then, a critical distinction to be made between lineage affairs— not "in the strict sense" of thok dwiel but in the only sense—and the affairs of a lineage community (one kind of cieng), where the latter is a local group that includes some members of the locally dominant lineage, some of their kin and in-laws, and perhaps some adopted or attached persons of Dinka origin. Evans-Pritchard (1951:23–24) goes on to say that within any lineage community social relations "are expressed not in the language of lineage structure but in the language of the kinship system." That goes also for social relations between co-resident members of a minimal lineage (whether or not that lineage happens to be dominant in the community), who have "an undifferentiated lineage relationship" only on those occasions when "the lineage acts or is thought of as a group." Otherwise, social relations between persons who happen to be lineage-mates, and whether or not they are members of the local dominant lineage, are, like all intra-community relations, governed by considerations of kintype or kin class. The clear implication is that it is seriously misleading on Evans-Pritchard's part to write, as so often he does, of each Nuer community as composed of a nucleus of a locally dominant lineage and of other small lineages that are attached to it. To judge from his data on village and cattle-camp composition, there are very few minimal lineages, much less any lineages of higher order, whose members—even male members—are not widely dispersed.

The difficulty is that lineages and lineage communities are two quite different (though not wholly unrelated) kinds of group, and, correspondingly, interlineage relations and intercommunity relations also are two quite different kinds of thing. Yet it seems, or so it did to Evans-Pritchard, that intercommunity relations are represented as, or as though they are, relations between lineages. The fact that many (but by no means all) territorial sections derive their names from the names of lineages does not, however, warrant the claim that when Nuer use those names in reference to local groups they are representing those groups as, or as though they were, lineages. Neither do we have to suppose that in the sentence *thok dwillan e cieng Rue*, "Our lineage is Rue," the thok dwiel and the cieng both have the sense of 'lineage.' There is no other suitable gloss for thok dwiel, but 'homeland,' surely, is the appropriate gloss for cieng in this context (that is, "our lineage, its homeland is RUE").

It is not evidence to the contrary that, in the questions that followed (1933:29), Evans-Pritchard and his informant continued to use cieng where thok dwiel would have been more precise, in an attempt to learn the name of the lineage of which Rue is a segment, and so on up. When it comes to purely formal relations of class inclusion, the relations between cieng may not be always exactly the same as the relations between their dominant lineages, but this appears to be one of those instances in which they are. Although the relations between cieng are spatial and the relations between thok dwiel are genealogical, in some instances it makes no difference which expression is used (cieng or thok dwiel) once the central topic of the conversation has been established. In any event, Evans-Pritchard himself several times wrote "cieng has always a residential [or spatial] and not an exclusive descent connotation" (1950a:364). Ipso facto, it could never be used more or less synonymously with thok dwiel. Howell (1954:21), whose representation of the forms of Nuer social life was much influenced by Evans-Pritchard's, also says "cieng is, in many contexts, synonymous with thok dwiel." But he makes it clear that, in his experience, cieng always has a spatial signification, as well as perhaps a genealogical connotation, whereas thok dwiel always has simply a genealogical signification.

V

We have seen that there is nothing in Evans-Pritchard's Nuer data to show that a thok dwiel, a patrilineage of one or another order, ever includes any Nuer other than agnatic descendants of its founder. That is not to say that recruitment from the outside is impossible. It is well known that a captured Dinka boy may be adopted into the kinship status of a son of his Nuer captor and, in the process, made a member of his captor's minimal lineage. That is possible, however, only because a Dinka boy does not already have an identity within the Nuer lineage system, that is, another identity of the same kind, of which he simply cannot rid himself. It is not true, though, that sons of Nuer women may and often do become members of their mothers' lineages. Although Evans-Pritchard does sometimes mislead his readers on that matter, sometimes the readers mislead themselves. For example, one of them writes:

> The absorption of sister's sons into the status of member of a dominant lineage is all the more remarkable in that Evans-Pritchard (1951:25) 'ventures to say that in the vast majority of cases they are Dinka' (Southall 1986:1).

This makes it appear that Dinka men marry Nuer women and their progeny become members of the lineages of those women. What Evans-Pritchard actually says, however, is quite different.

In the place cited the topic under discussion is how, other than by childhood adoption into Nuer families and lineages, Dinka and their progeny can be absorbed into Nuer communities and their social life. Evans-Pritchard then notices again that there are many small lineages that are not dominant in any tribal section, but each is "attached through a female" to a set of people who are members of the lineage that is dominant in the tribal section where they all reside. He then speculates that "in the vast majority of cases" these small, attached lineages are composed of Dinka, or rather of persons ultimately of Dinka agnatic origins. He does not say that these small, attached lineages are included in higher-order Nuer lineages, and it would have been quite inappropriate for him to say that, because he would not have been speculating about their probable Dinka origins had they been known as segments of higher-order Nuer lineages, in particular the minor lineages that include the minimal lineages to which they are "attached through a female."

Another and a rather curious misreading of *The Nuer* is by D. Schneider (1965:74, 79 n. 2), who says first that Evans-Pritchard was "faced with the odd fact that, although the lineages are territorial units, and although they seem to be as patrilineal as patrilineal can be, descent is traced through women and many people live matrilocally," and then "it becomes apparent on close inspection that the lineages as actual groups are not . . . so strongly localized as might be inferred from a hasty reading of his monograph." It takes a very hasty reading indeed to miss noticing that, far from seeing it as a "fact" that "lineages are territorial units," Evans-Pritchard was at great pains to stress the difference between local groups and lineage groups. That difference is essential to his representation of the nature of the Nuer polity.

The passage perhaps most often cited in support of the claim that, despite their professed agnatic principles, Nuer lineages do routinely recruit from the outside, and most especially from the offspring of their female members, is this:

> I suggest that it is the clear, consistent, and deeply rooted lineage structure of the Nuer which permits persons and families to move about and attach themselves so freely, for shorter or longer periods, to whatever community they choose by whatever cognatic or affinal tie they find it convenient to emphasize; and that it is on account of the firm values of the structure that this flux does not cause confusion or bring about social disintegration. It would seem that it may be partly just because the agnatic principle is unchallenged in Nuer society that the tracing of descent through women is so prominent and matrilocality so prevalent. However much the actual configurations of kinship clusters [i.e., local communities] may vary and change, the lineage structure is invariable and stable (1951:28).

Sahlins (1965:105), Schneider (1965:74), Holy (1976:110–111), Kelly (1977:290), and numerous others have represented the part about "the tracing of descent through women" and the prevalence of "matrilocality" as an open admission that Nuer lineages are in practice, even if not in principle, open to recruitment from the outside. It is, surely, most ironic that the paragraph as a whole is intended to make exactly the opposite point. That is difficult to see, however, if it is not realized that (like Fortes) Evans-Pritchard never endorsed Rivers's proposals about the use of descent and other technical expressions. By *descent* he meant nothing more or less than "ascending kinship," and he often made a point of noticing the prominence of "the tracing descent through women" in Nuer society precisely to counteract the old prejudice that, in a society with patrilineal descent groups, maternity and maternal kinship must "count for little or nothing."

If a Nuer cannot choose his lineage affiliation, can he choose between being an active or an inactive member of his lineage? It should be clear by now that when a Nuer elects to live elsewhere than in the homeland of his lineage, he may or may not be electing also to be an inactive member of his lineage. Whether or not he does so depends on the nature of the rights and duties of lineages and of persons as members of them, and, more specifically, on whether or not exercising those rights and fulfilling those duties is tied to a specific locale. It is unfortunate that it remains unclear just exactly what those rights and duties are.

Evans-Pritchard sometimes writes as though the rights and duties of lineage affiliation (at least at the minimal lineage level) are quite extensive:

A minor lineage like the PUAL lineage of the GAATBAL are a community really well knit by common residence and blood who lead a common economic, political and social life. If one takes a small lineage like the MÄR lineage, one reaches the strongest unilateral unit in Nuer society, a unit who herd their cattle by communal arrangements; who build their huts contiguously and cultivate gardens side by side; who act as a blood revenge group in case of the homicide of one of their kin; who assist one another in providing cattle for marriage or homicide payments; who act as assistants at all important ceremonies; and who will in general cooperate as a mutual assistance society for all purposes of social insurance (1933:39).

That, however, is a very overblown description of the significance of minimal-lineage affiliation. It appears in the earliest of Evans-Pritchard's publications on the Nuer, and it is followed immediately by this disarming observation:

At least this is how I understand the relative cohesion of clan segments, though I feel that there is a leaning towards theoretical conclusions not adequately supported by a strong foundation of facts in my presentation (1933:39).

The difficulty is not, as many observers have already noticed, that to judge from Evans-Pritchard's detailed accounts of the compositions of the several villages, it is perhaps rare for all or even many of the men of even a minimal lineage to reside together and to cooperate in the way indicated. It is instead that there is virtually nothing in Evans-Pritchard's data to indicate that the members of a minimal lineage have the right to expect such pervasive cooperation from one another. Indeed, throughout his writings on the Nuer Evans-Pritchard is continually reminding his readers that lineage affiliation per se governs a person's conduct generally not at all, but only in certain ritual or ceremonial contexts, in connection with exogamy, and to a limited extent in connection with the feud (and he is not altogether consistent about that). Certainly, small sets of closely related male agnates may from time to time live and work together, but such a small set does not a lineage make. The right and the duty to take revenge for a person's death does fall to his father, father's brothers, brothers, or sons (and in the case of a woman to her husband), and, by common anthropological usage, these are close agnates; and they and some more distant agnates are among the kinds of kin who are obliged to contribute to, and who are entitled to receive portions of, bridewealth. None of that, however, makes these the rights and duties of lineages or of persons as members of lineages. Moreover, Evans-Pritchard himself, in his later writings at least, continually stresses that they are the rights and duties of particular kinds of kin vis-à-vis one another, and that no good can come of mistaking them for the affairs of lineages.

Even more critically, and as already noticed, in a number of places Evans-Pritchard emphasizes that membership of a Nuer lineage is relevant only in contexts of inter-lineage relations. That is to say, the inclusion of any two persons, say A and B, in one and the same minimal lineage, say X, is jurally relevant to their conduct vis-à-vis one another only in relation to person C's inclusion in another minimal lineage, say Y, and also if and only if X and Y are both segments of the next-higher-order (minor) lineage P. Similarly, the inclusion of persons A, B, and C in minor lineage P is relevant only in relation to person D's inclusion in minor lineage Q, and then if and only if P and Q are both segments of the next-higher-order (major) lineage R; and so on up to the level of the clan. What all that implies is that there are no individual rights and duties entailed by lineage affiliation except those that can be deduced from the special rights and duties of lineages vis-à-vis one another. In short, the distinctive feature of a genuine segmentary lineage system is precisely the existence, at each level of hierarchical inclusion, of mutual and special rights and duties between immediately adjacent collateral lineages.[6]

It is here, however, that Evans-Pritchard's ethnography is disappointingly thin. Although he frequently asserts in very general terms that lineage affiliation is a determinant of behavior only in certain kinds of ritual and ceremonial contexts, in connection with exogamy, and to a very limited extent in the feud, he nowhere makes the topic the focus of an extended and detailed discussion. *The Nuer* focuses on "political organization" and deals only with those formal features of the lineage system that are relevant to intercommunity relations. *Kinship and Marriage Among the Nuer* (1951) focuses on intracommunity relations and emphasizes how differences of lineage affiliation are by and large irrelevant to ordinary, everyday social relations within villages and cattle camps. Given Evans-Pritchard's repeated emphasis on the ritual and ceremonial functions of lineages, we might have expected to learn more about them in *Nuer Religion* (1956); but they are mentioned there even less than in the other two books. Here and there in those three books and in Evans-Pritchard's many essays on the Nuer, there are at most only a few hints about the specific nature and extent of the rights and duties of lineages, and of persons as members of lineages, vis-à-vis one another.

We have seen already that the rights and duties of lineages do not encompass seeking revenge or compensation in the event of a homicide. Neither do they encompass giving or receiving bridewealth. Evans-Pritchard (1950a:366) is quite explicit that giving or receiving bridewealth is antithetical to lineage relations. That is not to say that persons who are members of the bride's and groom's minimal lineages do not contribute to or receive bridewealth cattle; certainly they do, but in capacities other than as members of those lineages. If membership of those lineages were the critical consideration, many additional persons would have to contribute or receive cattle on that occasion. The same goes for contribution to or receipt of blood compensation following a homicide.

In his earliest publications on the Nuer, Evans-Pritchard (1934:30–34) reports that each "small lineage" (or, later, each family) has its own *gwan buthni*, a sort of "master of ceremonies" who acts as its ritual officiate on various occasions and most especially when there is an animal sacrifice to be made and consumption of the meat is limited to members of the sponsoring lineage and to members of certain other lineages collateral to it. This gwan buthni is a member of a collateral lineage, maybe even a very distant one. He conducts the rituals of adoption (i.e., of "giving buth" to a Dinka boy so that he may share in the sacrificial meat of his Nuer adopter), of marriage, of the "breaking off" of kinship so that distantly related persons (but never members of the same clan) can marry, of paying bridewealth and blood compensation, the lengthy mortuary ceremonies, the building of new cattle biers, the division of highly valued elephant tusks, and so on. Any family may have more than one gwan buthni, and when a family's gwan buthni is not available one of his lineage mates may substitute for him, or someone else may be found to do the job. When he dies one of his sons may succeed him. As a consequence of that and of the possibility that the relationship may be (but is not necessarily) mutual, it sometimes happens that two families serve as one another's gwan buthni for several generations.

Howell (1954:47) reports that the first cow to be handed over in compensation for a homicide is the "cow of the axe" which is given to the buthni, or representatives of a collateral branch of the lineage of the slain person, by the gwan buthni of the slayer. That, Howell says,

> extends the processes of appeasement and compensation beyond the more immediate kinsmen of the killer and the killed to their lineages as a whole. The solidarity of the patrilineal descent group is thus emphasized, and the way in which all persons within it are involved is publicly acknowledged (1954:47).

Howell does not say whether or not this interpretation was volunteered by Nuer themselves; nor does he state the scale of the relevant lineages. We have already noticed that Evans-Pritchard sometimes writes in this connection of a "small lineage" or of a "family." Also according to Howell (1954:49), the compensation for a homicide is contributed by and distributed to much the same kinds of kin and in much the same proportions as is a payment of bridewealth. He and Evans-Pritchard make it quite clear that neither is the affair of a lineage, not even a minimal lineage.

Evans-Pritchard reports that buth itself means "to share," and jibuthni are people of collateral lineages who are entitled to a share of the meat from a sacrifice. Even clans may "have buth" with one another, and if members of one clan are present when some members of another make a sacrifice, the former will get their conventional share. The size of the share may depend, though, on the number of persons of that category who are present, because similar shares may be due also to various kinds of kin. There are similar relations between lineages within a clan. Evans-Pritchard (1950a:367) reports that the Nuer often explain these ceremonial buth relations "in terms of elephant tusks," which are difficult to acquire and highly valued as the source of ivory bracelets. Speaking in general and vague terms, some Eastern Jikany elders told him that the branches of the GAATGANKIR clan share the meat of each other's sacrifices. More precisely, they explained, when a man spears an elephant his minimal lineage is entitled to keep a part of the ivory for themselves; but the spearer is obliged to give some to the minimal lineage of his gwan buthni who would (or should?) belong to the other maximal lineage of the clan. Apparently, the more general point is that the ritual or ceremonial rights and duties of lineages vis-à-vis one another are realized via representative action on the part of one or more of their members—though, again, the details remain vague.

All in all, it appears that lineages and lineage affiliation are jurally of rather limited, though by no means minor, significance.[7] It is difficult to imagine how, if they were not, Evans-Pritchard could have avoided saying more about them and saying it more systematically. Yet, and this it seems is what Evans-Pritchard found paradoxical about Nuer social order, the lineage system remains structurally highly significant because, via the concept of lineage homelands, it serves as the "framework" or "skeleton" for jural relations between tribal segments at all levels of spatial segmentation. Nuer lineages are not corporate, in any sociologically useful sense of the term. They are jural entities, but the rights and duties they possess are not general or in rem but are special or in personam, are in relation to immediately adjacent lineages of the same structural order, and are usually, if not always, exercised by one or a few persons acting in a representative capacity.

VI

It was noted above that in some societies it is possible not for persons to change their own lineage affiliations, but for them to have those affiliations changed for them long after their deaths. To that it may now be added that there are also some societies in which a person's lineage affiliation may be altered while he or she is still a child. We deal first with this latter possibility.

In many African societies there is more than one kind of culturally constituted relation of patrifiliation. As explained in some detail by Evans-

Pritchard (1945) for the Nuer, for certain specified social purposes such as determination of lineage affiliation, the crucial social identity is that of the man in whose name the brideprice has been paid for the mother. As a consequence he holds genetricial (or reproductive) rights in relation to that woman and he has a right to be known as 'father' of any children born to her, to have physical custody of them, and to have them known as members of his lineage, regardless that it may be known that he is not the genitor of one or another of them. Evans-Pritchard (1945:19) describes this social identity as that of the pater (legal father), as against that of the genitor (physical or natural father), though they are not differentiated in the Nuer language. Many anthropologists contend that the latter identity is not in any way socially significant, but among the Nuer and many other peoples it is quite significant, though of course for purposes other than those for which the identity pater is socially significant (see especially Evans-Pritchard 1945).

In many African societies if the mother of a child is unmarried it is possible for the genitor to establish himself as the pater, either by paying the brideprice and marrying the mother, or by paying a lesser compensatory fee whereby the child belongs to his lineage. In some instances it is even possible for the genitor thereby to get custody of his child. Otherwise, unless some other man marries the mother, pays the appropriate brideprice for her and thereby becomes ex post facto the pater of her child, the child will belong by default to the lineage of its mother's father—he being the man who has jural control over (but of course not the use of) her sexual and reproductive capacities. If the mother is already married to another man, there is usually nothing an extra-marital genitor (or the mother's husband for that matter) can do to effect the jural status of the child. Even so, among the Nuer it is common for children to be reared by their genitors, rather than their paters, or for married men with families to live sometimes with their paters' kin and sometimes with their genitors' kin.

In the societies being discussed here, when a married couple separate but remain married any children the woman subsequently bears are members of the man's lineage and are entitled to inherit from him, regardless that it may be known that they were conceived by another man. Divorce, though possible, can be quite complicated because it requires return of the brideprice, or some part of it if the woman has borne one or more children to the man. If a man who engenders a child by a woman who is married to another man wants to secure custody of his child and make it a member of his lineage, his only option (not one always jurally available) is to get her marriage annulled. To accomplish that the husband and his kin who helped to pay the brideprice (part of which at least is in these societies also a childprice) must be fully repaid. Once that is done, and it is usually very difficult to do, the husband becomes not only an ex-husband but also an ex-father of any children born to the woman during the course of her marriage to him. The woman is returned to her legal guardian (her father if he is still alive or her brother), and he is then in a position to remarry her, if he so wishes, to the extra-marital genitor of her child. That man then becomes not only the husband of the woman and the pater of any children born to her afterwards, but also the pater of all her offspring, even those borne by her while she was married to the first man. Because the kind of patrifilial relationship relevant to inclusion in a descent group is, in these instances, that of a child to the bearer of genetricial rights in relation to its mother, all the woman's children then become members of the second husband's lineage (see e.g., P. Mayer 1950:50–52 on the Gusii of East Africa).

In short, there are social situations in which it is possible to annul not only a marriage but also the kind of patrifilial relationship that is established by a kind of marriage, specifically the kind of marriage in which the husband acquires not only uxorial or wifely rights in relation to a woman but also genetricial rights in relation to her—that is, the exclusive right to engender children by her. One consequence is that all social implications of the annulled patrifilial relation are themselves annulled and a person born automatically into one lineage can be reassigned to another lineage. The situation is made into one rather like that of a Dinka boy adopted by a Nuer man into the status of his son and thereby made a member of a Nuer lineage, which is possible only because the Dinka boy has no already-established affiliation with a Nuer lineage. Neither does the child whose mother has had her marriage completely annulled.

We now consider the evidence for the assimilation of persons into lineages other than those into which they were born, not during their own lifetimes, but as long-deceased ancestors. That is in effect a process of movement of a lineage segment from one lineage to another, where the two lineages may or may not be agnatically related. That process has been described by Paul and Laura Bohannan in relation to the Tiv of central Nigeria (P. and L. Bohannan 1953; P. Bohannan 1954, 1957; L. Bohannan 1952, 1958).

VII

Among the Tiv, as among the Nuer, there are two interdependent but distinct segmentary systems, one of patrilineally constituted groups and one of territorial units known as *tar*. Each minimal tar or "country" is controlled, governed, and exploited agriculturally by a lineage from which it takes its name. Ideally, adjacent minimal tar are controlled by immediately adjacent collateral lineages, which, again ideally, are more or less equally matched in manpower and land holdings. Two or more such minimal tar form a higher-level tar, and their associated lineages form a higher-order lineage; and so on up to the level of Tiv himself, the apical ancestor of the Tiv people. The apical ancestor of the lineage associated with a minimal tar is as much as five or six generations removed from the eldest living males. Although that lineage is itself usually segmented internally at several levels, that segmentation is described as "within the hut" and it is irrelevant to the external affairs of the minimal tar, though it is highly relevant to governance of social relations within that tar.

The composition of Tiv minimal tar differs significantly from that of a Nuer minimal territorial segment, because the Tiv are sedentary agriculturalists and it is a derivative right of membership of the lineage that controls a minimal tar that a man is entitled to sufficient farmland within that tar to enable him to maintain himself and his family. Although men and their families may reside and farm elsewhere, either temporarily or permanently, they can do so only as guests of relatives and friends, and not as a matter of right. Consistent with this jural arrangement, in the early 1950s, approximately 83 per cent of male family heads resided within the minimal tar of their own lineages.[8] Some 7 to 10 per cent resided in their mother's minimal tar; another 2 to 4 per cent in the minimal tar of their father's mothers; and a few more were residing elsewhere, some even with "strangers" (P. Bohannan 1954:12). There was, as already suggested, nothing improper, irregular, or contrary to some "agnatic principle" about these non-agnatic residential alignments. Tiv maintain that a person is always welcome in the place of his mother's or father's mother's lineage, which is of course not the same thing as having a simple, unqualified right as against those lineages to live in their tar, but is instead a simple matter of kinship hospitality and amity. A man living in the tar of his mother's lineage is "a child of a woman" and therefore "his jural (or citizenship) rights are limited as are those of a woman" (L. and P. Bohannan 1953:24).

Although at any one time most of the male household heads who are residing outside their own minimal tar are only temporary visitors or guests, each of whom has his own special reasons for residing elsewhere than his own tar at least for the time being and will sooner or later return to his own minimal tar, some of them will stay on to rear their children and grandchildren in those other tar. Eventually, some of them will come to form small lineages recognized as being "attached," most commonly as "children of women," to the lineage that controls that tar, and later still some of them may become jurally fully assimilated segments "within the hut" of that lineage. Tiv are well aware of that process. As one Tiv put it, speaking of the small lineage MbaChihin, which is attached via a woman to Iyon lineage and is living in its tar:

Iyon is their tar, and MbaChihin are becoming Iyon. When a man settles down and all his children grow up around him and he dies and they die, and their children's children live there until their children can say my father's father's father lived in Iyon—they have become Iyon: it is their ityo [or their own lineage] (L. Bohannan 1958:44).

As the ethnographer goes on to point out, it is not accidental that it takes something on the order of four generations for this process of assimilation to work itself out. One of the reasons is peculiar to Tiv social order, within which it is important for each person to have not only his or her "own lineage" or *ityo*, but also a mother's ityo (one's *igba*) and a father's mother's ityo (one's *igba ter*). It is through his mother's lineage that a man gains control of certain "magical forces" and can rise above the status of a "youngster," and a man's mother's lineage is obliged to support him if he and they believe he is being mistreated by his own lineage mates. Therefore, it is something of a social handicap not to have the full complement of one's own lineage, one's mother's lineage, and one's father's mother's lineage, and it would not be in the interest of any Tiv man, even if it were possible, for him to relinquish membership of his own (his father's) lineage to become a member of his mother's or father's mother's lineage. After three generations, though, a genuine minimal lineage may grow up within an alien minimal tar and it can then be transferred from one higher-order patrilineage to another without social disadvantage to its living members, all of whom will then have their own (father's) lineage, mother's lineage, and father's mother's lineage. The transfer occurs when the host lineage takes on the duties of ityo for all members of the attached segment and permits them to participate as equals in all lineage affairs (which include governance of social relations within the minimal tar).

It is not peculiar to Tiv society however that, as already indicated, the minimal scale of a unit recognizable as a patrilineage is not the unit of a man and his offspring but is at least three generations deep. In that light, we can speculate that the Tiv quoted above was indicating that, until a set of "children of women" residing in a community reaches the scale of a minimal lineage, the members of that set must remain members also of the lineage of the linking parent or parent's parent. The only way to fit the members of that set into the structure of that minimal tar is via their individual relations of kinship with their sponsor or sponsors in that community, usually their mothers' brothers or fathers' mother's brothers or their immediate offspring. As such they must continue to have duties to their natal lineages that may come into conflict with those they have to the people among whom they are residing. If, however, they remain long enough to establish a minimal lineage of their own, it is likely that they have ceased to be active members of their natal lineages and that it has become clear that they do not intend to "return" to the tar of those lineages. It is then possible to move that small lineage into the status of a segment "within the hut" of the lineage that controls the minimal tar within which it resides.

This process is not contrary to the constitutive principle that patrifiliation is the necessary and sufficient condition for inclusion in a group, because no living person's minimal-lineage affiliation is altered. Moreover, the Bohannans' genealogical data show that it may be many generations before the identity of the linking ancestor, if female, is altered to male. That is to say, jural incorporation of an attached segment does not require immediate genealogical revision (a "dogma of descent" that, a la Sahlins, quickly makes up for its own inevitable imperfections). Such revision does occur, but in the long run and not deliberately, in that middle zone of lengthy genealogies in which there is typically much confusion and disagreement about the genealogical facts and also a propensity to rework them ex post facto to fit present de facto social conditions.[9]

Here some of the relevant social conditions are that, because Tiv is an expanding and moving population, the ideal that territorially neighboring groups ought to be also genealogically neighboring groups is not always realizable, and there is a tendency among Tiv to interpret whatever genealogical information is available to make the (necessarily continually reconstructed) genealogical facts correspond to de facto territorial and consequent social relations (L. Bohannan 1952). Moreover, Tiv think that groups of the same structural order ought to be of roughly the same size and to control territories of comparable size; they ought not, that is, to be unevenly matched in resources or manpower. This structural principle enters into the interpretation (necessarily a political process) of genealogical information. So, to take an exceedingly simple hypothetical example (see figure 5.4), if three tar, A, B, and C, are known as brothers of one another and A increases substantially in size in comparison with B and C, then B and C may ally with one another when and if necessary against A, and eventually one, say B, may become incorporated into the other, not by losing its own identity but by becoming represented by some men as a son (rather than as a brother) of the apical ancestor of C. In this as in many of the examples reported by the Bohannans, there is no conversion of nonagnates into agnates and thus no violation of agnatic principle; there is merely reordering of agnatic relations between more or less distant ancestors to account for present-day spatial and social relations between the tar occupied by their descendants. Certainly, as Sahlins (1965) perceived, where there is a principled correlation between lineage groups and local groups, and the latter are of at least some politico-military significance, we can expect attempts to redress imbalances in manpower be-

Stage 1.   Brother Segments Same Size

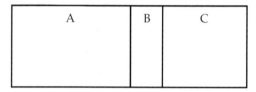

Stage 2.   Brother Segments Widely Disproportionate

Stage 3.   Segmentation Reconstituted

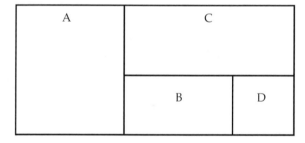

FIGURE 5.4   Realignment of Lineages, Tiv

tween them. That cannot be done, however, by recruitment from the out-side of "sisters' sons" and so on, but has to be done mainly by restructur-ing relations of inclusion between long-established lineage segments above as well as at the lowest levels of territorial segmentation. Often, the restructuring is of already-agnatic relations; but where it is otherwise, the result is not dogmatic insistence on agnatic purity. As recounted in some detail by the Bohannans, the Tiv are well aware to some considerable ge-nealogical depth that tar-within-tar relations do not correspond neatly with lineage-within-lineage relations (both of which are in any event mat-ters of serious political contestation), and assimilated lineages deriving from sisters' sons are openly acknowledged.

Just as Evans-Pritchard (also Fortes and Evans-Pritchard 1940:6) claimed that the lineage system of the Nuer serves to structure relations between territorial segments, which he stipulated are the political units of Nuer society, so also the Bohannans argue that the political units of Tiv society are the tar and that relations between them are, again, structured by the lineage system. This virtual equation of the political with social relations between territorial units, thus excluding among many other things, the processes of policy-making and governance within territorial units, has been severely criticized by M. G. Smith (1956) and others; and Fardon (1984, 1985) and others have been justly critical of P. Bohannan's (1965:523) hyperbole that Tiv social organization "utilizes a single principle . . . the agnatic lineage structure, based on the principle of segmentary opposition." We can acknowledge all that and still feel compelled to disagree with Kuper's (1982) claim that it has yet to be demonstrated that in any society a wide range of political and economic relations are ordered by a segmentary lineage system. Surely, if there is such a society, it is Tiv.[10] This is amply demonstrated in the Bohannans's rich ethnography, which there is no need to attempt to condense here.

Riches's (1979) lengthy argument to the contrary fails to convince. It depends on redescribing the groups described by the Bohannans as descent groups and lineages as, instead, agnatic *kin* groups, purporting to follow Scheffler's (1974) distinction between ancestor-oriented and ego-oriented social relationships. By so doing Riches can then assert "Tiv lineage groups do not exist." Instead of being "informed, sustained and sanctioned in terms of a relationship between members and some specified common ancestor," Tiv activities as members of social groups "are based on edicts associated with [agnatic] kinship ties" (Riches 1979:74, 75). Riches's redescription of Tiv nongo, described by L. Bohannan (1958:37) as a lineage segment, as instead an agnatic kin group, rests on the report that "*nongo* refers primarily to the living representatives of a lineage" and "a man identifies his nongo, not by the name of the lineage segment, but by the name of some prominent man amongst its living representatives." If asked the personal question "What is your nongo?," a man does not reply (e.g.) "I am MbaDuku," but (e.g.) "I am of Kiagba's nongo" (L. and P. Bohannan 1953:23). This, however, is hardly adequate evidence that the category nongo itself is egocentrically constituted, because the expression is used also to frame and answer questions from a top-down or ancestor-oriented perspective. One can ask, for example, the impersonal question "What are the nongo of MbaDuku [i.e., those of, or the descendants of the ancestor Duku]?" and the proper response is a list of MbaDuku's component units, for inclusion in each of which patrifiliation is the necessary and sufficient condition.

As for ityo, contrary to Riches (1979:70), the Bohannans do not "translate" it as "patrilineage" but say that it means "agnates," that its "meaning is always personal," that "one must always speak of someone's ityo," and that its range of reference may vary from one's full brother to the whole of the Tiv people (who have an eponymous common patrilineal ancestor). Thus there is reason to argue that ityo is a term of egocentric reference. But when one says "MbaDuku are my ityo," one does not by that act reconstitute MbaDuku itself as an egocentric category.

Notes

1. Although hardly at the outset, A. L. Kroeber's essay of 1938 (1952:210–218), "Basic and Secondary Patterns of Social Organization," starkly illustrates the relevant fallacies. Evans-Pritchard's early essays in *Sudan Notes and Records*, which were later rewritten into *The Nuer*, are plainly addressed to this issue and argue strongly against both the analytic reductionisms and evolutionisms that were influential at the time. For some enlightening commentary on these aspects of Evans-Pritchard's writings on the Nuer see A. Free (1990, 1991).

2. In a letter of December 1937 addressed to Meyer Fortes, Evans-Pritchard "explains that one of the difficulties of writing [*The Nuer*] is that 'I have not quite made up my mind what I want to show in it—what the plot is going to be—so to speak'" (J. Goody 1995:60).

3. Evans-Pritchard's fieldwork was done between 1929 and 1935, and much has happened in Nuerland since then, for an account of some of which see Hutchinson (1985, 1988, 1990, 1992, 1996).

4. See also Howell (1954:18). Evans-Pritchard (1933:42–43; 1940:217) does say that he was told by some Nuer that in the Eastern Jikany tribes the amount of compensation paid for killing an aristocrat would be substantially greater than the amount paid for killing a stranger. But, he added, he was not able to confirm the practice and other Nuer informants denied it was done. He speculated that he was being told what his informants hoped to have established as the rules to be enforced in the native courts then being established by the British colonial administration. Neither is there any confirmatory evidence in Howell (1954), though he does report (p. 34) that minor administrative posts in the colonial administration always went, by Nuer demand, to men of the locally dominant clan or lineage.

5. R. Fox (1967 [1983:163]) asserts that descent groups "are usually 'corporate' groups, that is, groups that exist independently of the individuals composing them," and that corporateness "implies that they act 'as a body'; thus if one of their members kills a man, the group as a whole is held responsible for the killing." This is an extremely incautious, wholly unwarranted empirical generalization.

6. There has been much disagreement (and vagueness) about the defining features of segmentary lineage systems (see e.g., Middleton and Tait 1958; Sahlins 1961). In part the difficulty is that most observers have not been careful to attend to the fundamental distinction between defining features and merely accidental features, and therefore they designate any system of lineages within lineages (or

even within clans) as a segmentary lineage system. In part, too, it has not been perceived that most of the features cited are corollaries of the way in which lineages of lower order are jural constituents of lineages of higher order. The "jural constituents" phrasing was first introduced, so far as I have been able to determine, by Goodenough (1961). See also Davenport (1963).

7. The role of lineage and lineage affiliation in the feud is, it seems, of considerable significance in the maintenance of social order via limitation of the spread of conflict and in its eventual resolution. This is discussed at length in Gluckman (1955) and Mair (1962, 1974).

8. The actual per cent of strictly agnatic affiliation may have been more on the order of 74 or 75 per cent. The 83 per cent figure may include men affiliated agnatically to "attached" segments, on which see below.

9. For a most useful general discussion of anthropological knowledge about "oral genealogies" and genealogical processes see Wilson (1977).

10. And Tallensi (Fortes 1945, 1949), though, curiously, hardly any of the self-styled critics of "descent theory" have undertaken to comment on Fortes's data and analyses, and the few exceptions are almost cursory in their treatment of, and do not inspire confidence in the critics' knowledge of, the ethnographic data or the subtleties of Fortes's analyses (see e.g., Anglin 1979 and Kuper 1982:85, who draws on Anglin; see also Fortes's brief reply, pp. vii–xii, in Holy 1979b).

6

PATRIFILIATION NECESSARY BUT NOT SUFFICIENT

I

Where patrifiliation is necessary but not sufficient for inclusion in a group, the groups include only patrilineal descendants of their founders, but they need not and perhaps cannot include all those descendants. As where patrifiliation is both necessary and sufficient, recruitment from the outside is not possible, but because affiliation requires credentials in addition to patrifiliation, it is not automatic by birth. Both kinds of group are nonoverlapping and mutually exclusive and their members are all agnatic kin of one another (again, if there is a single apical ancestor). However, where patrifiliation is a merely necessary condition, some proportion of any person's agnatic kin may not be members of his group and, therefore, of any such group. One consequence of that is that the rights and duties (if any) of group members vis-à-vis one another cannot be also the rights and duties (if any) of agnatic kin, or of persons of common patrilineal descent, vis-à-vis one another. An implication of that is that relations of descent can have no jural significance, in either the internal or the external affairs of groups.

Membership of such a group might or might not be a matter of choice. Within different systems of this kind a person might or might not have the option to acquire the additional credentials necessary to be reckoned a member of a group. If he has that option and acquires those credentials he is ipso facto a member of his father's group; if he elects not to have those credentials, he is ipso facto not a member of any such group. Where an individual has no choice in the matter of acquisition of the additional credentials, it may be that the group itself is able to confer or to withhold them. It might also be able to expel a member by depriving him of the additional necessary credentials. That person would then be "a man without a country," as it were, for he would not then be able to affiliate himself with another group of the same kind, because there can be no recruitment from the outside.

Where patrifiliation is necessary and sufficient and where it is only necessary, conflict between groups for members and their loyalties is not a possibility because change of group affiliation is not a possibility. But, where patrifiliation is a necessary condition, there can be intragroup conflict of a kind that may seriously compromise the possibility of group solidarity and make it difficult for group members to act in concert vis-à-vis outsiders. If the additional necessary credentials are in short supply and not all offspring of all members can acquire them, there may well be conflict within each group for those additional necessary credentials and, in effect, for retention or acquisition of membership status. One consequence of that possibility is that it may prove difficult, perhaps impossible, to institute a set of mutual rights and duties between co-members, especially those of a kind that would entail cooperation in defense and aggression. It will be difficult also for the groups themselves to be bearers of rights and duties or, in other words, to be jural entities, and it will even be difficult for them to be jural collectivities. A group of this kind is not likely to be anything more than a jural aggregate.

Despite the numerous significant differences, groups of this kind might easily be mistaken for genuine lineages, and nested, pyramidal sets of them for genuine segmentary lineage systems, if only because they can include only children of their male members and only patrilineal descendants of their putative founders. As in genuine patrilineages, their members are necessarily all agnatic kin of one another. Even so, because in such a system of groups relations of descent can have no jural values, in either the internal or the external affairs of groups, it would be a strategic error to describe the groups as lineages or descent groups and as the components of segmentary lineage systems. That description must in due course give rise to the question why these groups do not function or operate in the same ways as do lineages in other (especially certain African) societies. That question is, however, wholly spurious; it is not likely to prove amenable to coherent resolution, and attempts to answer it may well prove to be theoretically much more destructive than constructive. The question takes for granted the identity of the rule of recruitment in both kinds of situation, whereas the critical difference for explanatory purposes is precisely a difference between rules of recruitment or, in other words, rules of filiation and affiliation.

All these observations are verified in the several ethnographic sources on the *khel* of the Pukthun (Pathan) of northern Pakistan, especially those of the Swat Valley (Barth 1959a, 1959b, 1966, 1973, 1981; Ahmed 1980;

Lindholm 1982). In all sources the Pukthun are described as organized into an acephalous and patrilineal segmentary lineage systems, and two of the three ethnographers—Ahmed and Lindholm—characterize the khel as corporate, land-owning groups, between which there are relations of complementary opposition. Yet, as Barth (1959b) has shown, and as Ahmed and Lindholm acknowledge, Pukthun khel do not operate at all like lineages do in any of the classical acephalous segmentary lineage systems of various African societies. That, however, is only expectable because, as Fortes pointed out, "the way a lineage system works depends on the kind of legal institutions found in the society; and this, we know, is a function of its political organization" (1953 [1970:78]).

By way of explanation of the differences, Barth (1959b [1981:55]) suggests that it is essential to distinguish between "a purely structural arrangement of units defined by a unilineal descent charter" and "the manner in which these units are made relevant in corporate action." In brief, Barth's argument is that a unilineal and segmentary constitution does not entail any particular jural attributes for the groups so constituted, so we must be careful not to mistake the jural attributes of some African segmentary lineages for the jural attributes (if any) that are intrinsic to segmentary lineages in general. Also, shared interests, as where a group possesses a "joint estate," need not entail "corporateness" or, in other words, unity of action. About the Pukthun, Barth observes, although the members of each khel "share rights in a joint estate," that sharing does not imply a community of interests, but does in fact imply an overriding opposition or conflict of interests between group members, and that in turn prevents the khel from ever acting as unitary bodies. More than that, instead of uniting the members of a khel as allies, it tends to divide close agnatic kin and to pit them as rivals one against the other. Indeed, the prototypical rivals in Pukthun society are patrilateral parallel cousins, men related as father's brother's son one to the other. Their designation, *tarbur*, is virtually synonymous with "enemy," although in any genuine lineage system, they would be almost inevitably co-members of a minimal lineage. Because "lineage cousins" are the archetypical enemies, and not only in contrast with brothers, political alliances are with more distant agnates, and "in the pattern of these alliances the architecture of the unilineal descent system can be recognized, as if by its very negation" (Barth 1959b [1981:.67]).

Barth maintains that although the khel themselves do not emerge as "corporate" groups (that is, act as single bodies) in political action, "the genealogical charter is nonetheless relevant to the structure of the corporate groups that do emerge; essentially, it defines rivals and allies in a system of two opposed political blocs. Closely related descent units are consistent rivals . . . ." (1959b[1981:56]). In this context, however, "descent units" can refer only to sets of a man and his sons or to sets of brothers, and we have already seen that these are not "descent" units, at least not in any sociologically useful sense of the term. Moreover, although Barth plays it down, the kind of rivalry that is routinely expected between patrilateral parallel cousins (father's brother's sons) may and often does penetrate into sibling sets and into social relations between father and son. Some degree of ambivalence between brothers, sons of the same man, and between father and son is expectable in any "patrilineal" society; but, surely, it is indicative of some truly fundamental difference between Pukthun society and societies with genuine patrilineages that one Pukthun proverb counsels "When the flood waters reach your chin, put your son beneath your feet" (Lindholm 1982:161).

Barth takes it that the Pukthun rule of filiation and affiliation is the same as that found in the lineage systems of numerous African societies. Therefore, he argues, we must look to other than strictly formal features for an explanation of the differences between the Pukthun and those other "lineage systems." Yet as he explains in a number of places, it is not only "descent from the apical ancestor" that is necessary for inclusion in a khel; "actual land ownership is a necessary condition," too (Barth 1959a:21; also Lindholm 1982:74). Odd though it may seem in comparative perspective, it is not by way of his khel affiliation that a Pukthun man comes to have rights in land, but via his possession of rights in relation to one kind of land that he becomes a member of a khel. In other words, patrifiliation is not the necessary and sufficient condition, it is a merely necessary condition for inclusion in a khel. The implications of that difference are sufficiently profound to warrant saying that it will serve no productive sociological purpose, but will only further obfuscate matters, to continue to describe the rule of filiation and affiliation in the case of the khel as a rule of patrilineal descent, to describe the khel themselves as patrilineal descent groups or lineages, and to describe relations between them as constituting a segmentary lineage system.

II

In the following discussion the focus is on the Yusufzai Pukthun of the Swat Valley. The population of that valley includes members of several ethnic groups, the politically most dominant one being the Yusufzai branch of the Pukthun, descendants of immigrants who several hundred years ago conquered the indigenous inhabitants and reduced them to the status of dependents of the Pukthun men who took possession of their land. Each village includes some number (usually a minority) of Pukthun, each of whom holds some number of shares of the residential and cultivable land in the vicinity. Typically, the Pukthun residents of a village comprise one or two minimal khel, each of which is principally a unit of administration of utilization of land in the vicinity of the village. Several contiguous village communities constitute a district, which is itself the territory of a higher-order khel, also a unit of administration of utilization of land; and so on up, in principle at least, to the level of Yusuf himself, the apical ancestor of all Yusufzai Pukthun.

As described in detail in Barth (1959a:79), political alliance and opposition in Swat is factional, and the factions, led by big-men called *khans*, cross cut the khel at all levels. A man cannot be a khan without being a Pukthun because to be a khan it is necessary to own large quantities of land, which the khan as patron lets out to client-peasants who are ipso facto committed to being his allies in conflicts with other khans. In return the khan provides not only land to sharecrop but also protects it, the crop, and the body of the client.

Before 1930, the period dealt with in the following pages, no Pukthun minimal khel was permanently domiciled in any village. Instead, every five or ten years (depending on the region) the Pukthun inhabitants of several villages traded places with one another. Pukthun legend has it that one of their great khans or leaders conceived a system of land tenure that would guarantee each Pukthun man equal access to all kinds of land, even if not also an equal proportion of each kind of land. By this system, called *wesh* ('division'), each Pukthun man holds title, not to a particular parcel or parcels of land in or near a particular village, but to some number of shares in the area of land that is administered by a khel, and the particular area administered by any such group varies every five or ten years in a regular cycle. When the time arrives, all Pukthun residents of each village in a region pack their belongings and remove themselves to another village in that region. Typically, the number of villages participating in such a change of places is fairly small, and after at most a few decades people find themselves back where they started from. This system not only equalizes access to different kinds of land; it also has the (presumably unintended) effect of weakening bonds between particular Pukthun men and their non-Pukthun dependents, who do not migrate with them.

According to Barth (1959b [1981:65]), this system of re-allotment gives rise to few disputes at the higher levels of segmentation, because the equivalence in value of the relevant territories was worked out long ago and is not contested by the relevant higher-order khel. (We will see in due course that it is rather unlikely that any higher-order khel could transcend its usual state of internal friction, fraction, and faction long enough to make a protest.) Tension and conflict do arise, however, at the level of adjacent villages and within the khel of each village. At that level, where individual men are competing for actual, individual fields, there cannot be an established division of the land that immediately corresponds to the configuration of shares as it stands at the moment, because that configuration is constantly being revised. That correspondence must be worked out via negotiation and compromise by the men who hold those shares meeting as a khel council, perhaps supplemented by force or threat of force outside the council meetings. It is perhaps obvious that one implication of all this is that, the closer the agnatic relationship the more probable it is that there will be cause for conflict.

Land under the administrative control of a khel council (and not all land in the Swat Valley is under such control) is called daftar, and a man must hold some number of shares of such land if he is to be known as a member of a khel and as a Pukthun. Lindholm (1982:66, 56) writes of "the principle of lineage ownership of land," and he says "Land rights are granted through the patrilineal genealogy . . . ." This may give the impression that members of a khel merely divide up, for purposes of individual or family usage, an area of land that is group owned. In fact, however, and this is a point on which Barth and Lindholm agree, it is not via his membership of a khel that a man comes to have shares in daftar; it is, instead, via his possession of such shares that he becomes a member of a khel, and he must be a member of a such a group if he is to be a Pukthun. Initially at least, he can come into possession of such shares only via inheritance from his father. If a man falls on bad times and loses his shares by selling them, or if they are taken forcibly from him before he can pass them on to his sons, both he and his sons automatically cease to be members of any khel, and, what is more, they cease also to be Pukthun. Ownership of shares in daftar administered by a particular khel is the condition not only for participation in a khel council but also for maintenance of privileged Pukthun status.[1]

The sole right entailed by membership of a khel is to participate in the council of the group and, by so doing, to represent and defend one's own land interests. Such a council may be convened virtually at will by any member of the group. It has, however, no head or chief executive, and its powers of enforcement of its decisions are decidedly weak. It can find fault, impose a fine on a member, and dictate a course of action by way of resolution of a dispute between some of its members, but it has no recourse to physical sanctions and must leave it up to the parties to a dispute to abide by its decisions. If one of the parties to the dispute refuses to go along with the council's decision, the other party is licensed by that decision to resort to self help, in which process he may be aided by his dependents or even by other Pukthun from other villages who are co-members with him of one of the local political factions. If the dispute is between members of different minimal khel and is being dealt with by the council of a higher-order khel, neither party can count on having all or even any members of his khel on his side, and some of them may in fact side, either covertly or overtly, with the other party.

There are strong incentives for men not only to maintain the number of shares of daftar that they inherit but also to expand their holdings. The latter is the one way in which a man can assure the Pukthun status of his progeny, and it is also the only way he can expand his wealth and increase the number of his non-Pukthun dependents, and therewith his own security, power, and prestige. All that can be done, however, only at the expense of the other members of his minimal khel, even his own father and brothers. That is because although daftar may be sold within the khel that administers it, selling shares is regarded as a shameful and degrading act, and only in the most dire of circumstances will a Pukthun sell all his shares and, in the process, make himself no longer a Pukthun. Also, as a corollary of the same principle, it is not possible to expand one's daftar holdings by purchase from members of other khel. By and large, then, it is possible to expand one's land holdings either only temporarily by small encroachments on the holdings of one's neighbors, or permanently by somehow acquiring shares held by other members of one's minimal khel. Because, in the absence of an heir in the form of a son, a deceased's man's daftar shares go to his brothers, or failing a brother, then to his father's brothers, and then to his father's brother's sons, and so on, it is potentially to a man's advantage for his father's brother to die without a son. That, of course, is the root of the antipathy that Pukthun expect between patrilateral parallel cousins. Although it seems that they are less inclined openly to acknowledge it, this is also the root of much hostility and resentment between brothers, each of whom stands to benefit from the death of the other before he can engender his own male heirs; and between father and son, because the latter cannot become a fully adult and autonomous person until he acquires a definite number of shares in daftar via inheritance or premortem gift from his father. Elderly men are reluctant to retire, as it were, by dividing their land shares among their sons, for fear that if they do so their sons will not feed them.

In view of all this, it should not be surprising that no khel at any level of segmentation is or could be a solidary social group, much less a jural entity or even a jural collectivity; and the jural constituents of higher-order khel are not lower-order khel but are, again, individuals who represent their own interests, and who cannot represent anyone else's interests, in group councils.

Suppose, for example, that two men belong to two different minimal khel but to the same next-higher-order khel and they are farming adjacent parcels of land. One encroaches on the land of the other, attempting to expand his own plots at the expense of his neighbor. After trying a few times to re-establish the original border, the only recourse available to the offended party is to call a meeting of the council of the higher-order khel, the least inclusive administrative entity that encompasses both parties. Any adult male member of either minimal khel may attend that meeting and present his own views on the issue, and no one present is authorized to speak for anyone who is not present or for either minimal khel as a whole. The dispute is not one between those two khel but is one between persons who, as it happens, are members of those khel. Ipso facto, the jural constituents of higher-order khel are not khel of the next-lower order, but are single persons. In view of that indication that khel are not jural entities, that they have no special rights and duties via-à-vis one another, it is only expectable that immediately adjacent collateral groups do not and are not normatively obliged to ally with one another in opposition to genealogically more distant groups. By implication of their constitutive rule of filiation and affiliation, all khel at all levels of segmentation must remain nothing more than jural aggregates, that is sets of men each of whom has his own rights that he alone can exercise and that cannot be claimed by anyone else acting in a representative capacity.

It is not evidence to the contrary that Barth (1981:97) writes often of Pukthun "descent groups" holding "joint rights to territories" and "different types of joint estate"; of their members as "sharing joint rights" in relation to land; of access to agricultural and grazing land being obtained "by virtue of agnatic status"; and of each segment as becoming "corporate in the form of a council of its living male members who sit together as agnates with equal rights." Similarly, Lindholm (1982:xxvi, 62, 65, 80) says "individuals have their property rights and gain their social identity through their membership in a lineage" (i.e., khel); "the relatives in the patrilineage are connected by their common inheritance." He writes also of "the principle of lineage ownership of land" and of "the unity of blood groups . . . which is activated in cases of revenge," and he is insistent that Pukthun "lineages" exhibit "segmentary" or "complementary opposition."

Much of this is incautious and overblown phrasing. The facts are—as the same ethnographers make abundantly clear in other ways—that Pukthun khel are not land-owning groups and neither are their male members joint or common owners of anything. The land rights of Pukthun men do not derive from patrilineal descent or from membership of descent groups. They are acquired mainly by inheritance from fathers or other close agnatic kin, sometimes by purchase, and sometimes by stealth. Pukthun men do not "share land rights" at all; shares in the critical daftar are personal property. What the male members of a minimal khel do have in common (but of course do not own) is simply that each has a right to represent his own interests (his shares and allotments in the daftar that is administered by the group) in the council of that group, as well as to participate in proceedings that do not concern his own shares or allotments; and each has the corollary duty to abide by decisions reached by that council. The khel, as already emphasized, are nothing more than administrative bodies, and the fact of the matter is that the mode of land tenure and administration is virtually guaranteed to prevent them from ever becoming anything more than that. That is because it pits the members of each khel continually one against the other in competition either to maintain or to enlarge their individual land holdings.

Far from acting "corporately" or participating in relations of segmentary or complementary opposition, Pukthun khel are chronically, even congenitally, incapable of any kind of collective enterprise. The reason for that is not, as Barth (1966:24) appears to suggest, that in general "an offer of incorporation is not accepted, and a corporate group is not mobilized by a member, if that person's losses through membership are greater than his gains." It is not, that is, that by and large each Pukthun man has more to lose than he has to gain by attempting to "mobilize" the khel to which he belongs, or by responding to such an attempt on the part of another member; so that by and large men do not even attempt to "mobilize" even their minimal khel for concerted action against outsiders. That interpretation of the lack of "corporateness" (i.e., unitary action) on the part of the khel would be plausible if and only if there were rights and duties associated with those groups and with membership of them, on the basis of which persons could, if they wished to do so, attempt to mobilize their co-members for concerted action against outsiders. Yet it is clear enough from Barth's accounts, and also from those of Lindholm and Ahmed, that the rights and duties of the khel and of persons as members of them are severely limited and, certainly, do not entail that those groups should ever act as units in competition or conflict with one another. The difficulty that stands in the way of mobilizing a khel at any level of segmentation is not the probability of greater individual cost than benefit; it is the legal structure or constitution of the group itself. That is acknowledged by Barth (1981:39–40) himself when he says "the greater part of the rights and obligations which define the position of a Pathan in his various spheres of activity are the subject of private contractual agreements."

It is therefore quite striking that Barth and Lindholm seem compelled to argue, each in his own way, that in the political factions actually formed by Pukthun, khel affiliation is a significant determinant of who is on which side. As already noted, Barth (1959b [1981:67]) says, "in the pattern of these alliances the architecture of the unilineal descent system can be recognized, as if by its very negation." That is to say, the closer the agnatic relationship, even within the minimal khel, the more likely the two parties are to be on opposite sides of any political fence. According to Lindholm (1982:80), "the unity of blood groups" is not "obliterated" by the way in which the obligation to take blood revenge is restricted to the nuclear family of the deceased, aided by his tarbur or father's brother's son, who is not only the archetypical enemy but "may" be a friend. Lindholm says group "unity" is "activated in cases of revenge," *not* by "all of a man's lineage" gathering to take revenge on the lineage of the killer, but (again in an oddly negative fashion) by relatives of the victim refraining from giving direct support or aid to the killer and his family. Lindholm does not show, however, and it seems very unlikely that he could show, that the scale of the set of people who are obliged to refrain from giving aid to the killer is directly proportional to and is determined by the scale of the agnatic relationship between victim and killer. Nor does he show that the sets of people who are obliged to avoid giving aid to the killer are agnatically constituted. Finally, he says "complementary opposition does exist in Swat, since no man would support the murderer of his tarbur under any circumstances" (1982:80), even though a few pages earlier he observes that fathers' brothers' sons sometimes "do more than merely hope" that the other's line will die out (1982:62), and a few pages later (1982:82) he writes about disgruntled refugees who encourage their hosts to make war on their tarbur in their home village and who may even join in on the killing themselves.

The problem is that although the khel system is segmentary insofar as there are khel within khel, the inclusion is not of the required kind. Khel B and C may be two branches of higher-order khel A, and together make up A, but they are not the jural constituents of A. They have no special rights and duties vis-à-vis one another, certainly none of the kind that would enable them to act together in the name of A and vis-à-vis another khel of the same structural order, and, correlatively, none of the kind that would enable some one member of B to represent it in relation to C. Ipso facto, they cannot exhibit complementary opposition. The argument here is that this is a predictable consequence of the fact that although patrifiliation is a necessary condition, it is not also a sufficient condition, for inclusion in a minimal khel; or, in other words, it is a predictable consequence of the fact that khel are not patrilineages or, for that matter, descent groups of any kind.

This brings us to the last main point in this discussion. It was argued above that where patrifiliation is necessary but not sufficient for inclusion in a group, there can be no recruitment from the outside—just as where patrifiliation is the necessary and sufficient condition. This is confirmed by Barth's (1959a:28) report that, according to his Pukthun informants, "genealogical assimilation is inconceivable," and he adds that the claim "would seem to be borne out, rather than contradicted, by . . . two exceptional cases." The two cases are "exceptional," however, only insofar as both show that daftar, land administered by a khel, can be alienated from that administrative jurisdiction and still remain daftar by coming under the jurisdiction of another khel—but, critically, a new one. What Barth shows is that a very powerful and land-wealthy man may elect to make a gift of daftar to another Pukthun or set of Pukthun (usually as a reward for exceptional services rendered), such that the receivers may then constitute their own khel which is independent of and in no way assimilated to either the lowest-order khel from which the land was administratively detached or to the next-higher-order khel.

Additional case material cited by Barth, Lindholm, and Ahmed show that when daftar is transferred to a non-Pukthun either it ceases to be daftar and becomes *siri*, land that is not administered by a khel and is freely transactable, or the recipients are given Pukthun status but, instead of being made members of the khel that has been administering that land, they establish their own independent khel. At some level, of course, this new khel, if acknowledged to be a Yusufzai group, must be related patrilineally to the one that formerly administered its newly acquired lands. Similarly, a very powerful, land-wealthy man may give daftar to a Pukthun of another khel, but it is not possible thereby to change the group affiliation of the recipient or recipients. From Ahmed's (1980, chapter 5) account, it would seem that the recipients establish a new settlement and a new khel, but not a subgroup of the former administering khel. They do claim prior relationship to it, but at a fairly remote genealogical level, as co-members of a much higher-level khel (which relationship entails no particular social relationships between those khel per se).

III

Much has been made in the preceding discussion of the lack of jural significance, in Pukthun (and Pukthun-dominated) society, of relations of patrilineal descent. That is not to say, however, that Pukthun do not "recognize" relations of patrilineal descent and accord them some considerable social value, especially when they are backed up, as it were, by other more substantial "credentials." Elite khans maintain elaborate patrilineal pedigrees linking themselves to illustrious predecessors and, ultimately, to the apical ancestor Yusufzai, and they use these "to justify [their positions] in relation to the rest of the population" (Salzman 1978:59), including non-Pukthun and other Pukthun. Yet they "govern" not by virtue of any jural authority vested in them on account of their ancestry, but on account of their (transient) success in an often ruthless "game" of factional politics in which only Pukthun may play (with much help from non-Pukthun). It is, conversely, also a "game" in which only Pukthun can lose, in one way at least, largely on account of the actions of and to the benefit of other

Pukthun—that by losing their Pukthun status by losing their daftar shares, regardless that they may still be able to recite their lines of descent from Yusufzai. So, although Pukthun status is of considerable social value and does require demonstrated patrilineal descent from Yusufzai, that does not make patrilineal descent jurally significant in Pukthun or Pukthun-dominated society. It is not simply descent from Yusufzai that confers privileged Pukthun status, but also inclusion in a khel, and that is contingent on holding at least some shares of daftar (khel-administered land).

It has been stressed also that the specific way in which Pukthun khel are in fact constituted (with patrifiliation as necessary but not sufficient for inclusion and with inheritance of daftar land as another necessary condition) undercuts the possibility that the members of a khel may have genuinely shared interests that they will cooperate to develop or to defend. Instead, the tendency—as Barth and, following him, Lindholm, and Ahmed, have all shown—is for co-members of a khel (and especially the minimal khel) to compete with one another for more and more land shares, and, as a consequence, for the rights and duties entailed by group membership to be few and very limited in scope, and for the groups themselves to have no rights and duties vis-à-vis one another.

None of that is to deny the possibility that co-members of a khel, especially those of the lowest order, may at times find it expedient to cooperate with one another and to act as unitary bodies vis-à-vis outsiders. Barth (1959a:112) reports that in communities in the lower parts of the Swat valley the ratio of Pukthun to non-Pukthun runs as high as one to ten; average individual Pukthun land holdings are comparatively large; and so also is the number of non-Pukthun dependents for each Pukthun landowner. In contrast, in communities in the higher reaches of the valley, the ratio of Pukthun to non-Pukthun is more in the range of one to three or even one to two; individual Pukthun land holdings are comparatively small; and so also is the number of non-Pukthun dependents of each Pukthun land-owner. For our purposes here, the most notable consequence of this difference is that in the latter circumstance the tendency for closely related members of a khel to be opposed to one another and to take opposite factional sides is much reduced, and for "fairly large Pukthun descent groups [khel] to remain politically united" (1959a:112). That is to say, the tendency for political factions to crosscut the khel, and to divide paternal cousins and even brothers, is substantially reduced. As Barth explains it, given their small land holdings (which implies intense competition for land) and the few non-Pukthun dependents available to fight for them, Pukthun men in the upper reaches of the valley must cooperate more with other members of their khel or run the risk of not being able to defend their land holdings at all and of being reduced to the status of dependents of other Pukthun men.

Although all that affects the composition of the factional blocs that do develop, it does not result in the long-term political solidarity of khel (at any level of segmentation), or in anything like a segmentary lineage system. Indeed, Barth (1959b:122) goes on to remark that tension between collateral kin within a khel (for all the reasons already rehearsed) must lead sooner or later to conflict within the group and, moreover, to "a continual sloughing-off process, whereby Pukthuns who lose all their land [to their more crafty close agnatic kin and neighbors] forfeit their Pukthun status" and are reduced to being dependents of other Pukthun men. He speculates that, had it not been for that process, the rapid growth of the population among landowners would have resulted in the fragmentation of land estates and the progressive impoverishment of the Pukthun caste.

IV

Barth (1956) provides some evidence that similar systems of group organization occur elsewhere in the same general region of South Asia. It may also be that groups for inclusion in which patrifiliation is necessary but not sufficient are common in the Middle East, for "lineages" and "segmentary lineage systems" have become a common feature in the ethnographic literature of that region. Several of Emrys Peters' essays on the Bedouin of Cyrenaica are commonly cited to polemical ends by critics of descent theory; but, as pointed out by E. Marx (in Peters 1990:1–2), it was Peters who "challenged the view that the Bedouin are a tribal society, an acephalous segmentary political system," and who always stressed "that membership of groups, though initially conferred by birthright, is really voluntary and is retained as long as it serves members' interests." If so, Bedouin (at least Lybian Bedouin) "lineages" are groups for inclusion in which patrifiliation is a necessary but not sufficient condition, and it is hardly surprising that they do not conform to any generalizations that might reasonably be derived from ethnographic data on societies such as those of the Nuer, Tiv, and Tallensi. It is clear also from Dresch's (1986, 1989) observations on Yemeni "lineages," and Spencer's (1960) and Stirling's (1960) on Turkish "lineages," that they, too, are voluntary organizations, for inclusion in which patrifiliation is a necessary but not sufficient condition. The other conditions for and of group affiliation in these various societies differ significantly from the Pukthun, as do the larger political regimes in which the groups operate, but exploration of those differences must be left to others, as we move on next to consider some systems of grouping wherein patrifiliation is a merely sufficient condition for inclusion in a group.

NOTES

1. The statuses of women and children are not discussed in any detail by any of the ethnographers. It is clear enough that women and children cannot hold shares in daftar. It may be that women and children are regarded as Pukthun and as members of particular khel but also as jural minors whose khel affiliations are largely without social implications. It may be also that a man reaches seniority and thus full realization of his membership potential when he acquires, via inheritance from his father, a distinct individual interest in daftar. A man may give an adult son some of his daftar shares, thereby enabling him to participate in the khel council, but he does so at the risk of giving the son a degree of independence from himself.

7

PATRIFILIATION SUFFICIENT BUT NOT NECESSARY I

I

Where patrifiliation is a merely sufficient condition for inclusion in a group, membership is automatic by birth, but the groups are in principle open to recruitment from the outside and change of affiliation is possible. The groups are not in principle mutually exclusive but may overlap in membership, because it may in principle be possible for a person to be simultaneously a member of more than one such group. Another corollary is that the members of a group need not be related genealogically one to another in any particular way; indeed, unless it is stipulated as an additional constitutive rule, they need not be related one to another in any way at all, except voluntarily as co-members of a group. Also, there can be competition and conflict between groups for members and their loyalties; and there can be competition and conflict within groups on the matter of membership status. It is unlikely, though, that competition and conflict of that kind will result in the establishment of two or more different categories of group member, to which are attached different rights and duties. Given that patrifiliation is a sufficient condition for inclusion in a group, it is possible conceptually to differentiate between members whose fathers also were members and members whose fathers were not members; but it is not likely to prove possible to give to the former some kind of jural advantage within the group, at least not without at the same time discouraging recruitment from the outside and foregoing whatever advantages such recruitment might have. Moreover, it may prove difficult to establish much in the way of distinctive rights and duties entailed by group affiliation, or for the groups themselves to be right- and duty-bearing entities.

Groups of this kind are especially prevalent in the highlands of Papua New Guinea, and in the ethnographic literature on that area they are commonly described as agnatic, patrilineal, or quasi-patrilineal descent groups, and sets of them are often described as acephalous segmentary lineage systems. But such groups do occur elsewhere, and one of the best bodies of relevant ethnographic data is that provided by C. D. Forde (1938, 1941, 1950, 1963a, 1963b, 1964) on the Yakö of the middle Cross River region of Eastern Nigeria, West Africa. In one of those publications, Forde (1963b) addresses the question of the more general theoretical significance of his data, and that discussion provides yet another example of how failure to differentiate between the several ways in which a kind of relation of filiation may be a condition for inclusion in a group has led, not to theoretical advance, but to spurious analytical difficulties and spurious resolutions of them.

The Yakö data are, moreover, of rather special interest because they may provide an example of a situation in which there are not only groups constituted by the rule that patrifiliation is a sufficient condition for inclusion, but also groups constituted by the rule that matrifiliation is a sufficient condition for inclusion. That is to say, far from being one of the better described instances of "double descent," which it is often taken to be (see e.g., Fox 1967, Mair 1974), Yakö society may be good example of one that gets by quite well with no descent groups at all and in which relations of descent have no jural values.

II

C. D. Forde (1963b:38) observed that it has often been recognized that "anomalous and fictive incorporation into unilineal descent groups may in fact occur"; but, he added, "the effects of permissible disregard of [the principle of recruitment] have been little considered." Like Firth (1963) and Sahlins (1963, 1965), he questioned whether "any overall distinctions between lineal and non-lineal groups are ethnographically justifiable or adequate for the analysis of the factors involved in the composition and roles of descent groups." He proposed to show that, as he had put it some years before,

> The adaptation of a pattern of unilineal succession to vicissitudes both in particular households and in the larger community must be effected in all such societies, and is likely to result in discrepancies between theory and practice (Forde 1938 [1964:84]).

There is in fact, he argued, "a continuum as to the degree of rigidity and consistency" in the interpretation and application of rules of affiliation such that, as Sahlins was later to say, there is little or no correlation between group constitution and group composition, at least not in "major territorial descent groups."

Forde sought to show that, among the Yakö, a "doctrine of patrilineal affiliation" has not prevented, and has not been affected by, a considerable degree of recruitment from the outside in each of the several recent generations for which quantitative information could be acquired, with the consequence that on the average only 50 percent of the members of Yakö "patrilineages" claim to be patrilineal descendants of the apical ancestors of those groups. Even more remarkable, no attempts are made to obscure members' nonagnatic origins, and there are no jural disadvantages entailed by nonagnatic affiliation. Little wonder that Sahlins (1965:105), citing on the Yakö only Forde (1963a), was moved to proclaim: "As a matter of genealogical fact, the discernible cognatic bias can be as great in classic patrilineages as in recognized nonunilineal groups."

There is much, however, in Forde's extensive accounts of various aspects of Yakö society to cast serious doubt on the appropriateness of saying that the Yakö express "a doctrine of patrilineal affiliation" or "an ideology of patrilineal descent" (Forde 1963a:12; 1963b:56), or that the groups designated *yepun* in the Yakö language "can obviously be regarded as patriclans and as composed of a number of patrilineage" (Forde 1963b:39). The relevant data are not, it should be emphasized, the long-available numerical, genealogical data on "clan" composition (Forde 1938). It would be unsatisfactory, because of the possibility of circularity, to rely on such data to make the case that Yakö "clans" are not descent groups of any kind and are best understood as groups for inclusion in which patrifiliation is a merely sufficient condition. More to the point is Forde's final formulation of the Yakö rule of filiation and affiliation, which makes it quite clear that what we have to deal with is not "permissible disregard" of a rule of one kind but, instead, another kind of rule:

> The initial principle [is] that a child has a right through its father, but subject to its own fulfillment of obligations, to participate in the assets of the land-controlling group to which the latter belongs. . . . While a unilineal principle does characterize the natal potential rights of group membership for men and women . . . , these natal rights are defined not in terms of the natal but of the de facto affiliation of the parent at the time of birth, and those potential rights have in turn to be validated by appropriate adult performance. . . . Thus the principle of presumptive unilineal affiliation . . . is directly applicable only over one genealogical generation (Forde 1963b:54–56).

In short, at the time of his or her birth a child is reckoned a member of the "lineage" and of the "clan" of which his or her father is then a recognized member, but these need not be the groups with which the father became affiliated at birth. Therefore, "clans" are constituted, not by the rule

TABLE 7.1   Yakö Group Nomenclature

Inclusion via patrifiliation		Inclusion via matrifiliation	
Yakö term	Forde's gloss	Yakö term	Forde's gloss
kepun	patriclan	lejima	matriclan
yepun	patriclans	yakima	matriclans
eponama	patrilineage	kejimafat	matrilineage
yeponama	patrilineages	yejimafat	matrilineages

that patrifiliation is the necessary and sufficient condition, but by the rule that patrifiliation is a merely sufficient condition for inclusion. Once that is perceived we can no longer speak, as Forde (1963b:56) did, of recruitment from the outside as a matter of "accepted contravention of unilineal principle."

It remains to be shown that the social-structural corollaries of that rule, as outlined in Chapter 2 and in the first section of this chapter, are attested in Forde's accounts of various aspects of Yakö society. We may begin with consideration of the nature of the so-called patriclans and patrilineages. It will suffice here briefly to reiterate the main points made in Forde (1963b:39–47; see also Forde 1964:48–134).

First, on the matter of nomenclature, the most relevant Yakö expressions and Forde's English glosses of them are shown in Table 7.1.

Because it is a major contention of this discussion that these are not unilineally constituted groups, it is risking self-defeat to continue to employ Forde's glosses, rather than the Yakö expressions, but to employ all or even several of the Yakö expressions would put a nettlesome if not intolerable burden on the reader. The option chosen here is to continue with Forde's glosses but hereafter to set them off between quotes. We can later deal with the question of which if any general terms are needed to replace them.

III

In 1935 the 20,000 or so Yakö lived in five compact villages, two of which were quite large. Forde's data pertain mainly to the largest, Umor, which was then the residence of nearly 11,000 people. Like other Yakö villages, Umor is divided into four wards. Within each ward there are numerous distinct dwelling areas of groups called yepun, patriclans, and those groups control not only house sites within the ward but also scattered parcels of farm land lying beyond the ward on the outskirts of the village. These dwelling areas are further subdivided into the dwelling areas of smaller groups called yeponama, patrilineages, the members of which not only live together, but also engage in cooperative farming and in exclusive rituals.

At any given time, most of the component households of a "lineage" are headed by men whose fathers also are or were members of that group. According to Forde (1963b:39), that is in some large part a consequence of a man's obligation "to provide a house site and farm plots for his sons when they come to marry and establish households of their own." A man does that by helping his son build a house adjacent to or close to his own and by transferring to his son's use farm plots that he has been using within the area controlled by his clan. Where necessary, the son may be allocated other plots not currently in use, that "with public consent by the elder of the farm path" along which those plots are reached. Further, both kinds of group are in principle exogamous, and when a man marries it is expected that he will bring his wife to live with him and his parents. In short, the so-called patriclans and patrilineages are residential groupings and their adult male members tend to be related one to another through their fathers. Forde (1963b:45–46) argues, appropriately enough, that, strictly speaking, it is not simply residence that is at issue here because a man may reside with a "clan" into which he was not born while at the same time doing his farming on the land of the "clan" into which he was born. Also, both residing with a "clan" and farming on its land is not sufficient to make a man a member of that group.

There are several ways in which it may come about that a man does not reside or farm in the area of his "clan" and "lineage" of birth. Among them, a woman may be widowed or divorced and then return to her natal "lineage," taking her children with her. The ex-husband as genitor (or, if he is dead, his brother) may eventually demand the return of his children, but the right is difficult to enforce and, unless the children later choose to return on their own to their father's "lineage," they grow up in the "lineage" of their mother and mother's brother. Or, if the mother remarries, they may grow up in the "lineage" and "clan" of their stepfather. A young man who has come to maturity in one of those circumstances may, when it comes time to marry, be allocated a house site and given farm plots by his mother's brother or his mother's husband, and thereby become an acknowledged member of the "lineage" and "clan" of that man. The critical factor, Forde (1963b:39–40) reports, is "the application of the exogamic rules." If the young man wishes to be regarded as a member of the "clan" in which he has grown up, rather than as a member of the "clan" with which he became affiliated at birth, he cannot marry a woman of either group.

Another way to become a member of a "lineage" and a "clan" is for a boy to become a sort of "client" of a man, perhaps though not necessarily a close relative such as a mother's brother or even a sister's husband, for whom the boy works and from whom the boy expects to receive in return the necessary assistance to get married and, when he does get married, an allocation of farm land for his own use, thereby becoming a member of that man's "lineage" and "clan." In addition, until the 1920s it was possible to "purchase" a child from traders of other ethnic groups, and such children became full members of the groups of their adopters. Finally, because of internal strife a small "lineage" may split off from its "clan" and set itself up on available vacant land, eventually to become a "clan" divided into a number of "lineages." Alternatively, such an offshoot group may be joined by small groups that are offshoots of other "clans" and these will in due course establish a new "clan."

Some of the consequences of all this, as described by Forde (1963a; 1963b:40–41) are: Some 10 to 20 per cent of Yakö boys are reared outside the households and "clan" of their fathers. Not all such boys are eventually adopted or assimilated into the "clans" and "lineages" in which they are reared, but it does appear from census data that, at any given time, somewhere between 10 and 20 per cent of the adult male members of such groups are members of groups of which their fathers were not members. Of course, one implication of that is that the proportion of men who are members of such groups but not patrilineal descendants of the apical ancestors of those groups must be considerably higher. Expectably, Forde (1963b:41) reports that the group genealogies he constructed reveal that, on average, "rather less than half of the living adult male members" of any "clan" claim to be lineal descendants of the apical ancestor of that group. For five "clans" the range was between 8 per cent and 100 per cent (Forde 1963b:41; 1964:66–67).

Consistent with this readiness to recruit from the outside, Forde (1963b:41) reports "no doctrine of genealogically unilineal linkage is expressed even as an ideal." Although "clan" genealogies are maintained and do feature unique male founders, no stigma of any kind is attached to inclusion in a subset the members of which do not claim to be agnatic descendants of that founder. What is asserted is that assimilation, via the allocation of house and farming sites, makes the new members "brothers in a classificatory sense" (metaphorical?) of the already-established members, and from them the corresponding behavior (for example, co-operation and restraint in opposition) is expected. The new status must be ritually expressed (publicly established?) on the appropriate occasions by acknowledging the sanctions of the "clan" spirit (not an ancestral spirit), which can be invoked only by or through the "clan" priest-head.

Within a "lineage" or "clan" there is no differentiation of members according to mode of affiliation, either categorically or jurally. That is to say, the rights and duties entailed by membership are not contingent on the mode of affiliation. Forde (1963b:43) does say that in some contexts "descent from the founder of the kepun ['clan'] or of an early lineage segment may be significant," but it is not that anyone suffers some kind of jural disadvantage by being affiliated with a group other than by birth as the child of a male member. It is instead that members of founding groups sometimes demand and, if highly qualified, receive preferential treatment in succession to certain offices in village cults and associations. But the cults and associations elect their own officers, and they are free to choose whomever they will. The "lineages" have no property rights or formal offices, although they do usually appoint an elder as their representative in village affairs, and he need not be a descendant of the group founder. Similarly, neither is patrilineal affiliation a condition for being a village elder or for occupancy of the office of "clan" priest-head. Although an "adopted" member is in no position to lead his "lineage" or to become the priest-head of his "clan," his son, who is affiliated via patrifiliation, can become either or both.

IV

According to Forde (1963b:47) the situation with regard to membership of another set of groups is "broadly comparable." These are the "matriclan" and "matrilineage," both of which are, of course, not localized or residential groups. Forde (1963b:48) reports that "the first and most prominent of the rights which the members of a ['matriclan'] have with regard to one another . . . relate to the transmission of movable property." That statement is seriously misleading. What Forde goes on to relate is that the preferred heir of a man's personal property and, at the same time, the successor to many of his social obligations, is a sister's son or other close maternal relative, a person who is (perhaps most usually anyway) a member of the same "matriclan" as the deceased. As heir and successor, he must see that the sons of the deceased are allowed to keep some of their father's equipment, and he must supply meat and wine for mortuary and succession feasts if, as it happens, the deceased was a member of any of the many village cults and associations.

Otherwise, co-members of a "matriclan," especially if they are also close kin and friends, are obliged to assist one another via gifts or loans, to assist a young man's family by contributing to brideprice payments, and to help in the payment of fines by members judged guilty of offenses; and co-members are forbidden to marry one another. Each "matriclan" also maintains, or participates in the maintenance of, a fertility cult for the benefit of each of its members. The several hundred members of one "matriclan," though they regard themselves as kin of one another, cannot all specify exactly how they are related. In contrast, a "matrilineage" is a smaller set of people, related one to another solely through women, who trace their common ancestry back three or four generations to a common ancestress. A few elders from each of these groups constitute an informal council that may be led, when occasion arises, by the priest of the "matriclan" fertility cult, either to arbitrate disputes between members or to represent the group as a whole in affairs with outsiders.

The "matriclan" can be made to appear to be a matrilineal descent group, because "in principle both men and women belong by birth to the ['matriclan'] of their mothers." Again, however, "by no means all members of [such a group] belong to it by birth" (1963b:51), and because, unlike the "patriclan," these are not land-owning or land-administering units, the conditions that affect affiliation with them are bound to be at least partly different from those that affect "patriclan" affiliation. But, just as "purchased" children were inducted into the status of legal children of their purchasers and, ipso facto, into their purchasers' "clans," so also were they made full members of their purchasers' or, in the instance of a male purchaser, of his wife's or his sister's "matriclan." Significantly for our purposes here, not all purchased children were also formally adopted by their purchasers, so this mode of affiliation cannot be dismissed as merely a corollary of adoption.

Change of "matriclan" affiliation was possible also through a practice associated with the peaceful settlement of a homicide. The death by homicide of a "matriclan" member was believed injurious to the group as a whole, to its vitality and fertility. Recompense in the form of goods and currency was payable by the "matriclan" of the killer to the "matriclan" of the victim; and the killer took the place of the victim as a member of the deceased's "matriclan" until and unless the payment were made in full. Also (although perhaps not often done), a young woman of the killer's "matriclan" was transferred to the "matriclan" of the deceased, but without losing the right to inherit from her brothers. In that way the "matriclan" of the deceased would benefit from additional members as well as from the flow of wealth from one group to the other.

Change of "matriclan" affiliation is possible in another way. "Matriclans" in different villages sometimes share a tradition of common origin, although they are ritually autonomous. So, when a woman marries into another village, and comes to have only intermittent contact with her own "matriclan" and especially her own "matrilineage," she can compensate for that by participating in the mutual aid and ritual services of members of a corresponding "matriclan" in her husband's village. If she remains in that village for life, and if her sons do not return, for one reason or another, to her natal village, they will not be in a position to inherit from her brothers, and so they will seek to become identified with the "matriclan" and "matrilineage" with which she became identified via her marital residence.

As a consequence of all that, in one "matrilineage" genealogy analyzed by Forde (1963b:54), slightly less than 20 per cent of adult members claimed to be matrilineal descendants of the apical ancestor. About 50 per cent acknowledged affiliation via adoption, own or parental; and the remaining 30 per cent acknowledged affiliation as "purchased" children or as the children of "purchased" children.

V

Forde (1938 [1964:53]) describes Yakö "patriclans" as corporate, but by that he means only that each has rights to exclusive use of a dwelling area in the village and to administration of areas of farm land outside the village. We may wonder, however, if it would be more appropriate to describe such a dwelling area more modestly as a neighborhood subdivision of a village ward, exogamous and recruiting by birth (patrifiliation) from the inside, but open to recruitment from the outside. It has an internal organization that centers on a spirit-shrine and its rites, an assembly house wherein its affairs are conducted, and a priest-head who officiates at those rites and in meetings between the elders of the "patrilineages" (compounds?) and who is chief spokesman for members of the group in disputes between them and members of other neighborhoods in its ward. A person's duties as a member (or resident) of a neighborhood are to conduct himself with restraint in dealing with his neighbors and to cooperate in clearing and maintaining paths leading to and through the outlying gardens. Otherwise, says Forde (1964:30), "Within the kepun there is marked individualism, and except on ceremonial occasions few effective demands can be made on the individual for the benefit of kepun fellows outside his lineage." He must also acknowledge the sanctions of the group's spirit cult and agree to arbitration by the priest-head in disputes with his neighbors. It would be stretching a point to say that the group owns the land it occupies. There is no indication in Forde's ethnography that the issue of legitimate occupancy ever arises; what does happen from time to time is that a compound in neighborhood B is expanded onto land that someone in the adjacent neigborhood A takes to be his own house site, in which event the priest-heads of the neighborhoods may be called upon to compose the dispute.

As for farm land, the group itself can hardly be said to own any but does, via its priest-head and a "farm path elder," administer the use of the scattered parcels of land that are either under cultivation by or being kept in fallow reserve by individual men who reside, or did reside, in the neighborhood, and that are intermingled with those being used or kept in fallow by men of other neighborhoods. But this administrative control is rather limited by what Forde describes as the "preferential rights" of the "patrilineages," which seem to consist of recognized priority of access to fallow gone long unused—which is one of the ways in which men get land for their adult sons or sister's sons or other clients. In any event, there is no general shortage of land and there is ample room for expansion of gardens—which, significantly, makes it possible for men acting individually to recruit other men into their own neighborhoods as their clients. Apparently, the advantage in maintaining control of the fallow of one's "lineage" mates is that it is less difficult to clear and its proximity to land currently being cultivated by them makes for easier access to shared labor.

In the concepts and terms developed in Chapter 4, Yakö "patriclans" (or neighborhood divisions of wards) and "patrilineages" (or compounds within them) are both jural collectivities. Dwelling sites and parcels of farm land are individual property, though subject, as anywhere, to some kind and degree of community control. In this instance, it seems reasonable to say, the ultimate owner of the land surrounding the village is the village community itself, which in effect relegates estates of administration to wards, neighborhoods, and compounds, though without in the process establishing any special rights and duties between the entities at each level. As for the "matriclans" and "matrilineages," they have no property, not even exclusive cults, and are not even jural aggregates. They are significant mainly as mutual-aid societies.

Our conclusion must be that, whatever else they may do, Forde's Yakö data plainly do not support any of Sahlins's (1965) contentions about relationships between "the ideology" and the de facto composition of "major territorial descent groups." It is true that Yakö "patriclans" and "patrilineages" are "territorial" groups and that they are a very long way from being anything like 100 percent agnatic or patrilineal in composition. But far from having, as Forde (1963b:56) said, an "ideology of unilineal descent," these groups are heterogeneously constituted, because patrifiliation is not the necessary and sufficient condition, but is a merely sufficient condition for inclusion. Moreover, Yakö "patrilineages" lack the one critical feature on which Sahlins's argument turns. The several "lineages" of a "clan" do not ally with or oppose one another according to the closeness or distance of agnatic relations between them. That is because neither kind of group is agnatically constituted and because the several "lineages" included in a "clan" do not have (and, given their constitution, could not possibly have) any special rights and duties vis-à-vis one another.

One of the main sources of difficulty, for Forde as well as for Sahlins, is the habit that anthropologists have, and that Fortes warned so strongly against, of representing the relation of child to father per se as a patrilineal relation, and the relation of child to mother per se as a matrilineal relation. It is only by way of that habit that it could be made out that "the patrilineal principle" is operative in relation to Yakö "patriclans" and "patrilineages." or that those English glosses can be made to appear appropriate. Another source of difficulty is the habit anthropologists have of treating rules of filiation and of affiliation as prescriptive and regulative rules rather than as constitutive rules. So it was that Forde began his (1963b) discussion of Yakö "kin groups" by announcing his intention to show that, however different they might be in "ideology"(that is, constitutive principle), in practice or operation unilineal and non-unilineal groups are not as different as they are sometimes made out to be. The reason, according to Forde (and to Sahlins), is that unilineal principle has sometimes to be bent to accommodate "external factors of economy and demography." In the end, though, Forde (1963b:56) had to acknowledge that the effect of "permissible disregard" of "the principle of unilineal descent" is to "override" it and to make it "directly applicable only over one genealogical generation." It is curious, indeed, that at that point Forde did not conclude that there was something specious about his use of *unilineal* to begin with. Although he did not do that and went on to say that the Yakö themselves "recognize rights and obligations within such groups in terms of an ideology of unilineal descent," he did acknowledge, in effect at least, that relations of patrilineal descent, "in the sense of ascribed common descent from a single ancestor," are jurally insignificant in Yakö society.

> It is only where no countervailing factors affect the successive affiliations of parent and child over several generations, that a line of unilineal descent from a remote ancestor will exist. Such a line may be a matter of pride for an individual and may confer prestige and advantages in some contexts, but a principle of unilineal descent down the generations is not invoked with reference to the membership or formal status of individuals in the group (Forde 1963b:56).

All that and much more can be restated in a single sentence: Where patrifiliation or matrifiliation is a merely sufficient condition for inclusion in a group, relations of descent (as distinct from relations of filiation) can have no jural values, either in the internal or the external relations of groups.

VI

We may now confront the question posed earlier: If the Yakö groups under discussion here are not patrilineally or matrilineally constituted and, therefore, it is inappropriate to describe them as clans or lineages of any kind, what kind or kinds of group are they? Does our anthropological vocabulary already include something more appropriate? The possibility that they might be described as some kind of "kin group" may come immediately to mind, but must be resisted. Wherever a kind of filial relation is a (merely) sufficient condition for inclusion in a group (set, category, or whatever), the possibility is established that some proportion of the members of that group at any particular time will be kin of one another. It is not established, however, that any and all members at any and all times will be kin of one another, much less kin of any particular kind or kinds. So, if Yakö "clans" and "lineages," so-called, are to some degree "groups of kin," they are *not* also "kin groups" of any particular or even any kind.

A more probable candidate, at least in regard to Yakö kepun ('patriclan') and eponama ('patrilineage'), is something taken from the lexicon of local or residential groups. After all, what gives these groups any semblance of "patrilineality" is the obligation of a man to see to it that his sons have a place to set up their domestic units and access to land to till, and these he must get from the residential group of which he is a member when the time comes to do so. Indeed, the only thing that seems to stand in the way of describing these as some kind of local-residential grouping is that men do not automatically lose their affiliations by choosing to live and farm, at least for a time, as guests in some other place. But that is no real obstacle; all we need do is distinguish between residence and domicile, and say that he who is resident as a guest in one place (and who is not, or not yet at least, a member of the group domiciled there) may remain domiciled in and still a member of another (that is, it remains his "home").

Group structures somewhat similar to the Yakö "patrilineages" and "patriclans" (and "matrilineages" and "matriclans"!) appear to be not uncommon in West Africa. On some neighbors of the Yakö, see R. Harris (1969), and for some possible instances in Northern Nigeria see M. G. Smith (1969). See also S. Ottenberg's (1968) *Double Descent in an African Society: The Afikpo Village-Group.* Yet another instance, that of a set of Ewe-speaking villages in southeast Ghana, is described in some detail in Verdon (1983), albeit in a vocabulary and from a conceptual stance that are radically at odds with the ones being developed herein.

8

PATRIFILIATION SUFFICIENT BUT NOT NECESSARY II

I

At the same time as Forde was reconsidering his Yakö data, J. A. Barnes was reflecting on the difficulties that some anthropologists were having in conceptualizing the nature of groups and intergroup relations in the highlands regions of Papua-New Guinea (Barnes 1962, also 1967, 1971). In the 1950s, ethnographers began to encounter in the highlands societies in which there were—or so it seemed—nested hierarchies of patrilineal descent groups, and it seemed appropriate to turn for guidance in attempting to understand them to the concepts and generalizations that had been developed in studies of various African societies (as in e.g., Fortes 1953). As it turned out, though, most ethnographers found those "African models"—or what they understood of them—of little help and sometimes quite misleading.

There are only two possible reasons for that lack of fit. One is that there is something wrong with the concepts and generalizations derived from studies of African societies and they need to be revised, perhaps even radically, in the light of highlands data. The other is that classification of certain highlands groups as descent groups is mistaken, and therefore we should not expect the internal and external relations of those groups to conform to Africa-derived generalizations about genuine descent groups. The latter possibility was noticed in one or another way by a number of ethnographers, and doubts were sometimes expressed about the wisdom of describing certain highlands groups as patrilineal, as descent groups, or as lineages, clans, and so on. For the most part, however, those doubts were resolved in favor of the applicability of those designations.[1] The question then became how to reconcile established theory about the structure and function of unilineal descent groups with the New Guinea data. As pointed out in preceding chapters, some scholars have concluded that such a reconciliation is not possible and have recommended that the whole of lineage or descent theory be discarded without further ado.

Barnes (1962) argued for the other possibility. He pointed out that most highlands groups described as descent groups of one or another scale (that is, as phratries, clans, subclans, or lineages) are also local or territorial groups. The main reason why they have been described as patrilineal descent groups is that persons are assigned at birth to membership of their father's groups, in exactly the same way—or so it seemed—as they are among the Nuer, Tiv, Tallensi, and so on in Africa. But, Barnes went on to note, there are several significant differences. The most notable is that recruitment from the outside to membership of a local community and, therewith, to membership of "clans," "subclans," and "lineages,"[2] is quite common in the highlands. Also, persons recruited from the outside do not suffer any jural disadvantages as such; indeed, they may even become powerful within the group. Change of affiliation is possible, and in some instances it is possible to maintain simultaneous membership of more than one group. Genealogical knowledge is typically rather shallow and fragmentary, and little or no attempt is made (by way of genealogical revision) to represent groups (at any level) as made up wholly of patrilineal descendants (and their spouses) of a reputed apical ancestor. Finally, neither in principle nor in practice do groups within groups combine with or oppose one another in the fashion of segmentary or complementary opposition. Appearances to the contrary have been created, Barnes argued, by making the

> mistake of comparing the de facto situation in a highland community, as shown in an ethnographic census, with a nonexistent and idealized set of conditions among the Nuer, wrongly inferred from Evans-Pritchard's discussion of the principles of Nuer social structure. The New Guinea hamlet is found to be full of matrilateral kin, affines and casual visitors, quite unlike the hypothecated entirely virilocal and agnatic Nuer village (though similar to real Nuer villages) (Barnes 1962:5).

Despite this warning, and despite Fortes's repeated admonition against conflating lineage groups and local groups, many anthropologists have gone on, as we have already seen, to proclaim that the de facto composition of both Nuer and New Guinea highlands village communities only goes to show that patrilineal norms are, in at least some kinds of circumstance, quite unworkable and that departures from them are only to be expected.

Barnes argued instead that we need "to think twice before cataloguing the New Guinea highlands as characterized by patrilineal descent." It cannot be denied that "genealogical connection of some sort" is a criterion for membership of many social groups in the highlands, but, "if we follow Fortes and restrict the designation descent group to groups in which descent is the only criterion for membership," it is difficult, Barnes said, to discover descent groups in highlands societies. What it is not difficult to find are groups for inclusion in which patrifiliation is a merely sufficient condition, and that difference accounts for many of the ways in which social groups and intergroup relations in the highlands differ from genuine patrilineal descent groups and their interrelations elsewhere in the world.

Barnes pointed out that, because patrifiliation is a condition for inclusion in highlands' groups, there may be superficial similarities between them and groups described as lineages in the African literature. Most notable, to the degree that men act in ways that tend to perpetuate their natal affiliations until they have children of their own, those children will acquire the same affiliations as their fathers and their father's fathers. Barnes (1962:6) called that process cumulative patrifiliation.[3] He pointed out that via this process any group might become "similar in demographic appearance and de facto kinship ties" to a genuinely patrilineal group. But, he stressed, "its structure and ideology are quite different," and, again, he detailed a number of those differences.[4] Finally, he described the then common view that highland groups are comparable in the structurally most basic way but, curiously, not in other ways, to African lineages and lineage systems as "the African mirage in New Guinea." It was a mirage produced by failure to distinguish between situations in which patrifiliation is the necessary and sufficient condition and situations in which it is a merely sufficient condition for inclusion in a group (and, it may be added, by continued, almost willful refusal to attend to the difference between groups that are and groups that are not in principle localized; cf. Weiner 1982:6–8). It is that simple difference that accounts for why "highland societies fit awkwardly into African molds." It is also why, contrary to Meggitt (1965:5), "Fortes's Africa-derived generalizations" are not applicable to highland societies, and it is why, contrary to the opinion of many anthropologists, highlands ethnography cannot reflect negatively on those generalizations.

Despite Barnes's efforts, the mirage has persisted. If the focus of scholarly research and debate about highlands societies has passed on to other topics, as according to some authors it has (Feil 1984a; Lederman 1986), that is not because the conceptual problems and controversies of the 1960s and 1970s have been resolved to everyone's satisfaction and that resolution is now being built upon. Instead, a dominant tendency is still to complain about how "African models" and "classical descent theory" are inadequate, and not only in relation to highland societies, but also in relation to their African prototypes.[5]

II

In all the relevant African societies, certain apparent exceptions notwithstanding (for example, the Yakö dealt with in Chapter 7), there is a principled distinction made between lineages or descent groups and local groups, and, as Fortes always stressed, no good can come of confusing the two. Yet in much of the ethnographic literature on highlands societies and in much of the derivative literature, many arguments turn on just such a confusion. A large part of the reason is that, in dealing with highland societies, the distinction between lineage or descent group (so called) and local group is difficult to make, and it is precisely a territorial group, a geographically bounded entity, that is at issue when it is argued that nonagnates are often recruited to membership of groups that are agnatic in "ideology" or "dogma." As R. Salisbury (1956:5) put it, "All descent groups are also residence groups." Although he was referring to Siane in particular, the remark is much more generally applicable (see e.g., Barnes [1967:34] on Meggitt [1965]: "All Enga descent groups are effectively localized."). Andrew Strathern's (1969:37) suggestion that we ask not "Are there descent groups in the highlands?," but "To what levels of group structure are descent dogmas applied, and why?," was possible only on the condition that the groups in question are also local groups of one or another scale.[6]

It is not an oversimplification to say that the groups described as clans in the highlands literature are almost invariably groups associated conceptually with, and which occupy, a clearly bounded territory, and de Lepervanche (1967:157) has already suggested that they would be better described (following an earlier practice in New Guinea ethnography) as "parish groups" than as descent groups. The groups commonly described as subclans or subsubclans are generally groups that share a men's house located within a clan territory, and the so-called lineages are subsets of the so-called subclans or subsubclans. They are described as lineages most often because they are the lowest-level groups in an alleged hierarchy of groups or for no reason other than their small size (Salisbury 1956:3), which often makes them more aptly described as extended families (cf. Langness 1971:301).[7] There are, however, only two things to prevent us from describing all these groups, certainly the clans, virtually without qualification, as local groups.

One consideration is that the clan, so called, is typically an exogamous group and postmarital residence is typically, though by no means universally, patrivirilocal (the bride goes to live with the groom near his parents), but women retain their natal group identities, or, depending on the social context, they are identified with either their natal or their husbands' groups. The other reason is that the residence of a man in a community other than the one into which he was born does not in and of itself extinguish his membership in his natal group or immediately result in his identification as a member of the group with which he is resident. So, as named conceptual aggregates of persons, many highlands "descent groups" are not simply equatable with local communities. Yet the relationship between clan on the one hand and local community on the other is much closer in the highlands than in most African societies—one of the exceptions being, of course, the Yakö. If it were not, there would be no debate about whether certain highlands groups should or should not be described as descent groups.

Many ethnographers and theorists have found it sensible to argue that a group may or should be described as a descent group even if a form of filiation (they usually say descent) is not the necessary and sufficient condition for inclusion in it, provided that "a dogma of descent" is relevant somehow to its internal structure or to its external relations (e.g., Scheffler 1965). From that perspective, it has been argued repeatedly that it is difficult to dispense entirely with the term descent when describing highlands groups because the people themselves represent those groups as descent groups, even though they openly acknowledge that being a child of a male member is not the only way to become a member.[8] The claim is that, although highlanders do not discriminate jurally between agnatic and non-agnatic (or patrilineal and non-patrilineal) members of groups, in contexts especially of intergroup relations they often do represent those groups as patrilineally constituted or as sets of agnatically related males, and they do exhort fellow group members to conduct themselves as though they were all agnates.[9]

We must disagree, however, with the assessments of Holy (1976:120) and others that it has been "demonstrated convincingly" that highland peoples represent their groups at least partially in terms of agnatic or patrilineal descent. What has been shown repeatedly is, as Barnes (1962:6) put it, that when highlanders attempt to sanction a person's conduct in intra- or intergroup affairs, they appeal not "to the notion of descent [in Fortes's sense] as such but to the obligations of kinsfolk, differentiated according to relationship," that is, according to kin class. A very large proportion of the anthropological talk about highlanders' "dogma" or "ideology" of agnatic or patrilineal descent rests on little more than natives' talk about the male members of a group being 'brothers' or 'sons of one father.'[10] On the surface of it, such talk could be about patrilineal descent. Tallensi do talk that way about their lineages (cf. Fortes 1949:33), especially when considered in relation to collateral lineages related to them as "sons of one grandfather." They do that, however, in a society in which, as there is much other evidence to show, patrifiliation is the necessary and sufficient condition for inclusion in certain groups.

Such independent evidence has yet to be forthcoming in the highlands, and it is, therefore, rather unlikely that highlanders' talk about brothers or sons of one father must be interpreted as talk about patrilineal descent—unless, of course, we want to revert to using descent and filiation as synonyms. As Barnes (1967; 1971) has stressed repeatedly, it is sufficient to describe talk of that kind as talk about fraternal and paternal kinship, and such talk is consistent with the status of patrifiliation as a sufficient condition for inclusion in a group. If we must use *agnatic* here (and it is doubtful that we should), it ought to modify kinship, and not descent. Barnes (1967, 1971) suggests also that highlanders' talk about "brothers" and "sons of one father" may be a kind of taxonomic discourse, a way of talking about relations of inclusion in groups, either of individuals in groups or of groups within groups. He does not suggest that, in the highlands, "descent is not a criterion for group affiliation but, rather, an idiom of group unity" (Lederman 1986:58). Indeed, he argues directly to the contrary when he points out (1962:6) that "if the dogma [of descent] is absent, appeal to genealogy to validate present action is of no avail." Ethnographers working in the highlands have sometimes reported that a distinction is made by the actors themselves between "agnatic" (or "patrilineal") and "nonagnatic" (or "nonpatrilineal") members of social groups, although it is usually acknowledged by the same ethnographers that, curiously, members of the latter category are in no way jurally disadvantaged as such. Alas, many of the relevant ethnographic reports are disappointingly thin, in that data warranting the glosses agnatic and nonagnatic are not presented; but it is, even so, not difficult to show that this distinction is not between agnatic (patrilineal) and nonagnatic (nonpatrilineal) affiliation.

Writing of the Mendi, Ryan (1959:257, 281) reports the expression *shem* which, he says, "does in fact mean 'unilinear descent-group,'" and such groups range in scale from, at the upper end, "a clan-cluster of up to a thousand people" to, at the minimum, "a simple family of a man and his children." The phrase "a man and his children" should immediately arouse our suspicions about the accuracy of Ryan's confident assertion about the meaning of shem, especially in view of Evans-Pritchard's careful explication of the Nuer distinction between a family and a lineage (see Chapter 5). A Mendi minimal shem encompasses only a father-child set and is, therefore, not patrilineally constituted. Once that is conceded, it is no longer puzzling that although, according to Ryan (1959:265), the Mendi language does distinguish between agnatic and nonagnatic affiliation, expressions signifying the latter are "seldom used, because there are few situations in which a distinction between agnates and nonagnates is socially relevant." In other words, those categories have little or no jural significance. The relevant Mendi expressions are *shu moria, ol ebowa,* and *ebowan ishi,* which Ryan glosses as "born to the land," "newcomer," and "son of a newcomer" respectively. Ryan says the descendants of a newcomer are not established as persons born to the land until "the third generation," that is until the son's son's child of the newcomer. As Ryan sees it, it is because Mendi shem are patrilineally constituted that the process of conversion from nonagnate to agnate requires several generations. He acknowledges, however, not only that there are very few kinds of social context in which the categories noted above are "socially relevant," but also that they are not mutually exclusive.

Most important for our purposes here, the child of an immigrant male may be not only a child of a newcomer but also a person born to the land, if born after the immigrant's entry into the group. That is to say, being merely the locally born and reared child of an immigrant male (and often also of a locally born woman) is sufficient to make a person an acknowledged member of the group. Even more damaging to Ryan's claim that recruitment from the outside is a long, drawn-out, multi-generation process is the following. Each Mendi carries the name of his "patriclan" as a prefix to his personal name, and, according to Ryan (1959:269–270), "the general rule is that a nonagnate is known to his clan of residence by his patronym and to outsiders by the name of his clan of residence." Even so, an immigrant male who has no intention to return to his place of birth may insist on being known only by the name of his clan of residence, and so may his children, wherever and whenever they were born.

Similar distinctions, with similar lack of jural significance, have been reported by Meggitt (1965) for the Mae-Enga and by Strathern (1972) for Melpa-speaking peoples around Mount Hagen. Strathern's report, although published later than Meggitt's, should be considered first.

Among the Melpa, at any level of group segmentation the offspring of a male member of a group are known as *wua-nt-mei,* "born of a man" in relation to that group, and the offspring of a female member are known as *amb-nt-mei,* "born of a woman" (Strathern 1972:18–22). Because of the preference for and the prevalence of patrivirilocal postmarital residence, persons born of a man are usually also members of the group itself; and persons born of a woman are usually members of their fathers' natal groups. Even so, males and even females born of a woman are said to be welcome to become members of the group, and without jural differentiation. If a man born of a woman comes to reside with the group, be it as the child of a returning widow or divorcee or on his own initiative, his children who reside there with him are designated "born of a man." As Strathern (1972:19) points out, what we have here is plainly not a distinction between agnates and nonagnates (or even one between members and nonmembers). A woman's son's child who becomes a born-of-a-man member of her natal group is plainly not being "converted into an agnate." The operative distinction here is between patrifiliation and matri-filiation, and the former (but not the latter) is sufficient for affiliation—because the child of a male member is ipso facto a member, whether or not resident in the group's homeland.

To all appearances, the situation among the Mae-Enga is closely similar, although it may well be that recruitment from the outside is less common than it is among the Melpa. Meggitt reports that Mae-Enga phratries, clans, subclans, and lineages are patrilineally constituted but that "limited" recruitment from the outside—almost solely of the offspring of female members—is possible. Thus any group at any level of segmentation may include a set or sets of persons reputed to be descended from a woman, rather than from a man. Again, the members of such sets are not jurally disadvantaged as such. Meggitt (1965:31–32) reports that the children of female group members are known as "the children of a female agnate" regardless of where they and their mothers reside, but should they come to reside permanently in their mother's natal group and to rear their children there, those children "are regarded simply as clan agnates."[11] Departing from Enga usage, in which there is no special or intermediary category, Meggitt describes the resident offspring of the son of a female member as "quasi-agnates," that is, as nonagnates who have been "converted to agnatic status." In the typical instance, Meggitt (1965:32) says, a young man residing with his father and mother in his mother's clan parish is given land to use by his mother's brother or mother's father, and his child may "inherit" those rights. That child (the son's child of a female member) is no longer distinguished categorically, as "child of a female agnate."

> The quasi-agnate and true agnate of this patrilineage now share patrimonial land with equal validity. They all inherited it legally from their fathers. Therefore, according to the Mae, the quasi-agnate must be an agnate (Meggitt 1965:32).

Although Meggitt describes this process as one of conversion of nonagnates to agnates, the Mae-Enga, like the Melpa and the Mendi, do not trouble themselves to revise ancestral genealogies in the process. To all appearances, none of Meggitt's informants made any attempt to obscure the fact of matrifilial affiliation at any level of segmentation.

Assuming (on the basis of what he takes to be good evidence) that Mae-Enga groups are patrilineally constituted, but noting that they vary in degree of approximation to 100 per cent agnatic composition, Meggitt (1965:263) argues that "rules of land tenure, and with them recruitment norms, [become] more rigidly interpreted and supported" as, with a growing population, all available land is taken up for use, and men have fewer opportunities or inducements to change residence and group affiliation. That is, degree of adherence to agnatic principle is a function of one kind of ecological stress. Arguably, though, Enga groups are in principle not closed, but open to recruitment from the outside. Therefore, their variable composition from time to time and place to place and their variable willingness to recruit from the outside are wholly in line with constitutive principle. Neither requires variable "interpretation" or "support" of rules of land tenure and recruitment norms. If Enga become, under the stress of land shortage, less ready to admit persons from the outside, they are merely exercising one of the options made available to them by the rules constitutive of their groups. Being in principle open to recruitment from the outside does not oblige any group to absorb into its ranks any and every outsider who offers himself as a member, and in whatever circumstances. Groups may quite legitimately vary from place to place and time to time, and depending on various local economic and ecological or political conditions, in readiness to accept immigrants.

Among the Enga, it appears to be not so much a matter of being more or less rigid or flexible in interpreting rules or supporting adherence to them as it is of being more or less tolerant of the charity of one's neighbors. Generally in the highlands, anyone enters a group from the outside only as a guest of an established member and, moreover, only with the explicit or tacit consent of other members of the group. The host must provide the guest with land to cultivate from any to which he (the host) has special access (use rights); but this will be land to which other already-established members of the group would perhaps eventually have access, were it not given over to use by a newcomer. If a group increases in size without at the same time expanding the area of land it controls, increasing pressure is put on some members to let others cultivate areas over which they have use rights and are holding in reserve. Hence other members of a group may, quite within their rights, argue against a proposal to bring in from the outside additional mouths to feed.

In most highland societies, then, there is no condition other than patrifiliation that is sufficient for inclusion in a group. Matrifiliation is not a sufficient condition because a person becomes identified as a member of his or her mother's group when born and reared, or only reared in the midst of it, or by otherwise establishing residence within it. Thus, the one genealogical relationship that is formally related to group constitution is patrifiliation, and logically this implies that not only a man and his children but also paternal brothers are members of the same group, at least until one or more of them decides to arrange otherwise. It does not imply anything beyond that about group composition. Moreover, it seems that men are morally bound to reside with and to support their fathers and are entitled to benefit from the support of their fathers. Consistent with that, virtually all changes of group affiliation follow the death of one's father— when, that is, they do not result from movement with one's father (as perhaps a refugee from a raid or war) or with one's mother as a child of a widow or divorcee who may return to her natal community to live with her father or brothers. Thus, the one moral bond that is predicated on a relation of genealogical connection that is itself associated normatively with recruitment to groups is the moral bond between father and child. In such a context it makes good sense to exhort fellow members of one's group to conduct themselves as though they were fathers and sons or brothers, even if they know, as typically they plainly do, that they are not all even classificatory brothers or fathers and sons of one another.

In light of the preceding observations it must be regarded as one of the great sociological curiosities of the highlands literature that virtually no one (except Barnes)[12] has noticed that it would be decidedly odd—or, it is not too much to say, even absurd—for people to enunciate "dogmas of descent" in order to express group unity, solidarity, and continuity while, at the same time, openly acknowledging that they recruit members from the outside and, moreover, do not attach jural disability to affiliation with a group other than that of one's father. Efforts have been made repeatedly to show that when nonagnates are recruited from the outside, genealogical "revision" does eventually take place, and that has been alleged to show that the groups are agnatic in constitution. Salisbury (1956:5), for example, argues that "within three generations [Siane] genealogies have been 'clipped, patched, and telescoped' (Fortes 1953:32) to mask the changes under an appearance of stability." But his own and other data suggest to Barnes (1962:6) that it is more appropriate to say of the highlands in general that people "neglect their genealogies, either by not revising them or by simply forgetting them"; or, "where revision does take place it may be simplification [as in Siane] rather than the manipulation characteristic of the Tiv and Nuer."[13] Typically, although there is no attempt to encompass all persons in senior generations into a single genealogy, there does seem to be a tendency to reduce relations between men in senior generations to 'father-son' and 'brother' relations. Salisbury's description (see also Strathern 1972:47–51) suggests that this reduction comes about not through "manipulation" (that is, from creation of a legal fiction by elders which younger men are then obliged to accept as though it were fact), but simply through lack of public concern with genealogical detail and the consequent presumption on the part of the younger men that their predecessors in the group were by and large fathers and sons or brothers one of another. That presumption would accord with the perception of the de facto arrangements among the living members of the group. In any event, although it is sometimes claimed in the highlands literature that "assimilation of nonagnates" requires the passage of several generations, as among the Tiv (see Chapter 5), the data presented actually show or imply that even an immigrant male may be assimilated to de jure and not merely de facto membership; and in general the children of long-resident immigrant males are assimilated to full membership status.[14]

III

It was argued in Chapter 3 that where patrifiliation is a merely sufficient condition for inclusion in a group, it will be difficult if not impossible to institute distinctive rights and duties connected with affiliation via one's father versus affiliation in some other way, and, moreover, that the groups themselves are unlikely to be jural entities, especially of the kind that have special rights and duties vis-à-vis one another. The first point is validated by the demonstration that the distinction between affiliation via one's mother and affiliation via one's father has no jural significance. So far, the only within-group distinction that has been shown to be of any jural significance is that between recent immigrants and long-established members, and even that distinction is not relevant to the immigrant children of female members. It is sometimes reported that a man associated with a group other than that of his father is "jurally disabled," but it is clear from a number of accounts that the social disabilities that some such men may suffer are incidental to their group affiliations. They are those of any man whose father is deceased and who has yet to find a sponsor who will voluntarily do for him the things that his father would have been morally obliged to do (see e.g., Strathern 1972:149, 154, 164–165; Sillitoe 1979:41–42; Healey 1979; Lederman 1986:57).

It is clear also that the rights and duties of particular kinds of kin, especially fathers, sons, and brothers, have been systematically misrepresented as the rights and duties of persons as group members or as agnates. One example is provided by Ryan's accounts of who pays and who receives bridewealth among the Mendi. At first (Ryan 1959:269) it was described as though it were, at least in part, an affair of subclans or lineages (see also Ryan 1969:167). It finally emerged, however, that the principal contributors and recipients are the groom's and bride's father, mother, mother's brother, married sisters and their husbands and sons. In short, group affiliation is only accidentally and quite loosely related to participation in bridewealth payments.

Group affiliation may be more closely, but is still only accidentally, related to the making of "death payments" as well. Although commonly represented in the ethnographic literature as the obligation of the deceased's agnates or clansmen to his or her mother's agnates or clansmen, such payments are surely the obligations of specific types of kin and in-laws, and who pays whom hinges, for children anyway, on who has custody of and, therefore, responsibility for the deceased. This is confirmed in a curious way by Healey (1979). Among the Maring, if a widow returns with her children to live with her brother and one of the children later dies while in the custody of the mother's brother, he must make a death-payment to the brothers of the deceased father, though it would usually be they (if the deceased child were in their custody) who made the payment to him. Healey construes this to indicate:

> first, that a dead man's brothers relinquish their agnatic claims to his offspring and, second, the mother's brother's acceptance of the child into his own agnatic group, since in making the payment he is acting like an agnate of the child . . . . In other words, the reversal is expressive of re-aligned interests in the children of returning widows, and the transfer of clan membership of the children (Healey 1979:211).

What, however, warrants describing the dead man's brother's claims to custody of his children as agnatic claims, or if they had custody of the children, describing their obligation to make a death payment to the mother's brother (or his successor) as an obligation of agnates to mother's agnates? To warrant such a description it has to be shown either that the rights and duties in question are those of agnatic kin in general, or that the closest available agnatic kin act in a representative capacity. But none of that is shown. As it is, it seems that the only reason to write about agnates here is that fathers, brothers (at least father's sons), and men's children are, in anthropological parlance, agnatic kin. Yet, the local-language expressions we anthropologists gloss (reasonably enough) as 'father' or 'brother' are seldom if ever expressions that signify specifically agnatic relationship.[15] It seems, moreover, wholly unlikely that there are any expressions that signal agnation in any highlands language. To pick one from many possible examples, Goldman (1993:22) offers Huli *tene* as a candidate, but glosses it also as 'source', and he gives us no reasons to think that, when used (explicitly or implicitly) in contrast with *yamo wini*, "placed [in a clan parish] by [a] woman," it signals anything more than affiliation via patrifiliation in contrast to matrifiliation.

Group affiliation is only loosely, if somewhat less accidentally, related also to participation in many other kinds of activity such as warfare and ceremonial exchange, both of which are commonly described by ethnographers as activities undertaken jointly or corporately by groups, thus suggesting that participation is a matter of derivative right or duty. But, even allowing for some regional variation within the highlands, such descriptions seem generally overblown. Much ethnographic talk about joint or corporate activity and liability in the highlands rests on the observation that participants in fights, wars, raids, and large-scale ceremonial exchanges or prestations commonly speak of themselves, or are spoken of by others after the fact, as "the Xs" acting with or against "the Ys," as though, as some ethnographers see it, these named entities are "acting as single bodies." A close look at what is going on behind this kind of talk suggests that what we have to deal with are little, if anything, more than jural aggregates (see Chapter 4).

Some ethnographers make this transparent. In a refreshingly unpretentious account of the Wola, neighbors of the Mendi and Huli, Sillitoe (1979:20–46) is highly skeptical of most talk about descent, descent groups, and corporate action in the highlands. He observes (1979:22) that the members of a Wola *sem* (Mendi shem) "do not recognize any obligations to support the group in specific situations," and sem "do not constitute the action groups of Wola society." Certainly, he says, any ad hoc action group is likely to have a core or nucleus recruited from the members of a particular more or less permanent territorial group; but some of their various relatives from elsewhere may join in, and some of their immediate neighbors may, without penalty, elect not to participate. As Feil (1978, 1984b) shows for some Enga, Sillitoe shows that among the Wola all ceremonial exchanges are between single persons who coordinate or synchronize their activities so that by putting on a big show together they may enhance their own reputations individually. According to Sillitoe (1979:84) men prefer to act in unison with the people they live with "because it is in that way that they stand best to improve their status," that is their reputations as men who can handle wealth. "The advantage of [synchronizing] is that the more men who kill their pigs together the bigger the occasion, and those who take part in an event which attracts large numbers of people benefit from the reflected glory" (Sillitoe 1979:91). One consequence of that is that "sometimes the majority of participants [in an action set] are members of one semonda [clan]" and may be spoken of as such, even though they have no duty to participate as such (see also Joshepides 1985, chap. 7).

By way of contrast, Lederman (1986:21–23) claims that Mendi clans and subclans are corporate groups, the members of which have a joint, corporate, or collective responsibility or liability for actions "taken (or construed to have been taken) in the group's name" by past or present members. Yet her detailed accounts of how activities taken "in the name of a group" are organized (e.g., 1986:24, 163–164, 207) are strikingly similar to Sillitoe's and Joshepides's accounts of how similar activities are organized elsewhere. Moreover, she concedes (1986:207) that there is no group-owned as distinct from individual exchangeable property, and no more-or-less official representative of any group who could temporarily hold property in the name of the group. Thus, each and every activity carried out "in the name of a group" is one centrally organized (voluntarily, and opportunistically?) and financed by some number of its adult male members, with the tacit or express consent of some others who may or may not elect to participate, and the participants may, in the end, include persons associated with other such groups.

It may be that Mendi, but not Wola, make prestations such as death compensation "in the name of a group" (while at the same time conducting personal business), but it seems clear enough that the groups in question are jural aggregates at best, and certainly not any kind of jural entity or collectivity. Jural aggregates, perhaps, because it is possible to organize at least certain kinds of activity "in their names," activities in which each member has a right (but not an exclusive right, and not a duty) to participate; actions taken "in the name of the group" are not taken on behalf of the group; and those who do act "in the name of the group" are not acting as representatives of members who choose not to participate.

According to Lederman, virtually any potentially offensive act committed by any Mendi, for whatever reasons, may in the end be visited upon one of the groups he is identified with, even generations after the fact, and that group may accept (or dispute) its joint, collective, or corporate responsibility or liability. Absent the requisite joint or corporate property, this is rather improbable. What her detailed descriptions of particular events (e.g., Lederman 1986:21–25) seem to show is that for any member or members of a group to agree that certain actions of fellow group member, even a long deceased one, may have been "at the root" of a death is one of many ways for those individuals to accept a challenge to engage in a competitive exchange. Making the charge or accepting the challenge "in the name of a group" entails nothing whatsoever by way of liability on the part of any member of the nominally challenged group.

Violent intergroup conflict is a well known and widely studied feature of highlands societies, and it is often described by ethnographers, and apparently by the participants, too, as between clans or subclans. Again, however, appearances are deceiving. As accounted by Sillitoe (1979:86–91), intergroup conflicts arise from interpersonal disputes and sorcery and poisoning accusations that lead to deaths that must be revenged. Although the principal disputants are held to be "at the root of the conflict" and ultimately responsible for it, co-members of their clans and subclans, while not responsible for one another's actions, are morally obliged to defend one another and to revenge the wrongful death of one of their number. Also morally obliged in this way are relatives, especially close kin, and friends of a victim. The most injured and angry of these are likely to be some of the people with whom the victim lived and worked, and it is they who must propose a course of action. They recruit support from the people with whom they live and from other relatives and friends of the victim, who in turn recruit support from their relatives and friends, each of whom participates (or not) for his own reasons. When several men turn out from one clan or subclan, they are known as an "allied" clan or subclan, but they are in no sense representatives of those groups, because each man is recruited individually via a friend or relative closer to the principal party. As Sillitoe points out, one consequence of this network mode of recruitment of "action sets" is that it is possible for the clans of one region, or the various subclans of one clan, to become polarized into allied blocs; but that is a fleeting coincidental arrangement such that, if something like it were to arise again, the blocs would be very different in composition. It is an expectable consequence of this mode of organization that members of one clan or subclan, even brothers, may find themselves allied with opposite sides; in that event they avoid fighting directly with one another.

Again in relation to the Mendi, the situation appears to be little different; and much if not most or all talk about clan or subclan participation appears to be largely rhetorical. Even so, says Lederman (1986:46), it can come to have wider implications for the group of a participating person and "it acknowledges that sem potentially have multiple loyalties for the very reason that sem are actualized in historical circumstances by persons with diverse interests." The latter observation seems an especially roundabout way of acknowledging that sem per se have no enduring loyalties or interests (except in relation to the lands they occupy); the (fleeting) common interests and loyalties that they appear to summon up from time to time are in fact those of only some of their members (acting in a nonrepresentative capacity).[16]

Although highlands groups may be in some sense segmentary, it is wholly improbable that they could exhibit segmentary or complementary opposition. Again, the critical element is that immediately adjacent collateral segments have special rights and duties vis-à-vis one another, such that they may function as separate and opposed units in some situations but as a single unit in other situations (as against a higher-order collateral segment). It is critical, too, that no lineage ever functions on its own, as it were, for the only rights and duties the group has are vis-à-vis its immediately adjacent collaterals, and that is why it is often said that, in a segmentary lineage system, lineages emerge only in opposition one to another. Absent such special rights and duties, highlands lineages are not the jural constituents of subclans, and subclans are not the jural constituents of clans. Witness Lederman:

> In Mendi, the parts of a [clan] are not conceived to be subordinate to the whole any more than group members are thought to be subordinate to a leader. Rather than being a hierarchically organized structure, a [clan] is an affiliation of equivalent segments, each with strong (and diverging) loyalties and interests outside the group. Nor do the functions (or interests) of [clans] necessarily override those of its components (Lederman 1986:52).

None of this is to deny, as Merlan and Rumsey (1991:55–56), following the Stratherns, Lederman, and others, have recently insisted, that highlands "segmentary identities" do figure importantly in the "serious enough" business of the exchange of wealth, as well as in "warfare, residence, and the organization of economic production." The question, as Merlan and Rumsey themselves pose it, is: What exactly is the nature of that figuring or agency? No doubt it is variable from time to time and place to place, and no simple universal characterization is possible. My purpose here is to indicate as strongly as possible the unprofitability, indeed the largely obfuscatory effect on the precision of ethnographic description and on the coherence of ethnological comparison, of talking about jointness or corporateness in the context of highlands ethnography.

IV

If highland groups are not descent groups, what kind or kinds of group are they? The answer must be that there is little point in trying to subsume them all under one general designation. As de Lepervanche once pointed out, the so-called clans are typically describable as "parish groups," and the so-called subclans or subsubclans are often men's-house groups. The so-called lineages are certainly not lineages in the African (and Africanist) sense because they definitely lack the one essential, defining feature of lineages, that is, that patrifiliation (or matrifiliation) is the necessary and sufficient condition for inclusion.

In the terminology developed in Chapter 4, many highland groups, especially the territorial ones commonly described as clans, appear to be little more than jural aggregates, each member of which has certain derivative rights of use of the group-controlled land. That does not prevent, but is one of the preconditions for, some of their elements to cooperate and coordinate some of their activities and to do so "in the name of the group," but without making the group as such or all of its members jointly and severally responsible for any offense that may have been committed in the process. Because they are also communities of relatives and friends who afford one another many forms of support and are bound to be deeply implicated in many of one another's affairs, it is only to be expected that they sometimes exhibit some degree of unity vis-à-vis outsiders, especially when threatened with violence from the outside—but even then not always for long. Yet, because none of them have (or even could have) special rights or duties as against other groups of the same territorial and structural order, segmentary or complementary opposition, as formulated in so-called descent theory, is not a feature of highlands social orders.

V

The notion that highlands groups are agnatic in constitution but commonly recruit by other means as well has led to various attempts to explicate mechanisms whereby "nonagnates are converted into agnates," most of which, however unintentionally, provide good examples of the anthropological bad habit of mystification of the cultural other.[17] The by-now standard procedure is to confound the metaphoric with the literal, thereby impoverishing the object of analysis and all the while insisting that the literal/metaphoric distinction is in the first place the refuge of the incorrigibly ethnocentric.[18]

Perhaps the first mechanism posited for the conversion or transformation of nonagnates into agnates in the highlands was a propensity to maintain only shallow and fragmentary group genealogies, coupled with the structure of the local systems of kin classification, which is usually of the so-called Iroquois type (Cook 1970). One feature of this kind of system is that, for a male ego, brother's child is designated 'child' but sister's child is designated by a different expression; but one's own grandchild, brother's grandchild, and sister's grandchild are all designated by the same expression. This pattern is construed by some ethnographers as one in which, in the first descending generation, nonagnates are distinguished from agnates but in the second descending generation they are not; therefore, the difference between agnates and co-resident nonagnates is quickly lost sight of. Similarly, the son of a man who sponsors a sister's son as an immigrant is the father's mother's brother's son of the son of the immigrant sister's son, and these two are related terminologically as 'father'-'son'. Although they may know they are not really agnates, other members of their group may not and may think that, because they speak of one another as 'father'-'son', they are agnates. Certainly, it is argued, in subsequent generations it will be common knowledge that they were agnates of one another, and therefore so are their descendants within the group.

Demonstrably, however, none of the expressions of any Iroquois-like system of kin classification signals agnation, and appearances to the contrary can be produced only by the indefensible practice of self-serving selective attention to some few terminological facts while wholly ignoring others, especially the pattern of usage in relation to female ego.[19] Consider: Whereas for male ego brother's child is 'child' but sister's child is not, for female ego, sister's child is 'child' but brother's child is not and is designated by the same expression male ego uses for sister's child. Ipso facto, 'child' signals nothing about agnation. Conversely, the reciprocals of 'child'—that is, 'father' and 'mother'—signal nothing about agnation.

If there is nothing about the local systems of kin classification that can plausibly be said to facilitate the conversion of nonagnates specifically to agnates, there is equally nothing about them that can plausibly be said to facilitate the conversion of immigrants into full-fledged members of groups. There are no categories in the systems of kin classification the boundaries of which are coextensive with the boundaries of any social groups. Ipso facto, knowledge of kin-class relations between persons is a totally unreliable guide to inference about their group affiliations. Let it be recalled, too, that the co-resident child of a female member, though not included in the "born of a man" category, and even an immigrant in-law or a nonrelative can be accorded full membership status without it being lost sight of that they are not in fact 'brothers' or 'sons' of other members. We are not dealing here with a process that necessarily takes several generations, nor does it require some sort of conversion or transformation of nonkin to kin. The ethnographic presumption that it does arises only because of the fallacious assumption that there is something counter-normative or irregular about recruitment from the outside, not only of sister's sons and their progeny but also of nonkin, something that is being dealt with by means of various modes of ideological repression of the genealogical "facts" (cf. also Merlan and Rumsey 1991:37; J. B. Watson 1983:253–254).

Be that as it may, early on in the attempt to make anthropological sense of highlands social orders it was noticed that, irrespective of local genealogical knowledge to the contrary, it is common practice, not only in special situations where rhetoric flows freely but also in everyday life, for people to speak of members of their groups (clans or subclans) in general as 'brothers' or, more specifically, to differentiate between them by speaking of some as their or our 'fathers,' others as their or our 'brothers,' and still others as their or our 'sons' (even though some of them are, as is known to everyone, their sisters' sons or not even their relatives of any kind). The ethnocentric or otherwise impoverished anthropological imagination might have it that, surely, what we have to deal with here is "mere" metaphor (or, perhaps more accurately, a combination of metaphor and metonymy), that is, the treatment in speech and for special effect of one kind of thing as though it were another. A different anthropological imagination saw another possibility. Could it be that co-residence, not merely in and of itself but on account of all the cooperative social relationships it may well entail or in some other as-yet-undetected way is in the highlands of New Guinea one of the distinctive or defining features of "kinship" and, more specifically, of "agnatic kinship"? It could be only one of the distinctive features, because it had to be acknowledged that in highlands cultures, as elsewhere in the world, kinship is, in some part at least, a matter of genealogical relationship or relationship by birth.

It has to be acknowledged also, however, that there is more to it than that. (Who, after all, ever said there is not?) Kinship anywhere must be, for the locals, something more than merely relationship by birth as locally conceived and perceived, or it would be of comparatively minor interest to anthropologists (though that is, of course, hardly a good reason to think that we have to construct it as, by definition and at base, something more than that). But from the standard (ethnocentric, intellectually impoverished) anthropological point of view (or so its critics, at the same time its formulators, proclaimed) the "more than genealogical" is "merely" the superadded cultural specifications of what is entailed by the fact of being kin or kin of certain kinds. What about the possibility that "kinship" itself, by local definition, encompasses many of those features that the standard anthropological imagination has relegated to the status of the "merely accidental" or "incidental"?[20]

This possibility found its realization, tentatively at first, in the ethnographic observation that in some parts of the highlands people who live and work together, who "eat from the same land," and who cooperate with one another in intergroup affairs such as war and ceremonial exchanges, become, if they are not already, 'fathers', 'sons', or 'brothers' of one another, and so also do their children. Some ethnographers were not averse to regarding this as metaphoric—"Acting as though we were brothers makes us (like) brothers"—and to noticing that over the long run the bracketed "like" may be lost sight of and taken as the literal truth. In any event, it was often remarked, what matters for the locals is that you act like a brother, not that you actually be one. Others found this a disappointingly pedestrian, narrow-, even closed-minded response to the challenge posed by an "other" mode of thought.

One simple solution was to suggest that in the local schemes of things, "kinship" is by definition not merely a matter of relationship reproductively engendered (which is usually held to entail the sharing of flesh and blood), but can be established also postnatally by certain modes of social interaction, which may require co-residence. Perhaps, it was argued, in highlanders' conceptual schemes (their cultures), enacting brotherly social relations is, for purposes of inclusion in the categories "brother" and "relative," just another way of "making kin," no less valid or important, as it were than making kin by making babies by sexual intercourse. In that event, "kinship" in highlands societies would have not a distinctive feature, but at least two "alternative distinctive features."[21] One difficulty for this proposal is that the concept "alternative distinctive features" is logically incoherent. A category may have a distinctive feature, possession of which is necessary and sufficient for inclusion in it, or some set of distinctive features, possession of all of which is necessary and sufficient for inclusion (that is, which in conjunction define it). What was proposed, then, was not really a single category, "kinsman" or "relative," but the possible presence of two or more related categories each with the same designation, *kinsman* or *relative*, where one of the categories has for its distinctive feature a nondefining feature of one of the others. In effect, though it misrepresents itself as something else by confusing terms and categories, the proposal is that in highlands cultures there are two kinds of "kin"; one is predicated on relationship by birth, which normatively entails certain kinds of interpersonal conduct; the other is predicated on voluntary enactment of those kinds of conduct. That, however, is precisely what the concept "metaphor" is all about. Thus, the peculiarity of highlanders' concepts of kinship, at least as constructed in this analysis, is an artefact of a logical and terminological error on the part of certain ethnographers—those who persistently conflate terms and categories and are, therefore, unable to deal adequately or systematically with the facts of polysemy, whether it be by simple generalization or narrowing or by metaphoric extension (cf. Scheffler and Lounsbury 1972:3–12).

Another difficulty not lightly to be passed over is that there is a significant difference, which the argument previously reviewed does not take into account, between being spoken of as a 'brother' and being acknowledged to be a kinsman or a relative of that kind. The argument is (again in effect) that conducting yourself in a certain way (at least in certain circumstances) makes you a genuine brother and a genuine relative, not merely like a particular kind of relative, that is like a brother. But that would be true if and only if the parties to the relationship, and all other people they count as their kin or relatives, acknowledged that they are not only brothers of one another but also kin or relatives of one another and of all other people counted as their kin or relatives. Nothing like that has ever been demonstrated. What has been demonstrated is that many anthropologists (but few if any "natives"!) have a great deal of difficulty distinguishing between speaking of someone as though he or she were a particular kind of relative and speaking of someone as a relative of a particular kind.

Criticism of this kind of mystification of the "other" has gone, it seems, almost totally unnoticed; the practice has continued and "reconstruction" (LiPuma 1988, 1990) of alien others, via a kind of ethnographic archaeology, has become ever more elaborate—but no more ethnographically or logically defensible.

By the late 1960s at least, it was becoming widely noticed by highlands ethnographers that there is an interesting connection, in local thought (or, more accurately, in some of the things some people sometimes say) between ideas or theories about sexual reproduction and notions about how people become related via co-residence and various forms of social interaction.[22] It is commonly (though certainly not universally) held in high-

lands societies that each child is the product of repeated sexual intercourse between a woman and a man, the woman's contribution to the
child's bodily substance being its blood (or some part of its blood), the
man's being his semen (and perhaps some blood, too); and semen is only
one of several animal and plant oily substances locally classified as one
kind and designated in NeoMelanesian as *gris* (in English, *grease*). The locals perceive, we are told, that it follows that fathers and sons and, more
generally, men related through their fathers, "share the same grease," and
insofar as all male members of a clan are in some sense brothers or sons of
one father, they too share the same grease, and this is sometimes represented by the ethnographer as "clan substance" (without it being always
or even often clear from the report that this is an indigenous concept).
Being born into a clan is not, however, the only way in which a person
can come to harbor or share this clan grease and, therefore, to be a member of the clan because such sharing is of the essence of clanship. Semen is
only one kind of relevant grease. Other kinds include plant and animal
fats (especially taro and pig) and other bodily secretions. People replenish
their blood and grease, lost in various ways including labor and sexual
intercourse, by eating foods containing grease, the origin of which is in
their clan land. So, people who eat from the same land, as it were, and
who share food (via various forms of exchange) with one another, also
come to share the same grease, grease that derives from clan land, and
that in turn makes them fellow clansmen or, in other words, agnates. So
the process of conversion of nonagnates to agnates is not merely notional,
but is physical and substantive. As an immigrant gardens on and eats
from clan land and engages in the exchange of foodstuffs grown on clan
land, he or she and their children gradually become consubstantial with
other members of the clan: "production, exchange, and consuming of
food all become means for defining and creating kinsmen. The indigenous concept is that people who eat the same food or foods from the same
land construct a kinship" (LiPuma 1990:97).

There are reasons to be skeptical about much of this. First off, all the ev-
idential and logical difficulties mentioned above in criticism of the idea
that people "construct a kinship" by voluntarily interacting as though
they were kin of certain kinds re-present themselves here. It is of no avail
to insist, as LiPuma does, that there is a "sociocentric level" of use of
some Maring kinship terms wherein they signal agnation and, at least by
implication, also kinship or consubstantiality.[23] The claim that they signal
agnation rests not only on the claim that consubstantiation of agnatic
(male?) grease can be generated not only via sexual reproduction but also
in other ways; it rests also on the unexamined assumptions, despite cita-
tion of Barnes (1962), that there is no significant difference between patrifiliation and patrilineal descent and that patrilineal descent is, notionally

at least, the constitutive principle of certain social groups—when, again, Maring ethnography (including LiPuma's contribution) is replete with indications to the contrary.

What is perhaps most worrisome of all, however, is that this analysis is a product of a highly dubious enterprise. As already implied, various highlands ethnographers (e.g., Strathern 1972, Merlan and Rumsey 1991), even some working in other Maring communities (Lowman-Vayda 1971; Healey 1990), have reported elements of LiPuma's account and have found them intriguing, but few have tried to make as much out of them because the people themselves "do not appear to have an explicitly elaborated or coherent ideology of what constitutes substance and how it is transmitted" (Healey 1990:339).[24] But, as pointed out by Healey, LiPuma (1988:38, 39, 60) is quite explicit that his goal is to "reconstruct" a holistic model of Maring society based on a single "generative principle," and that principle and model would necessarily be one that no Maring could come even close to articulating. In the end, he concluded that "the social system is based on co-substance and thus encompasses production, exchange, and consumption from the start" (LiPuma 1988:106). Worrisome as all that will be to many anthropologists who can no longer sympathize with that kind of ethnographic enterprise or lend credence to its results, there is yet another question to be asked. Even if Evans-Pritchard, Fortes, the Bohannans, and heavens knows who else had committed the major anthropological sin of constructing holistic models of whole social orders centered on "the lineage principle" (cf. Schneider 1965; Weiner 1982), how is it that LiPuma's avowedly holistic enterprise has evaded similar criticism (cf. LiPuma 1988:x)? The answer appears to be that culturological holism is a virtue, whereas sociological holism (even if it has to be invented in order to be condemned) is not.

Merlan and Rumsey (1991:42–43), writing about peoples in the Nebilyer Valley (near Mount Hagen), remark that

> people who live, work, and eat together . . . become like siblings, and the effect multiplies over the course of generations, since in time it is irrelevant whether ancestors were brothers or merely 'like brothers'; descendants of co-resident men are 'siblings' in either case.

This suggests that, rather than saying that people who live and work together "construct a kinship" by extra-procreative means, we might more accurately say that, as they themselves see it, they enter into certain kin-like social relationships and thereby make themselves like certain kinds of kin. Plainly, over some span of time it can easily be lost sight of that these relations were metaphoric, and it may well be that in the absence of definite information to the contrary they are assumed to be genuine relations of consanguinity (that is, by birth). But, it is crucial to observe, structurally it is a matter of total indifference what they were, because being born into the group was never a necessary, but only a sufficient, condition for affiliation in any event, and the still co-resident, cooperating descendants of a immigrant male fulfill that condition. It is small wonder that highlanders have not come even close to articulating anything like the systematic doctrines attributed to their cultures, if not to them individually, by LiPuma and others. Given the local rule of filiation and affiliation, there is no motivational or logical foundation on which to develop such a system.

There is yet another culturological-holistic, total system model being purveyed in the highlands ethnographic literature, self-consciously in opposition to a factitious version of lineage or descent theory. As propounded by, for example, James Weiner (1982), it purports to show that "siblingship and exchange [but not descent are] fundamental organizing principles of social structure throughout New Guinea" and that there is "an underlying pattern of conceptualized structure of which each particular society in New Guinea manifests a specific variant" (Weiner 1982:6). Noting, as we already have, that it is common in the highlands for co-members of a group to speak of themselves as brothers or sons of one father, even while unable to demonstrate their common descent by means of pedigrees, and also that groups or sets of people are often represented as descendants of a pair of brothers (of unknown parentage), Weiner comes to the quite remarkable conclusion that in the highlands "siblingship" is a fundamental organizing principle that "does not presuppose common descent." To the contrary, "descent and filiation are calculated from siblingship and patrilineal ideology is 'backgrounded'" (1982:11). What siblingship does presuppose or take as its defining condition is sharing of male substance (that is, grease), acquirable in the process of physical-sexual reproduction from one's genitor or via the sharing of clan land and food grown on it, especially pork, which on Weiner's account is a most extraordinary entity: "Uniformly throughout the Highlands, . . . pork and other types of meat embody the continuity of male substance, the separate adjunct to masculine continuity or lineality" (Weiner 1982:9).

Descent, or simply parentage, figures in this construction as a variable the value of which is contingent on "exchange." It is said to be a "universal principle of Highlands societies" that "an individual will be recruited to his father's group" but that is not possible until and unless the father and his group more generally compensate his wife's agnates for the blood that the wife and child share with them. "Recruitment is thus contingent upon patrilineality and maternal compensation" (1982:9), the latter being described also as a form of intergroup exchange, such that it can then be said that groups are "defined" by exchange no less than by descent.

Clearly, or so one would hope, much of this is word play. In this word game, the statement "descent and filiation are calculated from sibling-ship" is an excessively jargon-laden, abstract, and rather ineffective and misleading way to make the simple observation that sets of people in the highlands often claim in a rather vague way that they are all descended from some pair of brothers; they are not much worried about how. But this does not even begin to justify, much less to imply the assertion "sib-lingship as an organizational principle does not presuppose common de-scent," especially insofar as descent for Weiner is nothing more or less than parentage. What siblingship or, more accurately, brotherhood does not presuppose when upheld as the epitome of genealogical-cum-moral bonds in contexts of intra- or intergroup relations is that common descent should be demonstrable by means of pedigrees—because, again, what is relevant is to act like a brother, not actually to be one. But no one can act like a brother unless there is such a thing as persons who simply are brothers of one another irrespective of how they conduct themselves vis-à-vis one another; even Weiner does not deny that in New Guinea, no less than in New York, two men who share one or both parents are ipso facto brothers of one another and, moreover, the very epitome of brothers at that. There is in any event entirely too much relevant linguistic data avail-able for highlands languages to permit serious questioning of that propo-sition.[25] Finally, to say that groups are defined also by exchange is merely to acknowledge, again in a language that obscures more than it reveals, the commonplace observation that paternity alone may not be sufficient to establish certain rights in relation to one's offspring; it may be neces-sary also to compensate certain ones of the mother's kin. It is, after all, here and elsewhere the mother's husband and presumed genitor who has the right and duty to do that. In the woolly-word world of this total sys-tem model, exchange and siblingship both presuppose descent, despite the author's insistence to the contrary.

NOTES

1. Another resolution that enjoyed some popularity for a short time was to characterize highlands social orders as "loosely structured" or "flexible"(e.g., Kaberry 1967). That merely begs the question of how they are structured and, in effect, admits defeat in finding a more positive and constructive characterization. It also makes the mistake of thinking that someone else has thought or said that only unilineal descent systems are well or tightly structured or that they are in-flexible.

2. Hereafter, the expressions *clan, subclan, lineage* are used only quotatively in relation to highlands ethnography, but without quotation marks.

3. Contrary to Holy (1976:112), Barnes did not say that highlands societies employ "cumulative patrifiliation . . . as a principle of group recruitment." Holy's dots represent a full eight lines of Barnes' text.

4. J. Weiner (1982:8) totally misconstrues these observations as "a recourse to [demographic or] functional evidence for descent and descent groups" or "descent phenomena," and says it is "exactly what we would expect to find if the ideological and conceptual nature of group formation is ignored." It was, however, the major point of Barnes's essay that ethnographers have misunderstood and misconstrued "ideological [ideational] nature of group formation" in the highlands.

5. See, for example, Holy (1976), Kuper (1982), Weiner (1982), Lederman (1986), Strathern (1982), Keesing (1975, 1987), Feinberg (1990) Masquelier (1993). For some refreshing exceptions compare Langness (1964) and (1971) and see Merlan and Rumsey (1991).

6. Jean La Fontaine (1973:37) represents one of Barnes's reasons for being doubtful about the existence of descent groups in the highlands as "the fact that local groups are heterogeneous with respect to the lineage affiliations of their members." What Barnes actually put into question is whether or not in the highlands there is any such thing as "lineage" affiliation that is independent of local group affiliation. He was, moreover, not criticizing "Fortes's conceptual scheme" (La Fontaine 1973:35, 37) but misunderstanding and misuse of it.

7. In standard anthropological usage, *clan* designates a unilineally constituted group or category, the members of which are unable to specify pedigrees that relate them step by step to the apical ancestor (if any); whereas *lineage* designates a unilineally constituted group that does have a specified apical ancestor to which each member is able to relate via a father-by-father (or mother-by-mother) pedigree. Subclan and subsubclan are employed in the New Guinea ethnography and elsewhere to designate named subsets of clans, the members of which claim but are not able to demonstrate descent from a common ancestor.

8. See e.g., de Lepervanche (1968:173), Strathern (1969, 1972, 1982), Holy (1976:119–120), Feil (1987:130–134).

9. Feil (1987:130–134) concedes most of the arguments of Barnes (1962) and Scheffler (1985) but says that, even so, we must not be too dogmatic about the nonexistence of patriliny in the highlands and must allow for the possibility of some local and regional variation. One can hardly disagree about the sociological undesirability of replacing one "dogma" with another. Be that as it may, Feil goes on to say it may be "difficult to do away totally with the language of descent and descent groups in the highlands," especially in relation to the Eastern Highlands where, he argues, "societies are boundary conscious" and "group oriented," there is "ideological emphasis on agnatic connections," and "group exclusiveness is stressed through idioms of masculinity" that are promoted via warfare. Yet all the arguments presented in Barnes (1962) and Scheffler (1985), and all those being developed herein, apply across the board, to Eastern as well as Western Highlands societies, and Feil presents no additional evidence to show that there is in fact "an ideological emphasis on agnatic [as something more than father-son and brother] connections" in any highlands society. He seems, moreover, to come perilously close to conflating masculinity , patriarchy, and patriliny and to inferring the pres-

ence of the last from the presence of the other two. In this he is not alone among ethnographers.

10. Some such talk is also about "lines of men." Merlan and Rumsey (1991:36) caution against construing this as indicative of "some notion of a line of descent by which each member of a group is linked to its apical ancestor." Usually there is no such hypothecated ancestor. Also the locally relevant image is "not a vertical genealogical line, but a horizontal, tactical one: the line of men who form a single flank on the battlefield and dance as a single row at ceremonial exchange events."

11. It is especially unfortunate that Meggitt does not report the Enga expressions he glosses as "child of a male agnate" and "child of a female agnate," seeing that the apparently comparable Mendi and Melpa expressions contain no elements that require translation as "agnate." One wonders, is Meggitt's use of *agnate* his own interpolation, unwarranted by the Enga forms themselves, however much it might seem warranted on other grounds? Is his use of *agnate* here an ethnographically gratuitous substitute for *member*?

12. And J. B. Watson (1983:253) who raises "the question why a fiction that repeatedly requires de facto contradiction should ever arise, trammeling a people who, if they need a dogma, would be better of with something credible, even a dogma without descent if descent is absolutely unconformable with practice."

13. J. B. Watson (1983:279) suggests that Tairora highlanders are not so much careless about their genealogies as they are constrained by the conditions of an "open social field," the nature of which, contrary to some ethnographers, they are not trying to conceal. Emphasizing the high degree off intergroup mobility in the highlands, Watson remarks that "keeping scrupulous genealogical records of begetters and begotten . . . under such conditions might be beyond the power of a nonliterate people, even if they had better reason to be dedicated to the task."

14. Healey (1979:114; see also Joshepides 1985:26) reports that among the Maring immigrant refugees "may be expected" to make "customary payment of pigs and other valuables" to their hosts, and that in one instance his informants said of a particular group of refugees that "from the moment [they] made their arrival payment they became assimilated as members of their host's subclan." The hosts, in turn made a counter presentation. "The refugees [were then] addressed by their host clansmen by agnatic kin terms and participate[d] fully in the exchange relations of their subclan." (On the matter of the so-called agnatic terms, see section V.) In part the "arrival gift" was in return for gifts of planting material, pigs to care for, and usufruct of land. Healey says it also "insure[s] their acceptance." It is not wholly clear whether "arrival payment" is the local designation, or a condition of incorporation (such that incorporation could not occur without it), or a signal of commitment to remain with and to cooperate with the hosts (or both of the latter); and Healey does not specify precisely to whom the payment is made. In view of his consistent reading of the doings of kinds of kin as though they were the doings of co-members of subclans or clans, it would be unsafe to assume that the subclan per se was the host and the recipient of the payment, even if, as it so happened, the set of hosts coincided with the set of subclan members.

15. This assertion might be denied by E. LiPuma, who argues that Maring speakers use a subset of expressions from their ordinary, everyday egocentric system of kin classification in a "sociocentric" fashion, specifically in reference to fel-

low clansmen and -women, and these he describes as constituting a special-register "agnatic terminology" (LiPuma 1990:103; 1988). It is striking, and is left unremarked and unexplained by LiPuma, that one of the expressions allegedly so used is *ama*, the only feasible gloss for which is 'mother,' an expression that would not normally be attributed agnatic signification. In any event, the proposition that these are expressions of agnation rests, somewhat circularly, on the presumption that the clans are agnatic in constitution, such that 'brother' used in the sense of 'clan brother' must signal agnatic relationship. Not unexpectedly, the Maring ethnographic corpus, which is now quite large, is overflowing with indications (though alas not conclusions) to the contrary (see also Lowman-Vayda 1971; Healey 1979, 1990, the bibliographies of which include most of the relevant publications). Moreover, in view of the fact that it is common knowledge in the Maring region that subclans and clans are not homogeneous (purely agnatic) in composition, indeed are not even groups of kin much less kin groups, it seems only prudent to conclude that 'brother' when used in the sense of 'clan brother,' even more so when used in reference to all the members of a clan, is being used metaphorically and without imputation of any sort of agnation or any values that might be associated with it. See Langness (1971:300–301) for a clear ethnographic statement to this effect.

16. G. Morren (1986), writing about Miyanmin in particular, points out that "loyalty is an issue in any group in which the objective price of joining is low," as it is among Minyamin where "most people are born into their groups [via patrifiliation] but others may join with few constraints and all can readily join other groups" (p. 160). Thus the "patrilineages" occupying a parish exhibit little in the way of solidarity, and Morren suggests that the parishes themselves generate loyalty on the part of their male members, and thus whatever solidarity they may exhibit, via elaborate rituals of initiation.

17. A highly literate, well informed, and very readable discussion of this practice is provided in Mark Schneider's *Culture and Enchantment* (1993). Note especially his remarks (in Chapter 3) on the much-overlooked difference between significance and signification.

18. The procedure is nicely codified in Sahlins's (1985:26–29) observations on what he calls "performative structures," a notion that, although thoroughly illogical, is credited with the potential to overcome "the limitations of Western social thought" and, finally, to make sense of, among other things, "the so-called loosely structured societies of New Guinea, which have so far defied anthropological explication" and "are monuments to the failure of the anthropological imagination." For more on the point about logic, see Scheffler (1976, 1991).

19. This is a widespread practice in anthropology and it vitiates many attempts to relate structures of systems of kin classification to other features of social structure. Any analysis that ignores patterns of usage in relation to the female ego or propositus ignores 50 percent of the relevant ethnographic data and, therefore, stands a much greater than 50 percent chance of being wholly wrong.

20. Notice that this relegation, at least in Scheffler and Lounsbury (1972) and Scheffler (1971, 1976), is quite explicitly stated to be logical or a matter of conceptual structure, and definitely not sociological. This caveat is ignored by exponents of the "social categories" and "cultural categories" theories of kinship, which is

convenient for the purposes of their polemics, but it leaves them thrashing their own straw man.

21. The phrase is taken from D. M. Schneider (1968, 1972), whose views are highly influential, indeed foundational, in analyses of the kind being explicated here. For more extensive discussion of this and other related points that cannot be taken up here see Scheffler (1976, 1991).

22. The line of interpretation now being outlined goes back at least as far as Lowman-Vayda (1971), runs through A. Strathern (1973), and reaches its epitome in the essays of LiPuma (1988, 1990). For the sake of brevity, I skip over earlier and less systematic developments of it and draw largely on LiPuma's version.

23. See again note 14, this chapter.

24. For a very thorough, down-to-earth debunking of this general line of argument via detailed consideration of his own Tairora data, see. J. B. Watson (1983:250ff.), and note especially his remarks on the "indigenizing effect" of the ingestion of food and water (p. 268).

25. See especially the many essays in Cook and O'Brien (1980) that contain detailed linguistic data on kin classification and kin-term usage in highlands societies, and that are sensitive to the difference between the metaphoric and the literal.

9

JOINT-FAMILY SYSTEMS

I

The very existence of the patrilineages of southeast China and Taiwan poses, it has been claimed, a major challenge to "established beliefs about the nature and forms of descent in human society" and "forces us to re-think the entire matter with fewer preconceptions" (Pasternak 1985:165–166).[1] The difficulty, or so it has appeared, is that conventional descent theory has it that the social environment most favorable to the de-velopment and persistence of corporate unilineal descent groups is a non-state, acephalous polity, little or no socioeconomic stratification, and a nonmarket, nonmonetary economy; yet the situation in southeast China and Taiwan is exactly the opposite and has been for a very long time. Also, these lineages exhibit a number of features that, again in compara-tive perspective, are rather odd. They vary greatly in number of mem-bers, in kind and quantity of property holdings (if any), and in modes of internal organization. The members of any one lineage may vary greatly in socioeconomic status, and not all members of a community are mem-bers of one of its lineages. Lineage segmentation, as condition and process, can be very irregular, so genealogical depth and span and degree of segmentation bear no orderly relationship to one another.

If lineage or descent theory, so called, does a poor job of accounting for all this, the problem is not with the theory; it is with the preconception, hardly questioned at all by anthropologists, that there is a "patrilineal principle" at work in Chinese society, one that is especially pervasive, strong, strict, or extreme (see e.g., Fried 1957; Fox 1967:116).[2] The groups in question are not in any theoretically significant sense of the expression corporate groups; the operative mode of ownership is either joint or in common, rather than corporate; membership is not ascribed because pat-rifiliation is at most a merely necessary condition for inclusion. In short, as pointed out by Ch'en (1983 [1987], 1990), Sangren (1984), R. Watson (1985), and others, these are voluntary associations. All this is ethnographically well established. It remains to be shown that patrilineal descent, as distinct from patrifiliation, is a relationship of little or no jural value or structural significance in Chinese society. A similar point was made by Maurice Freedman in the opening paragraphs of his *Lineage Organization in Southeast China* (1958:1–2). Freedman cited Fei Hsiao-tung's (1946:5) observation "I rather suspect that such an organization among the peasants is a local organization, not a kinship organization." To which Freedman added: "Lineages of the kind we see in south-eastern China are of course essentially political and local organizations. If we fail to realize this and think of lineages as inflated families, we must naturally wonder how they can persist in a complex and differentiated society" (Freedman 1958:2).[3]

The village communities of southeast China and Taiwan are populated by families that are joint in both the usual anthropological senses. It is conventional for a man's sons to bring their wives to live with him in his house or compound, and his sons are also joint owners with him of the family estate. Wives and unmarried daughters are not joint owners but, as dependents of the men who are, are entitled to maintenance and dowry from the family resources. Daughters marry out (except in the absence of a son) and have no further claim on the family estate. When the family head dies (or should he choose to retire or get nagged into retiring by his fractious male offspring and their wives) the family estate is partitioned into as many more or less equal shares as there are or perhaps were sons (the survivors of an already deceased son take his share and eventually divide it in the same way, that is, per stirpes). Alternatively, partition of the family estate may be delayed and the survivors may continue to exploit it jointly, at least for a time, under the leadership of the senior son. For reasons spelled out in Chapter 4, it is unlikely that such an arrangement will persist beyond the point at which the youngest brother is married and has children of his own (at which time the sons are at least legally, if not also morally, entitled to demand partition, even within the lifetime of the father). Domestic division and the division of joint property need not occur at the same time, and, of course, termination of the joint estate does not entail termination of the kin group. The deceased or retired father, his wife or widow, and their children continue to constitute a *chia* or family, and each son and his wife and children (while constituting their own chia) constitute a *fang* or division of their father's chia.

In principle this process of chia/fang proliferation goes on ad infinitum, soon giving rise to numerous lines of descent from a common and eponymous ancestor, which lines, taken together, constitute a *chia tsu* or family line.[4] Thus, again in principle, any person is a member of as many chia tsu as he has agnatic ancestors, and he is included in equally many tsu or lines of descent. These purely genealogical statuses and inclusions are, however, of little or no social significance (except in matters like surname exogamy). These tsu and chia tsu are not the entities commonly described as lineages in the ethnographic literature. Those organized groups arise from (or are constructed out of) this genealogical base in one or the other of several different ways: "There is no uniform process of lineage formation in China" (R. Watson 1985:33).

When a family estate is divided, some portion of it may be set aside in the name of the deceased family head to remain joint property. The amount varies greatly, depending largely it seems on the overall wealth of the family. The portion held back is then dedicated to the memory and worship of the deceased family head, or, if he is retired, to a pension income for him or his widow and later to his worship. If this is a large block of land capable of producing a substantial income, it may be let out to tenant farmers, the income being used to maintain a shrine for the deceased father and to make periodic sacrifices there. Any leftover income is usually divided per stirpes (per fang) among the survivors. Other arrangements may be made by general agreement and legal procedure. Sometimes the coparceners take turns managing this "sacrificial estate" for a predetermined period (commonly each fang for one year at a time), and if there is any surplus income after ritual expenses they either keep it or divide it per stirpes. Alternatively, some or all the income from the sacrificial estate may be expended in various ways for the common benefit of the joint owners and their dependents. The initial sacrificial estate may be enlarged, an ancestral hall erected, a school built, staffed, and maintained, various business enterprises established, and so on. In this way it is possible for a number of agnatically related men to become wealthy, well organized among themselves, and locally quite powerful. Such groups commonly set up ancestral halls or shrines, maintain formal genealogies, and write their own constitutions ("clan rules" [see Hu 1948, Hui-chen 1959]). It is possible also for little or nothing to come of the formation of such an estate, for these same families may fall on hard times or suffer from mismanagement and have to divide and sell their joint property.

Other arrangements are possible. At the time of partition, any son has the legal (if not the moral) right to opt out of the sacrificial-estate group created by his brothers in the name of their father, and he may if he wishes set up his own sacrificial estate in the name of his father. Or this man could, if he wished, either then or later create a sacrificial estate in the name of his father's father (whether or not one already existed), and he might or might not invite his brothers or father's brothers and their sons to join with him. Nothing compels inclusion in such a group of all agnatic descendants of the apical ancestor.

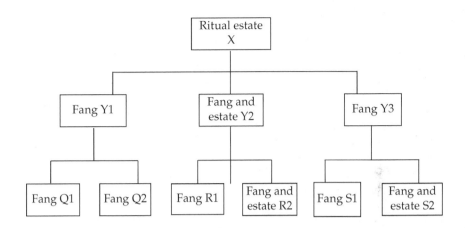

FIGURE 9.1   Chinese "Lineage" Segmentation

If a sacrificial-estate group persists for very long, it may expand into a multileveled collection of joint families (or, perhaps more accurately, joint-owner males, see below) within ever higher order joint families; and this is one of the social forms commonly described as a lineage in the ethnographic literature. In Taiwan it may be spoken of as X's chia or family, X's tsu or line, X's chia tsu or family line; or it may be described as X's *kung p'ai-hsia*, X's ritual-estate group, or X's *pai*, X's segment or faction. Although such a group is necessarily agnatic in de facto composition and may even include all male descendants through males of the man X, it is not patrilineal in constitution. Patrifiliation is a merely necessary condition for inclusion and relations of patrilineal descent do not figure in the internal or external relations of the group. Consider, for example, the matter of segmentation, so called. (See Figure 9.1.)

Exactly as the sons of X (or, as we have already seen, perhaps only some of the sons of X) may found a ritual-estate group in his name, any of their sons may (or may not) do the same thing in their names. Thus it can and does happen that as between Y-1, Y-2, and Y-3, all sons of X, only the sons R of Y-2 create yet another ritual estate in his name.

Every member of the ritual-estate group Y-2 is a member also of ritual-estate group X, but ritual-estate group Y-2 is not in any sense a segment of ritual-estate group X. The sacrificial estate of group Y-2 is not a part of the sacrificial estate of group X. The members of group Y-2 constitute a fang of and benefit from the estate of group X per stirpes along with the unorganized fang Y-1 and Y-3, but they benefit also from their own sacrificial estate. Moreover, even if the sons of Y-1 and Y-3 were also to create sacrificial estates in the names of Y-1 and Y-3, this would not bring them into any different formal relationship with the sons of Y-2. The groups Y-1, Y-2, and Y-3 would all be autonomous, having no special social relations with one another, other than each being also a fang of group X and therefore entitled to a per stirpes share of its benefits and liabilities. Nothing resembling segmentary opposition can arise in a situation like this, and as Ch'en (1983:232ff) points out, it is rather misleading even to speak of segmentation in this kind of situation. The sacrificial-estate group Y-2 is in no sense a constituent or component of the sacrificial-estate group X, even if as it may happen all the members of Y-2 are members also of X. Any appearance to the contrary is nothing but a diagrammatic illusion.

This is even more evident when we take into account that similar estates and groups also may be created in a man's name long after his death, this by voluntary subscription on the part of only some (a self-selected subset) of his descendants, and whether or not there is already such an estate existent in his name. Contributions to the creation of such an "organized estate" (*tsu-chih ti kung-yeh*) or "ancestral association" (*tsu-kung-hui*) are like stock and may be quite unequal; their modes of internal organization are highly variable (depending on the purposes for which they are formed); and the property may be held in shares by individuals or fang, or jointly, or in common, or as a beneficial trust (in which instance there is a corporation but no corporate group). Further still, such associations sometimes dispense with an eponymous apical ancestor and are thus nothing more–from the perspective of lineage theory—than voluntary associations of men with the same patronymic, which they take as sufficient reason to speak of themselves as constituting a tsu.

The position of women in all this is controversial. Some observers maintain that daughters, like sons, are born into their father's families and lineages, but at marriage become members of their husbands' families and lineages. So, it is argued, "adult membership is based on patrilineal descent for men and on marriage for women" (Goodenough 1970:66). Plainly, this is not generally true insofar as the reference is to organized social groups, for a great many men in southeast China and Taiwan have no such group affiliations, at least not above the level of the undivided joint family. What can be said is that women are jural minors, dependents of their fathers or brothers until married and then of their husbands, whose surnames they take.[5] According to Ch'en (1983:68–70), who writes about Hokkien speakers in western Taiwan, a daughter is born into and is a member of her father's chia, family, but she has no place in his chia tsu, organized or not, because she has no fang status. If she dies before marriage, she has no representation in any ancestral hall. On marriage she becomes a member of her husband's fang and of her husband's father's chia tsu—although it may be that Ch'en has in mind only the unorganized genealogical categories. J. Watson (1982:598, 615) is emphatic that Chinese women have no place at all in the system of organized, property-holding tsu or chia tsu (also Wolf and Huang 1980:63). If so, the jural constituents of these latter are not joint families (cf. Goodenough 1970:66).

What is there to be said in general about the role of patrilineal descent in the constitution of Chinese lineages, so called, or in Chinese society more generally? R. Watson (1985:16–17, 171–174) has noticed that where "lineages" exist in China, "descent from a specific ancestor is a necessary but not a sufficient condition for membership" and, moreover, that lineages were not so much a part of what might be called the "infrastructure" of the society as they were expressions of its class structure (being predominantly products and instruments of the economic and political elite). Still, she argues, "where descent groups are present they do play an important economic and political role," albeit "in maintaining a system of class privilege in the Chinese countryside"; and she argues that, even where there were no descent groups, there was a "definite patrilineal emphasis and ideology," a "belief that patrilineal descent itself carries considerable moral force"; that patrilineal descent was central to a complex system of ancestor worship and to the inheritance of property; and finally that it played a role in residence, household organization, ritual, and also in patronage relations.

There can be no doubt that the groups in question did indeed play important roles in and were integral parts of the economic and political development of the regions in which they developed. They did so, however, not as groups that were patrilineally constituted but as voluntary associations restricted in membership to men who were, nominally at least, related agnatically one to another—with the inevitable consequence that intra- and intergroup relations were of a strictly contractual nature. In what was surely the prototypical instance, relations of common patrilineal descent were not relevant at all, as when a set of brothers created a sacrificial or ritual estate in the name of their father. Here, clearly, what is necessary but not sufficient for inclusion is patrifiliation (and, of course, being a man). The same goes for inheritance, so called by Watson and others. First, there is no inheritance here but only survivorship and partition, and the only intergenerational genealogical relationship that is relevant is patrifiliation, not patrilineal descent. The first persons related by common patrilineal descent (that is, father's brother's sons) are already divided into their respective fang, and have no common interests by virtue of their common patrilineal descent. Similarly, it was patrifiliation (and the chia/fang relation), not patrilineal descent, that was significant in household organization (see e.g., Cohen 1970, 1976; Ch'en 1983 [1987]). The mere fact that the male members of large, complex, multigeneration, joint-family households are related agnatically one to another does not make relations of patrilineal descent structurally significant.

As for ancestor worship, on Ahern's (1973) account, there is no obligation to worship one's agnatic ancestors as such, although it is true that the persons who are worshipped are for the most part either parents, who must be tended to as such, or more remote agnates, who are worshipped very selectively, if at all. The obligation, on Ahern's account, is to filial piety and to remember the dead from whom one has acquired property interests, especially in land. The consequence is that people who leave no landed property don't get worshipped, except as parents, and the landless poor or people who do not make their living off the land do not have much if any use for ancestor worship. The fact that patrilineal ancestors get worshipped much more than others is, then, a reflex of the system of landed-property devolution, and not of any special moral value placed on relations of patrilineal descent per se. Of course, something else is going on when, long after the fact of some man's death, some of his descendants elect to get together and establish an ancestral association in his name but for their own benefit. Whatever the rhetoric may be, it is not fierce attachment to common patrilineal descent as a moral value that drives these associations.

II

In India, as in China, jointness is the most common form of family organization, and it is common for brothers who have divided a family estate to remain in the same village, to live as neighbors of one another, to share labor, to worship the same dieties as their father did, and so on. As a consequence, ethnographers have often found sets of varying size, and of varying genealogical depth and span, of coresident agnatically related men and their dependents, and they have often described these as lineages, as corporate, and even as comprising lineage systems (see e.g., Beck 1972, Dasgupta 1986, Dumont 1957b [1986], A. Mayer 1960). A few, however, have drawn attention to how these sets "differ from lineages as ordinarily defined" (Orenstein 1965:64, 73; Burkhart 1970, 1976, 1978). Most significant, women are considered to be members of their husbands' groups, and this for the simple reason that the constituents (physical though not jural) of these sets are joint-family households (even if the households are frequently also simple nuclear families). These are, then, as much local groups as they are kin groups; and considering that each has developed by successive and often troubled partitions of once-joint estates, it is hardly unexpected that conflict within these sets is commonplace and that they exhibit little solidarity in their relations with outsiders, which is to say that the sets per se do not have much in the way of relations with outsiders (though of course, their individual members do).

Social relations within these sets so often described as lineages (and as patrilineally constituted, despite their inclusion of in-marrying women) are governed, it seems, largely by an ethic of kinship amity and cooperation between individuals whose parents (or whose husband's parents) or grandparents were once coparceners. Mutual moral obligations between member households typically include consultation with regard to marriages and participation in one another's weddings and funerals. Moreover, the households are expected to ally with one another in disputes with outsiders, although as already noticed, this is a moral injunction that is often difficult to enact. In many instances these sets of joint-family households recognize a headman who adjudicates disputes between members and who represents them in a village council which adjudicates disputes between members of different sets; but he does not represent the group itself, which has no property of its own and cannot be held liable for any wrongs on the part of any of its members. These sets are sometimes described as at least ritually corporate, in some part because it seems that people do speak of "lineage" or "clan" dieties, and some co-members may on various occasions worship in concert. But Burkhart's (1976:51–58) observations about the situation in one Tamil community seem much more generally applicable: Lineages, so called, are not distinguished one from another by their worship of different dieties; co-members of such a set of families may worship the same diety as their father or father's father did and they may do so either individually or in concert. In short, there are no "lineage cults" and it would be stretching a point to represent worship in concert as an expression of "lineage solidarity."

NOTES

1. For similar observations see also Sangren (1984), J. L. Watson (1982, 1986), R. Watson (1985), A. Wolf (1985), and Chun (1996), who maintains that the existence of lineages in China "squarely contradicts the theoretical principles upon which lineage theory has been constructed." Again the bête noir is structural-functional theory and the inspiration for the criticism is D. M. Schneider (1965).

2. Most recently A. Chun (1996:438): "the existence of patrilineal descent and segmentary lineages . . . has been challenged even in 'classical' ethnography (Holy 1979, Scheffler 1985), [but] is not an issue in the Chinese context." But cf. Scheffler (1986: 348, n. 4) where the patrilineality of these groups is brought into question.

3. The following summary draws heavily on Ahern (1973), Baker (1968), Ch'en (1983), published in Chinese as Ch'en (1987), Cohen (1970, 1976), Freedman (1958, 1966), Hu (1948), Hui-chen (1959), J. Watson (1975), and R. Watson (1985), as well as on various essays in Ahern and Gates (1981), Ebrey and Watson (1986), and Freedman (1970). The practices described here are still prevalent in Taiwan and the Hong Kong region, but of course not in the People's Republic of China.

4. Tsu is commonly glossed as 'line' or 'lineage' in the anthropological litera-ture, but this may be very misleading. Chun (1985:92–94) gives a large number of examples that indicate that a better gloss would be 'group' or 'set,' but especially of living creatures, e.g. *han-tsu* 'the Chinese people.'

5. Again this is a matter about which there is some apparent disagreement. It seems, however, that a married woman was known by her husband's surname at least in his community, but might be spoken of by her own patronym in her own natal community. In any event, it is seriously misleading to say of married women that they were incorporated into their husbands' lineages or clans.

10

COGNATIC DESCENT GROUPS?

I

We may now consider whether, when simple filiation is a condition for inclusion in a group, it is possible for relations of descent to have jural or structural values in intra- or intergroup relations. We saw in Chapter 2 that there are good reasons to suppose it is not. Where simple filiation is either a merely necessary or a merely sufficient condition, the situation is clearly much the same as where patri- or matrifiliation is merely necessary or merely sufficient. The analogy fails, however, where simple filiation is the necessary and sufficient condition. That is because the sets constituted by that rule are not only not mutually exclusive, they are bound to be widely overlapping. Whatever the extent of the overlap, in any small-scale society it is bound to be sufficient to make it virtually impossible to institute a set of rights and duties between co-members that is distinctively different from the rights and duties entailed by two persons being kin of one another. Only if we were content to use *group* in a sociologically trivial fashion could we describe them as "descent groups de facto"; nothing would justify description of them as "descent groups de jure." Appearances to the contrary in ethnographic descriptions are likely to be consequences of misrepresenting the actions of persons as kin or as specific kinds of kin as the actions of groups or of persons as members of the same or different groups—which, as pointed out in Chapter 8, is a commonplace ethnographic error.

These general observations can be substantiated by brief reviews of a few relevant ethnographic examples. I begin with my own account of Choiseul Island social structure (see especially Scheffler 1962, 1965), in which I argued vigorously, and against Fortes (1959b), for the concept of cognatic descent groups. Agreeing then with Elman Service (1962:31), I argued (or rather merely asserted) that "descent group" is profitably used as a label for any group that is understood by the people concerned as being composed of descendants of a common ancestor or pair (Scheffler 1965:42). I did not then understand Fortes's (1959b) observation that in the absence of closure by a descent criterion, relations of descent can have no distinctive jural values or structural significance: However much they may be implicated de facto, they cannot be implicated de jure.

II

Choiseul is a forest-clad, mountainous island in the northwest corner of the Solomon Islands (formerly the British Solomon Islands Protectorate). Its aboriginal population was thinly and widely dispersed in small hamlets located strategically on inland ridges, although from time to time larger villages formed for purposes of defense or to fulfill feast and gift-exchange obligations between big-men and their followers. Subsistence was by slash-and-burn agriculture supplemented by mainly forest produce.

The most general term for kin group or category is *sinangge*. The exact reference of the term varies but is made specific by the addition of descriptive terms. One usage of sinangge is egocentric, referring to all persons with whom any specified person can trace cognatic connection and to whom he may, at least nominally, turn for support. This is his *sinangge lavata*, "big sinangge, " his "personal kindred" or "kinship circle." Another reference is to named cognatic descent categories (for example, *sinangge Kesi/Gabili/Sirosenga*) which comprise, again nominally, all the descendants, through both males and females, of an apical ancestor alleged to have originated that sinangge and its land estate by first clearing and occupying a tract of virgin forest. From the individual's point of view all the cognatic descent categories in which he is included converge upon him to form his sinangge lavata. Those members of a cognatic descent category who live together on its estate and who form the nucleus of a community also are known as a sinangge, more specifically a *sinangge sukasuka*, "little sinangge," or a *sinangge kapakapa*, "those who perch." Herein this unit is called a ramage.[1] Finally, sinangge may refer to any collection of people related among themselves by kinship or marriage, such as a task group for gardening, fishing, or warfare. In this context even in-laws are included, but in general sinangge signifies that the persons referred to trace common cognatic connection of some sort and they co-operate based on a cognatic kinship sentiment that enjoins them to *vari tavisi*, "help one another." None of these different kinds of sinangge is either exogamous or endogamous by cultural prescription.

A land estate founded by a distant ancestor may be subdivided at two or more levels into lesser estates that are the properties of branch sinangge. Some of these branches and their estates were founded when a leader—*batu* or manager—of the "truncal" or even another branch segment made a gift of a part of the main estate to a female member of the group and her in-marrying husband. Or the truncal segment might split into two segments, each under the leadership of a big-man who had been a member of it. Branches achieved their distinctiveness from the original unit as well as from other groups through participation in such activities as revenge, warfare, and potlatch-like gift-exchanges that were accompanied by large-scale feasts. These processes ended with pacification and the termination of competitive feasting and gift-exchange in the 1920s (see Scheffler 1964b).

In attempting to explain their sinangge to me and in talking among themselves, people often asserted "The important side is that of the father; we follow our fathers." When men marry, they said, they stay with their own sinangge and bring their wives to live with them and their fathers—"women go out, men stay put." That is to say, through patrivirilocal residence the men of a sinangge come to form the nucleus of its kapakapa, local group, or ramage. Within the overarching cognatic descent category, and within its ramage, a distinction is made between *popondo valeke* and *popondo nggole*, those who are "born of men" and those who are "born of women." This, unlike the terminologically similar distinction often encountered in the New Guinea highlands (see Chapter 8), is genuinely one between patrilineal and nonpatrilineal descendants of the founder. Its significance is that the former are "strong" within the group; the latter are "weak," they are "guests" who "dwell under" the agnatic affiliants, especially the ramage leader, batu or big-man, and they must "keep the peace, live quietly and cause no trouble," or they may be expelled from the group (a condition that holds no less, by the way, for any agnatic affiliant).

So far this may seem to be merely a system of localized patrilineal descent groups, albeit with explicit provision for occasional recruitment from the outside, even something of a segmentary lineage system. It would not be evidence to the contrary that the genitor of an out-of-wedlock child has no claim to custody of it because he paid no brideprice, and the child belongs solely to its mother's sinangge. And it is perhaps a minor difficulty that there is an alternative form of marriage, *tamazira*, in which no brideprice is paid, uxorilocal residence is required, and the offspring are said to belong primarily to their mother's "side"; it is their "strong" side. The father's sinangge retains an interest in them (it is not "thrown away"), just as does the mother's sinangge in brideprice marriages, and the children are always welcome with either group.

That, however, is only one side of the story, for people (often the same people) sometimes told another and sometimes apparently contradictory tale. Even when stressing that "the father's side is most important, we follow our fathers," people usually added, "We keep two sides because it is not good to lose the mother's side" and "we do not throw it away." The reference was to both one's matrikin in general and to one's mother's ramage of premarital origin in particular, to which, it is said, a person may "chose" (*vine*) to "return" at any time. It is said, moreover, that any person "keeps" (*miasoka*) not only his father's and mother's sinangge but also any one to which he is connected as an acknowledged descendant of the founding ancestor, regardless of how far removed spatially or genealogically that may be. At their most expansive, people said that anyone born of a sinangge—its *sasangi*—is welcome at any time to become an active member of its ramage. Often left unstated was the proviso that he be otherwise an asset to the group and not a person who would generate intra- or intergroup conflict.

As long as sassangi remain nonresident they are not obliged to participate in group activities but may do so from time to time. They are expected, however, to refrain from conflict (as in warfare in the past) against group members or, for that matter, any relative. They are said to "keep" the sinangge, but most often the reference is clearly to mere inclusion in a cognatic descent category and implies little or nothing about the quality of association with the ramage itself. To ramage members, its sasanggi are all relatives, and they may be close relatives. They are persons who may be called upon for all sorts of assistance, and as relatives, they should not refuse. When it is said that any person belongs to or keeps many sinangge it is meant that he or she has interests in the personnel and estates of many cognatic descent categories.

If any person may have several sinangge affiliations or associations, one is primary and his ties with other groups, which confer upon him at least nominal interests in their property and personnel, are of varying quality and utility depending largely upon his proximity to those groups but ultimately on many other factors. Persons are born (or adopted or introduced in childhood) into operating groups and become identified with them by virtue of parental connection. Later, the establishment of active interests in the group's personnel and property develops through protracted residence in or near the ramage and the relatively greater intensity of interaction with neighbors that follows from that residence. Ramage affiliation is most frequently through one's father (though not by that fact patrilineal) but not infrequently, and quite legitimately, through one's mother, and it is not so much chosen as it is conferred by birth or parental choice or residence.

Although (in one representation of the situation) ramages are always open to their sasangi, this openness is (as already noted) conditional, and it has to be negotiated between the would-be entrant and those persons who are already established members. In the past, stressing openness facilitated maintenance of a large and potentially more powerful group, one better able to protect itself and to function effectively under the leadership of a big-man. There would have been little point in turning away any peaceable person, much less a known and familiar relative. There would have been equally little point in insisting on the privileges of agnatic status, though one can readily imagine that the point did sometimes arise in the course of heated interpersonal competition.

In the past ramages were not stable units. The residential and political status of branches was not a direct function of their order of segmentation but rather of the political statuses of their managers. Relative status and, as a corollary, relative attractiveness, was worked out in competition and often violent conflict with other managers and their groups. Segments of one major sinangge had no special rights and duties in relation to one another and sometimes did ally with outsiders against companion branches. Mortality in warfare was apparently quite high, and there was a corresponding high rate of mobility to avoid those conflicts. The composition of local groups was therefore varied and fluid, cognatic and marital ties being utilized to obtain shelter and protection among close or distant kin and with a powerful manager. Periods of peace allowed the ramages some degree of stability and, unless nearly annihilated in warfare, a ramage maintained at least a core of its membership resident on its estate to keep its claims alive. This general situation encouraged the recruitment of kin to ramages if for no other reason than to increase military potential and ability to perform gift-exchanges resulting from revenge and warfare alliances. It encouraged a rhetorical emphasis on group openness and egalitarian intragroup relations at the expense of the rhetoric of agnatic hierarchy and privilege.

High mortality occasionally left a ramage without an agnatic line, and nonagnates were then left with the use and management of the group estate. But extensive participation in and help with ramage affairs were the more usual effective basis of a claim to an active interest in a group and its resources. A nonagnate might be able to point to several generations of continuous affiliation by his ancestors and cite their significant activities in support of the group when requesting support (such as in brideprice, revenge, and rights to land usage). Ideally, this support could not be refused. However, if a man were a troublemaker his nonagnatic status would be thrown up at him at every opportunity and his privileges refused on genealogical grounds. If he were hardworking and helpful to his relatives and did not alienate the ramage through lack of co-operation or by attempting to extend his interests in its estate at the expense of others, the fact that he was not an agnate would not arise, and if it did would be minimized by his supporters. Nonresident members of the cognatic descent category were in a similar position. The property of ex-members, such as land (in fallow) and groves, remained the property of their descendants who were reputed to be able to resume them at any time, and this was a common basis of a choice to affiliate elsewhere. Alternatively, a person might go on using such property without residing with the larger group holding custodial rights over the segment in which he had more particular interests. This often happens since there is a preference for marriage between proximate groups and a person may come to have interests in and to be called a member of two or more relatively contiguous groups at the same time.

Today there is little change of affiliation, in part because the Christian missions and protectorate government discouraged changes of residence. It is also because there are few areas of land that are economically attractive, and the people who have consolidated interests in them are reluctant to recognize the claims of others. Even in the past persons did not change affiliations arbitrarily or even very freely, and only people who establish and maintain active interests in the property or personnel of a ramage may be fairly sure of being able to exercise fully the privileges of membership. Changes of affiliation require the consent of those who have already established themselves in a group through domicile or proximate residence and all the activities implied therein, and, moreover, protection of one's own property interests requires that one establish and maintain a clear-cut allegiance to one ramage in particular. The openness of a ramage to everyone who appears in its cognatic descent category is not generally taken literally, and it is often no more than a way of talking about kinship and its duties and obligations. The dispersion of persons who have at least nominal rights in relation to various ramages had important consequences for the larger social order, especially in relation to the maintenance of a modicum of peace in aboriginal times (see Scheffler 1964a, 1964b).

A ramage is composed, then, of descendants of its founder who live together with their spouses and guests on the *sinangge* estate. They need not be agnatic descendants of the founder except, presumably, for limited purposes, particularly leadership status. However, even this much significance of agnatic status is undermined by the fact that the common Melanesian pattern of the acquisition of prestige through competition and public gift-exchange prevailed here too, and no man could be a manager in the fullest sense unless he were markedly successful in competition with other men, even those of his own ramage. He had to earn renown in the political sphere with which to back up the powers acquired by agnatic status and primogeniture. All other ramage members, regardless of their genealogical status, were said to be only his "hands." Yet, the manager was as much dependent upon their continued allegiance as they were upon his political talents. The position of the ramage within the larger society and its own internal operations demanded, therefore, that distinctions be glossed over except in situations having to do only with the internal affairs of the group itself. In external relations, such differences faded into insignificance, being matters of no interest to outsiders.

I have emphasized that sasanggi could become active members of a ramage only by permission of the group itself; change of affiliation was a matter for negotiation, not one of simple choice on the part of a would-be affiliate. Where the claim is contested, as doubtless it seldom was in the past but may well be today, the onus of proof of the worthiness of it is upon the claimant. Almost any incident in the past and present relations between the claimant and his ancestors and the established members of the ramage may be deemed relevant or irrelevant to his claims. Its relevance depends on the total quality of his relations with the ramage (that is, his desirability as a member) or other considerations such as the availability of primary resources, today, coconut land. The principal rationalizations for refusing the privilege of residence include the group being "too full," that is, the area cannot support additional persons, and also that "the tie has been covered by the passage of too many generations." Population pressure may have been something of a factor in the past, for enduring large groups were not possible given the aboriginal ecology. Yet, one suspects that room could always be made for a desirable member.

Threat of withdrawal of one's co-operation, sorcery, or, if one were a big-man, actual violence were the sanctions available to those refused what they took to be their rights. Property disputes have always been the most common grounds for sorcery accusations. Fear of sorcery or accusations of it were common reasons for opting to change affiliation, while such factors as persistent quarreling, consistently poor gardens, personal health, and fear of violent conflict also led persons to make temporary or permanent changes of affiliation.

By the 1950s much of this had changed. Ramages lacked whatever solidarity they may have had in the past, for there was no intergroup conflict, and they could not have the political and economic significance they once had. The modern economic situation has also been detrimental to group solidarity because it tolerates nuclear or small extended-family production, which the Choiseulese prefer for various reasons. Modern ramages are more stable in composition but also far fewer in number than their earlier counterparts, but this is partly artificially imposed. Interest in a stable crop like coconuts seems likely to have a stabilizing influence too. However, many ramages have become entirely defunct or exist only as cognatic descent categories merged with one or more other local groups and off their own lands. Between 1910 and 1925 the missions and government, for purposes of their own convenience, persuaded and pressured the people to leave the interior hills and settle on the coasts. A desire to enter the copra trade also stimulated this movement.

One consequence has been that the genealogical qualifications for managerial status are now stressed and practical qualifications are no longer important—the former are the only means of validating claims to such status. Ramage membership today means little for anything other than interests in land. There seems also to be a tendency for fragmentation of land interests in a more definitive manner than in the past. Men attempt to establish separate and exclusive rights over what was once group property and to deprive others of their rights of usage. Partly this is because control over land (management of a group estate) has traditionally been one of the ways of validating claims to managerial status, and thus many men may become managers, big-men, at least in their own eyes. The problem is particularly crucial in relation to good coconut land.[2]

III

If there were any descent groups in Choiseul society they were the ramages, the sinangge kapakapa or sets of co-resident descendants of the founding ancestor of a cognatic descent category. For inclusion in such a set, descent from that ancestor is a necessary condition, *but it is necessary only in a derivative fashion.* Insofar as the unit has a local or residential dimension, it is as much a local group as it is a descent group, if, that is, there is any compelling reason to describe it as a descent group. In 1965, I chose to agree with Elman Service (1962:31) that "'descent group' is profitably used as a label for any group which is understood by the people concerned as being composed of descendants of a common ancestor or pair" (Scheffler 1965:42); and the Choiseulese sinangge kapakapa certainly qualifies, provided that it is not important whether the group includes all or only some such descendants. But these groups include only some such descendants, and it is not simply descent, or even descent plus something else ('residence' is the usual simplistic plug-in here) that is the source of anyone's entitlement to inclusion.

Sinangge kapakapa are not mutually exclusive sets. It is possible for a person to maintain two or more affiliations by maintaining more-or-less extensive and intensive social relations with the two or more groups with which his father or mother, or both, were socially identified. Fulltime co-residence with the local nucleus of such a set is not necessary for that purpose. If a person participates in such social relations and thereby maintains for himself two or more such identities, that person's child has a right to do the same, and through either or both parents. If the parent omits to maintain such relations with any one set, the child does not acquire that particular parental identity. What the child acquires by virtue of filiation is not a single such identity but a set of them, and that set may or may not be the sum of the sets acquired natally by his father and mother. In short, the right possessed natally by anyone to participate in the assets and affairs of any one group is the result of a series of parental natal accumulations and of parental maintenances or losses. Continued possession of that right is contingent on exercise of it. Therefore, the necessary but not sufficient condition for inclusion in a group is filiation, and not descent.

Sinangge kapakapa do have general or property rights in relation to land estates, and membership of such a group does entail a duty on the part of each member to assist other members in defense of that estate (it does not entail a duty to assist in revenge or redress for a personal injury). But a person has that duty only so long as he chooses to remain a member, and he may at any time refuse to fulfill it and, in effect, withdraw from the group. As a corollary of this open-endedness, and of the lack of mutual exclusivity, these groups have no special rights or duties in relation to one another. That is to say, relations of descent are structurally insignificant in the field of intergroup relations, which are wholly contractual (see Scheffler 1965:chap. 7).

What, finally, are we to make of the distinction between agnatic (or patrilineal) descendants and nonagnatic descendants of the ancestral founder? It appears to establish an order of precedence and deference on genealogical grounds between two kinds of group member, subordinating one to the other (increasingly, in the postcolonial period, as "guests" versus "owners"). But, as pointed out by Fortes (1959b:212) in relation to the Maori *hapu*, "its internal composition is immaterial to its structural relations with other like, or subordinate or superordinate segments." It may be represented by a chief or defended by an army, but how the chief is chosen and the army recruited are strictly internal matters that are not of concern to other allied or opposed groups of the same sort. Insofar as such groups sometimes allied with one another, they did so contractually or voluntarily (Scheffler 1965:chap. 4), and without regard to possible differences in composition or leadership. Moreover, it appears rather unlikely that, in the precolonial period, the distinction between agnatic and nonagnatic affiliates could ever have been consistently and persistently applied; to invoke it at all is to fly in the face of kinship amity and to risk alienation of a broad category of potential group members, not only as group members but also as dependable kinsmen.

IV

Comparable arrangements are quite common in Polynesia, in particular in Samoa and, as already noticed, among the Maori of New Zealand, although both those situations are complicated by considerations of competition for "titles" and "rank" (as noticed in Fortes 1959b), and by somewhat larger scale polities and larger and more permanent settlements. Also notable are the ethnographic accounts by Roger Keesing (e.g., 1968, 1970, 1971, 1982)[3] of the Kwaio region, and by B. Burt (1993, 1994) of the Kwara'ae region of Malaita Island in the Central Solomons. Some African instances are provided by Allan Hoben (1973) for the Amhara of Ethopia, by A. P. Caplan (1969) for Mafia Island, Tanzania, and by P. Lloyd (1966) for some Yoruba. It would be tedious for the reader if we were critically to examine any of these in any detail, so we pass over the opportunity except to take notice of some especially significant information provided for Samoa by F. Grattan (1948:chap. 2) and R. P. Gilson (1963, 1970:chap. 2), and Epling and Eudy (1963).[4] Here, too, there is a formal relationship of dominance/subordination between the "male" and "female sides" of the *aiga*, "family" and "descent group," and it is commonly argued that a *matai's* or titleholder's son should succeed him. Nevertheless, father-son succession has no legally privileged status. Samoan courts have consistently turned back claims to the contrary. It is a value especially prized by men who would like to see their sons succeed them and by those sons, both of whom (and their supporters) may argue strongly for its status as a rule. But legally it is only one of a number of considerations that the electors—members of the "family"—are free to take into account when choosing a successor. In short, on Samoa as on Choiseul, agnatic affiliation and father-son succession are valued but not jurally sanctioned.

V

Cognatic or ambilineal descent groups have been described for a number of small islands in Micronesia and Polynesia. Two of the most detailed accounts are Lambert's (1966) on the northern Gilbert Islands and Huntsman's (1971) and Huntsman and Hooper's (1986) on Tokelau. Both provide ample evidence that although *some* of the groups in question, at *some* stages in their developmental processes, could be described as descent groups de facto, in none of them are relations of common descent structurally significant. Because the argument is the same for both, we deal only with Tokelau.

Like the Choiseul expression *sinangge*, the Tokelau expression *kaaiga* (cognate with Samoan *aiga*) may be used in reference to a cognatic stock or to a personal kindred. Some of the former, according to Huntsman and Hooper (1986:109), are "corporate units, . . . cognatic descent groups with exclusive rights to an estate, which is jointly exploited by its members and its produce distributed among them." These are known more specifically as *kaukaainga*. We are told also, however, that kaukaainga are short-lived, that they "rarely persist longer than two or three generations" and that some include only a married couple, who pool their inheritances, and their offspring (Huntsman 1971:327). In 1968, on one atoll with a population of about 500 people there were thirty-three widely overlapping kaukaainga. These "were identified by the name of the elders who represented them in the village council or [by] the name of their founders, who were occasionally the same person." Their properties were "estates inherited by a founder or founders, who were occasionally great-grandparents or grandparents of elders, [but who] were most frequently parents of elders, and are often the elders themselves" (Huntsman 1971:327).

Clearly, kaukaainga property is not at all corporate, at least not in the sense specified in Chapter 4, and, indeed, it is difficult to grasp in what sense a kaukaainga may accurately be said to own or possess any property. To the contrary, it appears that productive property here is by and large individually owned (otherwise it would make no sense to talk about it as being inherited) but is exploited cooperatively by family or (overlapping) extended family groups. Married couples pool their resources, exploit them cooperatively with their children, and later these resources are divided among their children, sometimes not until the grandchildren are adults. Whenever the assets are divided, there is ipso facto termination of one kaukaainga and formation of several new ones. Presumably, what an elder represents in a council meeting is not a corporate interest but an individual interest in assets (what has to be shown is the fact of an inheritance) that, because they are exploited cooperatively, are of interest to the larger set of cooperating kin.

Another indication of the inappropriateness of the appellation *descent group* is that a minimal kaukaainga comprises a married couple and their unmarried offspring. What the ethnographers call its "corporate estate" is just the set of properties owned by each of the spouses, and the elements of those sets are eventually reallocated among the offspring. This is no more a descent group than is the Mendi shem discussed in Chapter 8. It appears, moreover, neither is it a property-owning entity of any kind. It would be wrong to say that there is ownership in common of an estate, because there is no group estate to begin with, but only the sum of individually held estates. What the members of a kaukaainga have in common, as it were, is that they work together to exploit the various estates that belong to each one of them (or to their parents or grandparents if they themselves have yet to inherit). Neither is a kaukaainga a jural aggregate like the Rungus tree-owning unit mentioned in Chapter 4—again because there is no group estate to begin with, but only the sum of individually held estates.

Notes

1. I have no special attachment to this expression, first used in this sense by Sir Raymond Firth (1957, 1963), and I use it reluctantly; but it does help to avoid talk about descent where such talk is inappropriate.

2. These matters are discussed and analyzed at length in some recent ethnographies of other Solomon Island peoples. See e.g., G. Schneider (1996) on the Roviana region of New Georgia; E. Hviding (1994) on the people of the Marovo region of New Georgia; and B. Burt (1993, 1994) on the Kwara'ae people of Malaita Island.

3. When reading Keesing on Kwaio one should be aware that Keesing's concept of the "contextual definition of status" is really about the contextual realization of status, and that the statuses being enacted are not, as Keesing makes them out to be, matters of group affiliation but of interpersonal kinship. Also, the foci of the practices described by Keesing as ancestor worship might better be described as ghosts.

4. Epling and Eudy are virtually the sole ethnographers who avoid describing the Samoan aiga as a descent group. They describe it as "a corporation-like 'kindred group'," a usage they attribute to Fortes (1959b).

REFERENCES

Ahern, Emily
1973   The Cult of the Dead in a Chinese Village. Stanford: Stanford University Press.

Ahern, Emily, and Hill Gates (eds.)
1981   The Anthropology of Taiwanese Society. Stanford: Stanford University Press.

Ahmed, Akbar S.
1980   Pukthun Economy and Society. London: Routledge and Kegan Paul.

Aiyar, N. C.
1953   Mayne's Treatise on Hindu Law and Usage. 11th ed. Madras: Higginbothams.

Anglin, Andrew
1979   Analytic Models and Folk Models: The Tallensi Case. *In* Segmentary Lineage Systems Reconsidered. L. Holy, ed. Pp. 46–67. Queens University Papers in Social Anthropology, 4. Belfast: Queens University.

Appell, George N.
1974   The Analysis of Property Systems: The Creation and Devolution of Property Interests Among the Rungus of Borneo. Unpublished Ms.
1976   The Rungus: Social Structure in a Cognatic Society and Its Ritual Symbolization. *In* The Societies of Borneo. G. N. Appell, ed. Pp. 66–86. Washington, D.C.: American Anthropological Association.
1983   Methodological Problems with the Concepts of Corporation, Corporate Social Grouping, and Cognatic Descent Group. American Ethnologist 10:302–311.
1984   Methodological Issues in the Corporation Redux. American Ethnologist 11:815–817.

Augé, Marc (ed.)
1975   Les Domaines de la parenté: filiation/alliance/résidence. Paris: Francois Maspéro.

Baker, Hugh D.
1968   A Chinese Lineage Village: Sheung Shui. Stanford: Stanford University Press.

Barnard, Alan, and Anthony Good
1984   Research Practices in the Study of Kinship. London: Academic Press.

Barnes, John A.
1962   African Models in the New Guinea Highlands. Man 62:2–9.
1967   Agnation Among the Enga. Oceania 38:33–43.
1971   Agnatic Taxonomies and Stochastic Variation. Anthropological Forum 3:3–12.

Barth, Fredrik
1956   Indus and Swat Khoistan: An Ethnographic Survey. Oslo: Forende Trykkerier.
1959a   Political Leadership among the Swat Pathans. New York: Humanities Press.
1959b   Segmentary Opposition and the Theory of Games. Journal of the Royal Anthropological Institute 89:5–21.
1966   Models of Social Organization. London: Royal Anthropological Institute.
1973   Descent and Marriage Reconsidered. *In* The Character of Kinship J. Goody, ed. Pp. 3–20. London: Cambridge University Press.
1981   Features of Person and Society in Swat: Collected Essays on Pathans. London: Routledge and Kegan Paul.

Beck, Brenda
1972   Peasant Society in Konku: A Study in Right and Left Subcastes. Vancouver: University of British Columbia Press.

Black, Hebry C.
1983   Black's Law Dictionary: Definitions of the Terms and Phrases of American and English Jurisprudence, Ancient and Modern. 5th ed. St. Paul, MN: West Publishing Co., First edition 1891.

Bohannan, Laura
1952   A Genealogical Charter. Africa 22:301–315.
1958   Political Aspects of Tiv Social Organization. *In* Tribes Without Rulers: Studies in African Segmentary Systems. J. Middleton and D. Tait, eds. Pp. 33–66. London: Routledge and Kegan Paul.

Bohannan, Laura, and Paul Bohannan
1953   The Tiv of Central Nigeria. Ethnographic Survey of Africa: Western Africa, part VIII. London: International African Institute.

Bohannan, Paul
1954   Tiv Farm and Settlement. Colonial Research Studies No. 15. London: Colonial Office.

1957   Justice and Judgement Among the Tiv. London: Oxford University Press.
1963   Social Anthropology. New York: Holt, Rinehart and Winston.
1965   The Tiv of Nigeria. *In* Peoples and Cultures of Africa J. Gibbs, ed. Pp. 515–546. New York: Holt Rinehart.

Buchler, Ira, and Henry Selby
1968   Kinship and Social Organization. New York: Macmillan.

Burkhart, Geoffrey
1970   Agnatic Groups and Affinal Relations in a South Indian Caste: Udaiyaars of Salem District, Tamilnadu. Ph.D. dissertation, University of Rochester. Rochester, N.Y.
1976   On the Absence of Descent Groups Among Some Udayars of South India. Contributions to Indian Sociology 10:31–61.
1978   Marriage Alliance and the Local Circle Among Some Udayars of South India. *In* American Studies in the Anthropology of India. S. Vatuk, ed. Pp. 171–209. New Delhi: Manohar Publications.

Burt, Ben
1993   Tradition and Christianity: The Colonial Transformation of a Solomon Islands Society. Chur, Switzerland: Harwood.
1994   Land in Kwar'ae and Development in the Solomon Islands. Oceania 64:317–335.

Caplan, Ann P.
1969   Cognatic Descent Groups on Mafia Island, Tanzania. Man 4:419–443.

Ch'en, Ch'i-nan
1983   Fang and Chia-Tsu: The Chinese Kinship System in Rural Taiwan. Ph.D. dissertation, Yale University, New Haven.
1987   T'ai-wan ti ch'uan t'ung Chung-kuo she hui (Traditional Chinese Society of Taiwan). Taipei, Taiwan: Youn ch'en wan hua shin yehku fen yu hsien.
1990   Chia tsu yu she hui: T'ai-wan yu Chung-kuo she hui yen chiu ti chi ch'u li nien (Family and Society: Basic Ideas of the Study of Taiwan and Chinese Society). Taipei, Taiwan: Lien ching cha'u pan shih yoh kung sso.

Chun, Allen
1985   Land Is to Live: A Study of the Concept of Tsu in a Hakka Chinese Village, New Territories, Hong Kong. Ph.D. dissertation, University of Chicago, Chicago, IL.
1996   The Lineage-Village Complex in Southeastern China. Current Anthropology 37:429–450.

Cohen, Myron L.
1970   Developmental Process in the Chinese Domestic Group. *In* Family and Kinship in Chinese Society, M. Freedman, ed. Pp. 21–36. Stanford: Stanford University Press.

1976   House United, House Divided: The Chinese Family in Taiwan. New York:
       Columbia University Press.

Cook, E.
1970   On the Conversion of Non-Agnates into Agnates Among the Manga.
       Southwestern Journal of Anthropology 26:190–196.

Cook, Edwin, and Denise O'Brien (eds.)
1980   Blood and Semen. Ann Arbor: University of Michigan Press.

Critchley, John.
1978   Feudalism. London: George Allen and Unwin.

Cunnison, Ian
1956   Perpetual Kinship: A Political Institution of the Luapula Peoples. Rhodes-
       Livingstone Institute Journal 20:28–48.

Da Matta, Roberto
1973   A Reconsideration of Apinaye Social Morphology. In Peoples and Cultures
       of Native South America. D. Gross, ed. Pp. 277–291. New York:
       Doubleday.

Dasgupta, Santal
1986   Caste, Kinship, and Community: Social System of a Bengal Caste. Madras:
       Universities Press.

Davenport, William
1959   Non-Unilineal Descent and Descent Groups. American Anthropologist
       61:557–569.
1963   Social Organization. Biennial Review of Anthropology 1963:178–227.

De Lepervanche, Marie
1967   Descent, Residence, and Leadership in the New Guinea Highlands. I.
       Oceania 38:134–158.
1968   Descent, Residence, and Leadership in the New Guinea Highlands. II.
       Oceania 38:163–189.

Diwan, Paras
1978   Customary Law (of Punjab and Haryana). Chandigarh: Punjab University.

Dresch, Paul
1986   The Significance of the Course Events Take in Segmentary Systems.
       American Ethnologist 13:309–324.
1989   Tribes, Government, and History in Yemen. New York: Oxford University
       Press.

Dumont, Louis
1957a   Hierarchy and Marriage Alliance in South Indian Kinship. Journal of the
        Royal Anthropological Institute pp. 3–45.
1957b   Une Sous caste de l'Inde du sud: organisation sociale et religion des
        Pramalai Kallar. Paris: Mouton. English translation 1986.
1971   Introduction a deux théories d'anthropologie sociale. Paris: Mouton.

Ebry, Patricia, and James L. Watson (eds.)
1986   Kinship Organization in Late Imperial China. Berkeley: University of
        California Press.

Edgerton, Robert B.
1985   Rules, Exceptions, and Social Order. Berkeley, Los Angeles: University of
        California Press.

Elias, T. O.
1956   The Nature of African Customary Law. Manchester: Manchester University
        Press.

Epling, P. J., and Ardith A. Eudy
1963   Some Observations on the Samoan Aigapotopoto. Journal of the
        Polynesian Society 72:378–383.

Evans-Pritchard, E. E.
1933   The Nuer: Tribe and Clan. I. Sudan Notes and Records 16:1–53.
1934   The Nuer: Tribe and Clan. II. Sudan Notes and Records 17:1–58.
1935   The Nuer: Tribe and Clan. III. Sudan Notes and Records 18:37–87.
1940   The Nuer. London: Oxford University Press.
1945   Some Aspects of Marriage and Family Among the Nuer. Livingstone:
        Rhodes-Livingstone Institute.
1950a   Kinship and the Local Community Among the Nuer. In African Systems
        of Kinship and Marriage. A. R. Radcliffe-Brown and C. D. Forde, eds. Pp.
        360–392. London: Oxford University Press.
1950b   The Nuer Family. Sudan Notes and Records 31:21–42.
1951   Kinship and Marriage Among the Nuer. London: Oxford University Press.
1956   Nuer Religion. London: Oxford University Press.

Fardon, Richard
1984   Sisters, Wives, Wards and Daughters: A Transformational Analysis of the
        Political Organization of the Tiv and Their Neighbours. Part I: The Tiv.
        Africa 54:2–21.
1985   Sisters, Wives, Wards and Daughters: A Transformational Analysis of the
        Political Organization of the Tiv and Their Neighbours. Part II: The
        Transformations. Africa 55:77–91.

Fei, Hsiao-tung
1946   Peasantry and Gentry: An Interpretation of Chinese Social Structure and Its
        Changes. American Journal of Sociology 52.

Feinberg, Richard
1990   New Guinea Models on a Polynesian Outlier? Ethnology 29:83–96.

Feil, D. K.
1978   Straightening the Way: An Enga Kinship Conundrum. Man 13:380–401.
1984a   Beyond Patriliny in the New Guinea Highlands. Man 19:50–76.
1984b   Ways of Exchange. St. Lucia: University of Queensland Press.
1987   The Evolution of Highland Papua New Guinea Societies. Cambridge:
        Cambridge University Press.

Firth, Raymond
1957   A Note on Descent Groups in Polynesia. Man 57:4–8.
1959   Social Change in Tikopia. Allen and Unwin: London.
1963   Bilateral Descent Groups: An Operational Perspective. In Studies in
        Kinship and Marriage. I. Schapera, ed. Pp. 23–37. London: Royal
        Anthropological Institute.

Forde, C. D.
1938   Fission and accretion in the Yako patriclan. Journal of the Royal
        Anthropological Institute 68:311–338.
1941   Marriage and the Family among the Yako in South-Eastern Nigeria.
        London School of Economics Monographs in Social Anthropology 5.
        London: London School of Economics.
1950   Double Descent Among the Yakö. In African Systems of Kinship and
        Marriage. A. R. Radcliffe-Brown and C. D. Forde, eds. Oxford: Oxford
        University Press.
1963a   On Some Further Unconsidered Aspects of Descent. Man 63:12–13.
1963b   Unilineal Fact or Fiction: An Analysis of the Composition of Kin-Groups
        Among the Yako. In Studies in Kinship and Marriage I. Schapera, ed.
        London: Royal Anthropological Institute.
1964   Yako Studies. London: Oxford University Press.

Fortes, Meyer
1945   The Dynamics of Clanship Among the Tallensi. London: Oxford University
        Press.
1949   The Web of Kinship Among the Tallensi. London: Oxford University
        Press.
1953   The Structure of Unilineal Descent Groups. American Anthropologist
        55:17–41, Reprinted in Fortes 1970.
1959a   Descent, Filiation, and Affinity: A Rejoinder to Dr. Leach. I. Man
        59:193–197, Reprinted in Fortes 1970.
1959b   Descent, Filiation, and Affinity: A Rejoinder to Dr. Leach, II. Man
        59:206–212, Reprinted in Fortes 1970.

1963   The 'Submerged Descent Line' in Ashanti. *In* Studies in Kinship and Marriage. I. Schapera, ed. Pp. 58–67. London: Royal Anthropological Institute.

1969   Kinship and the Social Order. Chicago: Aldine.

1970   Time and Social Structure and Other Essays. London: Athlone Press.

Fortes, M. and E. E. Evans-Pritchard, eds.

1940   African Political Systems. London: Oxford University Press.

Fox, Robin

1967   Kinship and Marriage. London: Penguin. Reprinted 1983.

Free, Anthony

1990   Written or Living Culture? Journal of the Anthropological Society of Oxford 21:51–65.

1991   The Politics and Philosophical Genealogy of Evans-Pritchard's 'The Nuer.' Journal of the Anthropological Society of Oxford 22:19–39.

Freedman, Maurice

1958   Lineage Organization in Southeastern China. London School of Economics Monographs on Social Anthropology No. 18. London: Athlone Press.

1966   Chinese Lineage and Society: Fukien and Kwangtung. London School of Economics Monographs on Social Anthropology No. 33. London: Athlone Press.

1970   Family and Kinship in Chinese Society. Stanford: Stanford University Press.

Freeman, J. D.

1958   The Family System of the Iban of Borneo. *In* The Developmental Cycle in Domestic Groups. J. Goody, ed. Pp. 15–52. Cambridge Papers in Social Anthropology, 1. London: Cambridge University Press.

1960   On the Concept of the Kindred. Journal of the Royal Anthropological Institute.

Fried, Morton

1957   The Classification of Corporate Unilineal Descent Groups. Journal of the Royal Anthropological Institute 87:1–29.

Gilson, R. P.

1963   Samoan Descent Groups: A Structural Outline. Journal of the Polynesian Society 72:372–377.

1970   Samoa 1830 to 1900: The Politics of a Multi-Cultural Country. Melbourne: Oxford University Press.

Gluckman, Max

1950   Kinship and Marriage Among the Lozi of Northern Rhodesia and the Zulu of Natal. *In* African Systems of Kinship and Marriage. A. R. Radcliffe-

Brown and C. D. Forde, eds. Pp. 166–206. London: Oxford University Press.
1955   Custom and Conflict in Africa. Glencoe, Ill.: The Free Press.
1965   The Ideas in Barotse Jurisprudence. New Haven: Yale University Press.

Goldman, Laurence
1993   The Culture of Coincidence: Accident and Absolute Liability in Huli. NY: Oxford University Press.

Goodenough, Ward
1955   A Problem in Malayo-Polynesian Social Organization. American Anthropologist 57:71–83.
1961   Review of G. P. Murdock, ed., Social Structure in Southeast Asia. American Anthropologist 63:1351–1357.
1965   Rethinking Status and Role. In The Relevance of Models for Social Anthopology. M. Banton, ed. Pp. 1–24. London: Tavistock.
1970   Description and Comparison in Cultural Anthropology. Chicago: Aldine.

Goody, Jack
1966   Introduction. In Succession to High Office J. Goody, ed. Pp. 1–56. London: Cambridge University Press.
1985   Under the Lineage's Shadow. Proceedings of the British Academy 70:189–200.
1990   The Oriental, the Ancient, and the Primitive: Systems of Marriage and the Family in Pre-Industrial Societies of Eurasia. London: Cambridge University Press.
1995   The Expansive Moment: Anthropology in Britain and Africa, 1918–1970. London: Cambridge University Press.

Gottlieb, Alma
1986   Cousin Marriage, Birth Order, and Gender: Alliance Models Among the Bung of Ivory Coast. Man 21:697–722.

Grattan, F. J. H.
1948   An Introduction to Samoan Custom. Papakura, New Zealand: R. McMillan.

Harris, C. C.
1990   Kinship. London: Open University Press.

Harris, Rosemarry
1969   Unilineal Fact or Fiction: A Further Consideration. In Man in Africa. M. Douglas and P. Kaberry, eds. Pp. 138–152. London: Tavistock.

Healey, Christopher
1979   Assimilation of Nonagnates Among the Kundagai Maring. Oceania 50:193–217.

1990   Maring Hunters and Traders: Production and Exchange in the Papua New Guinea Highlands. Berkeley: University of California Press.

Hoben, Allan
1973   Land Tenure Among the Amhara of Ethiopia: The Dynamics of Cognatic Descent. Chicago: University of Chicago Press.

Holy, Ladislav
1976   Kin Groups: Structural Analysis and the Study of Behavior. Annual Review of Anthropology 5:107–131.
1979a   Nuer Politics. *In* Segmentary Lineage Systems Reconsidered. Pp. 23–47. Queens University Papers in Social Anthropology, 4. Belfast: Queens University.
1979b   The Segmentary Lineage and Its Existential Status. *In* Segmentary Lineage Systems Reconsidered. L. Holy, ed. Pp. 1–23. Queens University Papers in Social Anthropology, 4. Belfast: Queens University.
1996   Anthropological Perspectives on Kinship. London, Chicago: Pluto Press.

Howell, P. P.
1954   A Manual of Nuer Law. London: Oxford University Press.

Hu Hsien Chin
1948   The Common Descent Group in China and Its Functions. Viking Fund Publications in Anthropology No. 10. New York, NY: Wenner-Grenn Foundation.

Hui-Chen Wang Liu
1959   The Traditional Chinese Clan Rules. Monographs of the Association for Asian Studies. New York, NY: J. J. Augustin.

Huntsman, Judith
1971   Concepts of Kinship and Categories of Kinsman in the Tokelau Islands. Journal of the Polynesian Society 80:317–354.

Huntsman, Judith, and Antony Hooper
1986   Tokalau: A Historical Ethnography. Honolulu: University of Hawaii Press.

Hutchins, E.
1980   Culture and Inference: A Trobriand Case Study. Cambridge, MA.: Harvard University Press.

Hutchinson, Sharon
1985   Changing Concepts of Incest Among the Nuer. American Ethnologist 12:625–641.
1988   The Nuer in Crisis: Coping with Money, War, and the State. Ph.D. dissertation, University of Chicago.

1990   Rising Divorce Among the Nuer, 1936–1983. Man 25:393–411.
1992   The Cattle of the Money and the Cattle of the Girls Among the Nuer, 1930–1983. American Ethnologist 19:294–316.
1996   Nuer Dilemmas: Coping with Money, War, and the State. Berkeley: University of California Press.

Hviding, Edvard.
1994   Indigenous Essentialism: 'Simplifying' Customary Land Ownership in New Georgia, Solomon Islands. Bijdragen tot dem Taal-, Land- en Volkenkunde 149:812–824.

Josephides, Lisette
1985   The Production of Inequality: Gender and Exchange among the Kewa. London: Tavistock.

Kaberry, P. M.
1967   The Plasticity of New Guinea Kinship. *In* Social Organization: Essays Presented to Raymond Firth. M. Freedman, ed. Athelone: London.

Keesing, Roger
1968   Nonunilineal Descent and the Contextual Definition of Status: The Kwaio Evidence. American Anthropologist 70:82–84.
1970   Shrines, Ancestors and Cognatic Descent: The Kwaio and the Tallensi. American Anthropologist 72:755–775.
1971   Descent, Residence, and Cultural Codes. *In* Anthropology in Oceania: Essays in Honor of Ian Hogbin. L. R. Hiatt and C. Jayawardens, eds. Pp. 121–138. Sydney: Angus Robertson.
1975   Kin Groups and Social Structure. New York: Holt, Rinehart, and Winston.
1982   Kwaio Religion: The Living and the Dead in a Solomon Island Society. New York: Columbia University Press.
1987   African Models in the Malaita Highlands. Man 22: 431–452.

Kelly, Raymond
1977   Etoro Social Structure. Ann Arbor: University of Michican Press.

Kroeber, Alfred L.
1952 (1938)   Basic and Secondary Patterns of Social Structure. *In* The Nature of Culture. Pp. 210–218. New York: Columbia University Press.

Kuper, Adam
1982   Lineage Theory: A Critical Retrospect. Annual Review of Anthropology 11:71–95.

La Fontaine, Jean
1973   Descent in New Guinea: An Africanist View. *In* The Character of Kinship. J. Goody, ed. Pp. 35–52. London: Cambridge University Press.

Lambert, Berndt
1966   Ambilineal Descent Groups in the Northern Gilbert Islands. American Anthropologist 68:641–664.

Langness, L. L.
1964   Some Problems in the Conceptalization of Highlands Social Structures. American Anthropologist 66:162–182.
1971   Bena Bena Political Organization. *In* Politics in New Guinea. R. Berndt and P. Lawrence, eds. Pp. 298–316. Nedlands: University of Western Australia Press.

Leach, E. R.
1962   On Certain Unconsidered Aspects of Double Descent Systems. Man 62:12–13.

Lederman, Rena
1986   What Gifts Engender: Social Relations and Politics in Mendi, Highland Papua New Guinea. NY: Cambridge University Press.

Lindholm, Charles
1982   Generosity and Jealousy: The Swat Pukthun of Northern Pakistan. New York: Columbia University Press.

LiPuma, Edward
1988   The Gift of Kinship: Structure and Practice in Maring Social Organization. Cambridge: Cambridge University Press.
1990   The Terms of Change: Linguistic Mediation and Reaffiliation Among the Maring. Journal of the Polynesian Society 99:93–121.

Lloyd, Peter C.
1966   Agnatic and Cognatic Descent Among the Yoruba. Man 1:484–500.

Lowman-Vayda, Cherry
1971   Maring Big-Men. *In* Politics in New Guinea. R. Berndt and P. Lawrence, eds. Pp. 317–361. Nedlands: University of Western Australia Press.

Mair, Lucy
1962   Primitive Government. Harmondsworth: Penguin.
1974   African Societies. London: Cambridge University Press.

Malinowski, Bronislaw
1922   Argonauts of the Western Pacific. London: Routledge.
1929   Kinship. Encyclopedia Britannica 14th Ed. 13:403–409.
1930   Kinship. Man 30:19–29.
1935   Coral Gardens and Their Magic. 2 vols. London: G. Allen and Unwin.
1963 [1913]   The Family Among the Australian Aborigines: A Sociological Study. NY: Schocken Books, Reprint of the original 1913 edition with an introduction by J. A. Barnes.

Masquelier, Bertrand M.
1993   Descent, Organizational Strategy, and Polity Formation in the Cameroon Highlands (Bamenda Grassfields). Anthropos 88:443–458.

Mayer, Adrian C.
1960   Caste and Kinship in Central India. London: Routledge and Kegal Paul.

Mayer, Philip
1949   The Lineage Principle in Gusii Society. International African Institute Memorandum 23. London: Oxford University Press.
1950   Gusii Bridewealth, Law and Custom. Rhodes-Livingstone Papers 18. London: Oxford University Press.

McArthur, Margaret
1967   Analysis of the Genealogy of a Mae-Enga Clan. Oceania 36:281–285.

McDowell, Nancy
1991   The Mundugumor: From the Field Notes of Margaret Mead and Reo Fortune. Washington, D.C.: Smithsonian Institution Press.

Meggitt, Mervyn
1965   The Lineage System of the Mae-Enga. London: Oliver and Boyd.

Merlan, Francesca, and Alan Rumsey
1991   Ku Waru: Language and Segmentary Politics in the Western Nebilyer Valley, Papua New Guinea. Cambridge: Cambridge University Press.

Middleton, John, and David Tait
1958   Introduction. In Tribes Without Rulers. J. Middleton and D. Tait, eds. Pp. 1–32. London: Routledge and Kegan Paul.

Moore, Sally F.
1972   Legal liability. In The Allocation of Responsibility. M. Gluckman, ed. Pp. 51–108. Manchester: Manchester University Press.

Morren, George E. B., Jr.
1986   The Miyanmin: Human Ecology of a Papua New Guinea Society. Ann Arbor, Mich.: UMI Press.

Needham, Rodney
1971   Remarks on the Analysis of Kinship and Marriage. In Rethinking Kinship and Marriage. R. Needham, ed. Pp. 1–34. London: Tavistock.
1975   Polythetic Classification: Convergence and Consequences. Man 10:349–369.

Orenstein, Henry
1965   Gaon: Conflict and Cohesion in an Indian Village. Princeton: Princeton University Press.

Ottenberg, S.
1968   Double Descent in an African Society: The Afikpo Village-Group. Seattle: University of Washington Press.

Parkin, Robert
1997   Kinship: An Introduction to the Basic Concepts. Oxford: Blackwells.

Pasternak, Burton
1985   The Disquieting Chinese Lineage and Its Anthropological Relevance. *In* The Chinese Family and Its Ritual Behavior. Hsieh Jih-Chang and Dhuang Ying-Chang, eds. Pp. 165–191. Taipei: Institute of Ethnology, Academia Sinica.

Peranio, Roger
1961   Descent, Descent Line, and Descent Group in Cognatic Social Systems. American Ethnological Society, Proceedings :93–113.

Peters, Emrys
1990   The Bedouin of Cyrenaica: Studies in Personal and Corporate Power. London: Cambridge University Press.

Radcliffe-Brown, A. R.
1929   The Mother's Brother in South Africa. South African Journal of Science 21:542–555. Reprinted in Radcliffe-Brown 1952.
1935   Patrilineal and Matrilineal Succession. Iowa Law Review 20. Reprinted in Radcliffe-Brown 1952.
1950   Introduction. *In* African Systems of Kinship and Marriage. A. R. Radcliffe-Brown and C. D. Forde, eds. Pp. 1–85. London: Oxford University Press.
1952   Structure and Function in Primitive Society. Glencoe, Ill.: The Free Press.

Riches, David
1979   On the Presentation of the Tiv Segmentary Lineage System: Or, Speculations on Tiv Social Organisation. *In* Segmentary Lineage Systems Reconsidered L. Holy, ed. Pp. 69–90. Queens University Papers in Social Anthropology, 4. Belfast: Queens University.

Rivers, W. H. R.
1924   Social Organization. London: Macmillan.

Robbins, Sterling
1982   Auyana: Those Who Held onto Home. Seattle: University of Washington Press.

Ryan, D'Arcy
1959   Clan Formation in the Mendi Valley. Oceania 29:257–289.
1969   Marriage in Mendi. *In* Pigs, Pearlshells, and Women. R. M. Glasse and M. J. Meggitt, eds. Pp. 159–175. Englewood Cliffs, NJ: Prentice-Hall.

Sahlins, Marshall
1961   The Segmentary Lineage: An Organization of Predatory Expansion.
       American Anthropologist 63:322–345.
1963   Remarks on Social Structure in Southeast Asia (A review article). Journal of
       the Polynesian Society 72:39–50.
1965   On the Ideology and Composition of Descent Groups. Man 65:104–107.
1985   Islands of History. Chicago: University of Chicago Press.

Salisbury, Richard
1956   Unilineal Descent Groups in the New Guinea Highlands. Man 56:2–7.
1965   New Guinea Highland Models and Descent Theory. Man 65:168–171.

Salzman, P. C.
1978   Does Complementary Opposition Exist? American Anthropologist
       80:53–70.

Sangren, P. Steven
1984   Traditional Chinese Corporations: Beyond Kinship. Journal of Asian
       Studies 43:391–415.

Scheffler, Harold W.
1962   Kindred and Kin Groups in Simbo Island Social Structure. Ethnology
       1:135–157.
1964a The Genesis and Repression of Conflict on Choiseul Island. American
       Anthropologist 66:789–804.
1964b The Social Consequences of Peace on Choiseul Island. Ethnology
       3:398–403.
1965   Choiseul Island Social Structure. Berkeley, Los Angeles: University of
       California Press.
1966   Ancestor Worship in Anthropology. Current Anthropology 7:541–551.
1974   Kindship, Descent, and Alliance. In Handbook of Social and Cultural
       Anthropology J. Honigmann, ed. Pp. 747–793. Chicago: Rand McNally.
1976   The 'Meaning' of Kinship in American Culture: Another View. In Meaning
       in Anthropology K. Basso and H. Selby, eds. Pp. 57–92. Albuquerque:
       University of New Mexico Press.
1985   Filiation and affiliation. Man 20:1–21.
1986   The Descent of Rights and the Descent of Persons. American
       Anthropologist 88:339–350.
1991   Sexism and Naturalism in the Study of Kinship. In Gender at the
       Crossroads of Knowledge. M. di Leonardo, ed. Pp. 361–382. Berkeley:
       University of California Press.

Scheffler, Harold W., and Floyd G. Lounsbury
1972   A Study in Structural Semantics: The Siriono Kinship System. Englewood
       Cliffs, NJ: Prentice-Hall.

Schneider, David M.
1965   Some Muddles in the Models: Or, How the System Really Works. *In* The
       Relevance of Models for Social Anthropology. M. Banton, ed. Pp. 24–86.
       London: Tavistock.
1972   What Is Kinship All About? *In* Kinship Studies in the Morgan Centennial
       Year. P. Reining, ed. Pp. 32–63. Washington, DC: Anthropological Society
       of Washington, DC.
1984   A Critique of the Theory of Kinship. Chicago: University of Chicago Press.

Schneider, David, and Kathleen Gough (eds.)
1961   Matrilineal Kinship. Berkeley: University of California Press.

Schneider, Gerhard
1996   Land Dispute and Tradition in Munda, New Georgia, Solomon Islands:
       From Headhunting to the Quest for the Control of Land. Ph.D. disserta-
       tion, University of Cambridge, Cambridge.

Schneider, Mark
1993   Culture and Enchantment. Chicago: University of Chicago Press.

Searle, John
1969   Speech Acts: An Essay in the Philosophy of Language. London: Cambridge
       University Press.
1995   The Construction of Social Reality. New York: The Free Press.

Service, Elman
1962   Primitive Social Organization: An Evolutionary Perspective. New York:
       Norton.

Sillitoe, Paul
1979   Give and Take: Exchange in Wola Society. New York: St. Martin's.

Smith, Michael G.
1956   On Segmentary Lineage Systems. Journal of the Royal Anthropological
       Institute 86, part 2, pp. 39–80. (Reprinted in M. G. Smith, 1974
       Corporations and Society. London: Duckworth.)
1969   Differentiation and the Segmentary Principle in Two Societies. *In* Man in
       Africa. M. Douglas and P. Kaberry, eds. Pp. 152–176. London:
       Tavistock.
1974   Corporations and Society. London: Duckworth.

Southall, Aidan
1986   The Illusion of Nath Agnation. Journal of Anthropological Research 25:1–20.

Spencer, Robert F.
1960   Aspects of Turkish Kinship and Social Structure. Anthropological
       Quarterly :40–50.

Stirling, A. P.
1960   A Death and a Youth Club: Feuding in a Turkish Village. Anthropological
       Quarterly :51–75.

Stoljar, Samuel
1973   Groups and Entities: An Inquiry into Corporate Theory. Canberra:
       Australian National University Press.
1984   An Analysis of Rights. New York: St. Martin's.

Strathern, Andrew
1969   Descent and Alliance in the New Guinea Highlands: Some Problems of
       Comparison. Proceedings of the Royal Anthropological Institute
       1968:37–52.
1972   One Father, One Blood: Descent and Group Structure Among the Melpa
       People. Canberra: Australian National University Press.
1973   Kinship, Descent, and Locality: Some New Guinea Examples. In The
       Character of Kinship. J. Goody, ed. Pp. 21–33. London: Cambridge
       University Press.
1982   Two Waves of African Models in the New Guinea Highlands. In Inequality
       in New Guinea Highland Societies. A. J. Strathern, ed. Pp. 35–49.
       London: Cambridge University Press.

Verdon, Michel
1983   The Abutia Ewe of West Africa. Berlin: Mouton.

Wang, Sung-Hsing
1985   On the Household and Family in Chinese Society. In The Chinese Family
       and Its Ritual Behavior. Hsieh Jih-chang, and Chuang Ying-chang, eds.
       Pp. 50–58. Taipei: Institute of Ethnology, Academia Sinica.

Watson, James B.
1983   Tairora Culture: Contingency and Pragmatism. Seattle: University of
       Washington Press.

Watson, James L.
1975   Emigration and the Chinese Lineage: The Mans in Hong Kong and
       London. Berkeley: University of California Press.
1982   Chinese Kinship Reconsidered: Anthropological Perspectives on Historical
       Research. China Quarterly Dec.:589–622.
1986   Anthropological Overview: The Development of Chinese Descent Groups.
       In Kinship Organization in Later Imperial China. P. Ebry and J. L.
       Watson, eds. Pp. 274–292. Berkeley: University of California Press.

Watson, Rubie
1985   Inequality Among Brothers: Class and Kinship in South China. London:
       Cambridge University Press.

Weiner, James F.
1982 Substance, Siblingship and Exchange: Aspects of Social Structure in New Guinea. Social Analysis 11:3–34.

Wilson, Robert R.
1977 Genealogy and History in the Biblical World. New Haven: Yale University Press.

Wolf, Arthur
1985 The Study of Chinese Society on Taiwan. *In* The Chinese Family and Its Ritual Behavior. Hsieh Jih-chang and Chuang Ying-chang, eds. Pp. 3–16. Taipei: Institute of Ethnology, Academia Sinica.

Wolf, A. and C. Wang
1980 Marriage and Adoption in China 1845–1945. Stanford: Stanford University Press.

INDEX